Praise for *The Race to Save Our Century:*

"Jason Jones has given us a valuable tool for rebuilding our culture, and I urge you to read it!" —Fr. Frank Pavone, national director, Priests for Life, and president, National Pro-Life Religious Council

"The true ascent of man over the centuries has been the steady recognition and embrace of the truths about human nature and the good society that the Creator wrote upon our hearts. Forget these, the authors tell us in this prophetic book, and our new century will more than replicate the horrors of the one we just left behind." —Patrick J. Buchanan

"I am inspired by Jason Jones's courage to speak truthfully and write unequivocally in defense of Life. He is also a brilliant filmmaker, who uses powerful persuasive movies to publicly challenge calcified minds. Jason Jones's loud drumbeat for people to stand up and courageously speak truth to power evokes the spirit and words of Robert F. Kennedy, 'Few men are willing to brave the disapproval of their fellows, the censure of their colleagues, and the wrath of their society. Moral courage is a rarer commodity than bravery in battle or great intelligence. Yet it is the one essential, vital quality for those who seek to change a world which yields most painfully to change.'" —Kwame Fosu-Shabazz, policy director and director of international affairs, the Rebecca Project

"In this book, Jason Jones and John Zmirak employ vast historical knowledge and deep Christian insight to show how the confident secular humanism that props up Western society has crumbling feet of clay. . . . Read this book to find out how that happened and what you can do to help reverse the collapse before it's too late." —Joseph Farah, CEO and editor, *WorldNetDaily*

"Jason Jones is a passionate, brilliant, and incisive advocate for saving the culture and saving souls from self-destruction. He does more in a few minutes than many do in a lifetime." —Ted Baehr, publisher and editor in chief, *Movieguide*

"As a victim of the Chinese Cultural Revolution, I found hope for human dignity after reading Jason's book. The book is a must read for college students." —Dr. Kate Xiao Zhou, professor of political science, University of Hawaii

"I encourage anyone concerned about our country to read this book. You will be motivated, encouraged, and inspired." —Abby Johnson, author, *Unplanned: The Dramatic True Story of a Former Planned Parenthood Leader's Eye-Opening Journey across the Life Line*

"In many ways, the core event of the twentieth century was the attempted suicide of Western civilization. But even now, as Jason Scott Jones and John Zmirak demonstrate, there is hope. And it involves going back to the roots of that civilization: not for nostalgia's sake, but for the sake of breathing life back into the civilization that gave full meaning to human dignity and human freedom. This book shows us how." —Samuel Gregg, research director, the Acton Institute for Religion and Liberty

"Jones and Zmirak have compiled an incisive history that reveals so much of the connectedness in the atrocities since World War I, but it becomes more than a mere history when we realize that there is a normative ethics that can be reaped from all of the pain and suffering in a century of subhumanism. This book shows that the intrinsic value of human beings—this immutable worth—is really something that can be seen and comprehended not because one is a Republican or a Democrat, nor a Christian or an atheist, but simply because one is human. This will without question be required reading for our staff members: this is a monumental step in the right direction for the pursuit of a culture of peace and a culture of life." —Aimee Murphy, executive director, *Life Matters* Journal

"An important book and just in time. John Zmirak is one of the most insightful writers in this still young century. He sees the ongoing perils of the decaying republic, yet offers hopeful remedies for its ills." —Fr. C. J. McCloskey, research fellow, Faith and Reason Institute

"I share Jason Jones's view that denial of transcendental moral principles would lead to 'subhumanism,' which reduces us to a subset of mere lowly animals. Also, even though pleasure or happiness as such is good, human dignity as the highest principle cannot be placed under hedonistic utilitarianism. This book has discredited relativism, the prevalence of which has been corrupting the human intellect for many decades. Jason

Jones defends human life and freedom powerfully in this insightful book, and I encourage people from every part of the world to read it and take it seriously." —Zhenming Zhai, professor of philosophy, Sun Yat-sen University, Guangzhou, China; author, *The Radical Choice and Moral Theory*

"John Zmirak was brilliant when I met him at Yale thirty years ago, but to now see that brilliance in full flower in this magnificent book written with Jason Jones is a deep joy. Simply put, *The Race to Save Our Century* should be taught in every college in America. Do yourself a huge favor: chuck the newspapers for a while and read this book! You'll learn infinitely more about what is happening in the world today." —Eric Metaxas, *New York Times* bestselling author of *Bonhoeffer: Pastor, Martyr, Prophet, Spy* and *Miracles: What They Are, Why They Happen, and How They Can Change Your Life*

"Jason Jones and John Zmirak break down some clear solutions to help us make the most of our generation. This book could not come at a better time." —Josh Duggar, executive director of Family Research Council Action and reality star on TLC's *19 Kids & Counting*

"Jason Jones, a human rights activist and filmmaker, and John Zmirak, a scholar of economics and theology, have combined to create a book that is prophetic—not in the sense that it pretends to tell the future. No, *The Race to Save Our Century* speaks truth to power as Amos and Elijah did, and points to the deepest truths about God and man. The authors expose the antihuman ideologies that created the twentieth century's genocides and warn us how these moral viruses still lurk within our culture. Best of all, the book gives a cogent five-point program for defending human dignity, freedom, and peace in the twenty-first century." —Governor Mike Huckabee

"A fresh and provocative countercultural argument that transcends and challenges conventional political categories. People of good will from all points on the ideological spectrum will appreciate and profit from *The Race to Save Our Century*." —O. Carter Snead, director, Center for Ethics and Culture, and professor of law, University of Notre Dame

The Race to Save Our Century

Five Core Principles to Promote Peace, Freedom, and a Culture of Life

by
Jason Scott Jones and John Zmirak

Bob -

thank you for standing
for Life.

A Crossroad Book
The Crossroad Publishing Company
New York

The Crossroad Publishing Company
www.crossroadpublishing.com
© 2014 by Jason S. Jones and John Zmirak

Portions of this book have been adapted from the following articles:

"Breaking Stained Glass Windows," © 2011, John Zmirak. Reprinted and adapted with permission of *Crisis Magazine*.

"Conservatives Can Learn Latino," © 2012, Jason Jones. Reprinted and adapted with permission of the *The Blaze*.

"Flying Into the Abyss on John Brennan's Drone," © 2013, Jason Jones. Reprinted and adapted with permission of *Aleteia*.

"Killing Women and Children First," © 2005, John Zmirak. Reprinted and adapted with permission of *GODSPY*.

"Life Lessons from Joseph Stalin," © 2011, Jason Jones. Reprinted and adapted with permission of *Crisis Magazine*.

"Modern Insights and Ancient Virtues," © 2011, John Zmirak. Reprinted and adapted with permission of *Crisis Magazine*.

"A Nation with the Soul of a Church," © 2011, Jason Jones. Reprinted and adapted with permission of *Crisis Magazine*.

"Of Human Dignity and Shoes," © 2012, Jason Jones. Reprinted and adapted with permission of *Crisis Magazine*.

"Patrick Buchanan and the Necessary Book," © 2008, John Zmirak. Reprinted and adapted with permission of *Taki's Magazine*.

"We Proud Sons of Onan," © 2011, Jason Jones. Reprinted and adapted with permission of *Crisis Magazine*.

"Worse than a Crime," © 2004, John Zmirak. Reprinted and adapted with permission of the *The American Conservative*.

Library of Congress Cataloging-in-Publication Data available from the Library of Congress.
ISBN 978-0-82452019-9
    1. Current Events   2. Politics   3. Religion

First Edition

Books may be purchased in quantity and/or special sales by contacting the publisher, The Crossroad Publishing Company, at sales@crossroadpublishing.com.

Printed in the United States of America in 2014

10 9 8 7 6 5 4 3 2 1 20 19 18 17 16 15 14

Contents

To Micah, Marion, Maximilian, Jacob, Eva Marie, Isabella, and Andrew.
And to Faye.

Introduction

It's Always August 1914

We all love the stories about Sherlock Holmes. We enjoy the masterful storytelling and vivid characters, and the ingenious plots that only Holmes's razor-sharp mind can untangle. But there's another reason why we treasure them. They remind us of another world, just a hundred years ago, one in which so much appalling evil had not yet reared its head.

In the world before August 1914, you could travel without a passport. Economies were booming, and science promised a future of seemingly endless growth. Labor unions were rising to blunt the sharpest edges of capitalism, and in most of Europe voting rights for citizens were expanding. Frenchmen, Germans, Englishmen, and Russians met for scientific and literary conferences, studied at each others' schools, and their aristocrats intermarried. The diverse ethnic quilt that was central Europe was held together peacefully under the Austro-Hungarian empire, where Catholics, Protestants, Jews, and Muslims enjoyed religious freedom. While a few crank parties favored racist or ultranationalist platforms, minorities in Europe were mostly protected from the bigotry of their neighbors. Even in troubled Russia, rapid economic and technological progress were offering hope that the country's hard-pressed workers and land-starved farmers might join the modern world—with guidance from an Orthodox Church that was experiencing a spiritual renaissance.

If a character had tried to warn Sherlock Holmes about what was coming, would that brilliant detective have believed him? Could Holmes have imagined that Germans and Englishmen would soon be gassing each other with human pesticides? That a bitter world war would destroy three European empires and hand half of the continent over to hateful extremists? That the Russian government would try to wipe out Christianity, private property, and every vestige of freedom, and engineer famines that would exterminate some ten million people? That this first war's millions of dead would have died in vain? That another and bloodier war would come in its wake, and this time entail the murder of half of Europe's Jews? That this war would only end when terror weapons blotted entire cities off the map?

Surely Holmes would have asked Dr. Watson to treat this "prophet" for hysteria. Horrors like those were confined to the violent fantasies of the rare, sociopathic criminals Holmes hunted. Such schemes of evil would never become the policies of civilized governments in Europe. It was simply unthinkable.

The world of Arthur Conan Doyle's characters was eerily like our own. The world's superpowers, once locked into conflict, were now committed to peaceful coexistence. New technologies were annihilating distance, uniting mankind, and globalizing the economy. The English language had leaped far beyond its island home, and now knit together hundreds of millions of people on four continents. Medical advances were saving millions from infant mortality and infectious diseases, while new agricultural methods offered the hope of eradicating hunger. Transnational organizations in defense of human rights were striving to eliminate forced labor and torture, and reform movements in tyrannical countries promised to introduce democracy. At the same time, popular science and biblical criticism had weakened the hold of religion, leaving man as the measure of all things. We had entered the final phase of human development, an age of perpetual worldly progress. The sun that dawned on June 28, 1914, in Sarajevo shone bright as all our hopes in a sky almost clear of clouds—a day much like September 11, 2001, in New York City. A day much like today.

What would you think if we told you that all the horrors that marked the twentieth century might happen all over again? That this time the cruelties and casualties would be even greater, since our weapons are even deadlier. That the next genocides would face less resistance, and generate fewer "rescuers," because the West is less restrained by religion. That the twenty-first century could be remembered not for Twitter, but for total warfare? You might think that we were paranoid. Then you might remember August 1914, and think again.

It's a truism that history repeats itself, because the human heart is profoundly imperfect and torn between good and evil. Study of man's repeated lapses into cruelty and chaos can tempt us to lapse into cynicism, when what we really need is hope.

Hope is not optimism. Stock analysts are optimistic. Worldly optimism is a brittle dream that can be shattered by a single act of terrorism. But hope can survive in cancer wards and concentration camps, as Aleksander Solzhenitsyn and Victor Frankl have testified. Hope exists in a fourth dimension that cuts across the world we see at an angle we cannot imagine. It rises from secret places in the heart, where the torturers cannot find it, and spreads through quiet gestures or silent prayers they cannot quash. Hope is what Winston Smith hungered for in Orwell's *1984*.

If we wish to save the twenty-first century from repeating the crimes of the twentieth, we must face some very hard truths. We must realize that there is no salvation in our accumulated "stuff," in political programs, or in technological fixes. We have spent the last several centuries asking only "how" to do things to nature and to man. We must step back and ask again "why" and even "why not." We need to recover a dignified vision of the human person, or else it will cease to exist.

Such a vision will help us resist many temptations, of the sort our race falls into so very easily, to use the superhuman powers we gain in inhuman ways; to treat the weak, the "other," the Enemy, as subhumans; or even to embrace a subhuman vision of ourselves.

Subhumanism lay just beneath the civilized skin of life in 1914. Each of the toxic ideas that would make the twentieth century so inhospitable to innocent human life was already present, ready to turn a political or military crisis into a humanitarian catastrophe:

Total war, the theory that in time of military conflict any means can and should be used to bring about victory, however destructive to civilian life among the enemy or liberty at home. This principle had not been practiced in the West itself since 1648, but Western nations had been employing genocidal tactics against civilian populations in their African and Asian colonies. It was only a matter of time before Europeans turned their machine guns and gas against one another.

Racism and nationalism, the false religions that emerged with the decline of Christian faith. They offered an alternate principle of unity to rootless and economically vulnerable citizens, and directed the masses' anger away from their own upper class, outward to foreign enemies or to "untrustworthy" minorities in their midst.

Utopian collectivism, a collection of messianic political movements that promised to solve the economic problems that arose from modern technology and mass production by using the bullets and bayonets of the state to transform human nature itself. It promised to wipe out selfishness and re-create society on the model of a monastery, establishing a kingdom of perfect and permanent justice by rooting out the "exploiters" and forcibly sharing the wealth.

Radical individualism, a theory that takes the fragile, fallible human person and makes of him a self-creating god, who owes nothing to parents, children, or neighbors, and who may rightly keep as much wealth as he can accumulate, and scoff at the claims of the poor and the weak.

Utilitarian hedonism, a philosophy that tries to make respectable the old despairing slogan "eat, drink, and be merry, for tomorrow we will die." It denies that suffering or self-sacrifice has any significance, and uses every technological means to create a "brave new world" in which human beings can accumulate as many happy and comfortable moments as possible before they are annihilated.

Each of these principles was firmly rooted in one place or another in 1914, and each one would emerge to claim its share of the millions of human lives that were destroyed or snuffed out in the bloody twentieth century. And each of these principles still exerts an appeal today. The surface calm that pervades contemporary life is even more fragile now than it was a hundred years ago—a reality that rises to haunt us with each international crisis, from revolutions in the Muslim world to fitful aggressions by Russia, from nuclear tests in North Korea to clashes between the Japanese and Chinese.

To restrain ourselves and each other, to prepare a livable future, there are certain nonnegotiable principles we need to accept as the bedrock of human rights and lasting peace. We do not need an infallible authority to reveal them. Any honest student of twentieth-century history could piece them together by looking at those perennial truths that totalitarian movements and ruthless governments sought to deny:

Personalism, or the absolute value of every human person, whom we must treat as an image of God.

A transcendent moral order by which we judge every human law, public policy, cultural norm, and every decision we make in our own lives.

Subsidiarity, or the truth that a good society guarantees ordered liberty through a limited, decentralized government that preserves civil society, instead of trying to usurp its functions.

The solidarity of all human beings, regardless of race, class, nation, religion, or other criteria.

A free, humane economy that fosters individual enterprise and protects private property rights, within the limits imposed by human nature, human rights, and social cohesion.

In this book, we will unfold the implications of each of these irreplaceable moral principles, which blocked the progress of every "pure" ideology that has emerged in the course of modernity, of each partial truth about man that claimed his absolute loyalty. If we live out these principles day to day, let them direct how we do business, how we spend money, and how we vote, we can rebuild our society as a more humane place for our children. If we neglect them, the next hundred years will prove even more horrific than the last. The options are clear. It is time to choose.

PART ONE

Modern Ideologies of Evil

Chapter One

Subhumanism: Modern Man's Suicide Note

It is rare for a single book to make a difference. And many books that do have an impact change the world for the worse. Some of the "Great Books" that appear on college curricula became famous not for challenging reigning myths, but for undermining old truths and replacing them with sleek, efficient half-truths or outright errors. Niccolo Machiavelli's *The Prince* rejected the heritage of some two thousand years, during which political philosophers felt constrained to seek the Good. Thomas Hobbes's *Leviathan* helped raze the last bulwarks against authoritarian government. Thomas Malthus's *Essay on the Principle of Population* was cited to justify British inaction during the Irish Potato Famine. It also inspired many later initiatives around the world aimed at forcing the poor to bear fewer children, as part of what Edwin Black called "the war against the weak." There are many more examples of books that had toxic side effects.

But sometimes a book can act as a vaccine. Great examples include Orwell's *1984* and Huxley's *Brave New World*. Considering the near-collapse of marriage forces us to add Pope Paul VI's *Humanae Vitae*, which warned in plain language where the sexual revolution was leading—to the hookup culture we live in today, in which barely half of children grow up in intact families, and unwed mothers are mired in multigenerational poverty.

This book aims to warn us of the false theories of human life that pervade our culture. Put bluntly: Most Western men and women, including many who consider themselves conventionally religious, think of human beings as less than truly human. They accept without reflection theories of human life that reduce mankind to brainy animals or that let us play at being gods. These modern ideologies render suffering meaningless and urge us to live like cowards; they teach us to scorn the weak but train us in habits of avoidance; they speak about progress but encourage the lowest of human instincts; they claim to have surpassed Judeo-Christian ethics, but really they have slumped below the standards of ancient paganism. The picture of man they present is distinctly unheroic and has no claim to ultimate meaning—a far cry from the noble Renaissance man. The only proper term for this view of mankind is "subhumanism."

This view of man distrusts the bold reason that inspired the Enlightenment and has shrugged off the dreams of transcendence that beguiled the Romantics. When we speak of humanity now, too often we think in terms of ecological damage, excessive numbers, and intractable hatreds; ecologists have even taught us to see ourselves as a plague on the planet, with our generation's task to limit the damage we do to the biosphere. And yet, somehow and from somewhere, we are said to possess a set of things called "human rights"—which can be expansive enough to include the right to plastic surgery funded by our neighbors, yet simultaneously so narrow as to restrict the right of terminal patients to food and water.

Subhumanism simultaneously asserts a noble, high-minded view of human dignity that calls for a deep respect for human rights—which, in fact, exaggerates them and even makes up additional rights—and a deeply cynical, disillusioned view of man as just another mammal.

Subhumanism is not a coherent worldview with clear assertions that we can subject to the strict test of logic, much less to double-blind testing in the laboratory. It is not a single ideology that we could picture as a cypress tree and imagine cutting down. It is much more like the swamp, where plants of a thousand species grow. It is the mother of ideologies. But we can test the toxic chemicals in the soil and figure out why the trees that grow there all look so . . . ghostly.

The subhumanist simultaneously claims that each human being is endowed with inalienable rights, which begin with life, liberty, and the pursuit of happiness, but continue through infinite, tortuous emanations to include freedom from want, freedom from fear, freedom of choice, then extend to things like a living wage, health care, housing, educational opportunities, racial and gender equality, and handicapped-accessible restrooms—while also holding that human beings are the accidental result of billions of years of random cosmic and planetary accidents, followed by millions of years of undirected genetic mutations; that our brains are organic computers that generate all our thoughts for us and leave us no free will; and that our altruistic instincts are really only our DNA striving to replicate itself; that the most successful human being in history must have been Genghis Khan, who left behind several million direct descendants; that the biggest failure had to be Jesus Christ, who lived without sex or money, and died without having children.

We really cannot believe both things at once about ourselves or about the whole human family. Such perfect examples of what George Orwell called "doublethink" are not possible for the sane. But still we pick and choose, as if from a takeout menu, items from Column A (Western liberal humanism) and Column B (post-Darwinian scientific pessimism). Or we pick certain groups of people (starting with ourselves) to whom we will serve up the respect and esteem from Column A, and other groups who have to make do with the scorn from Column B. Of course, such choices are arbitrary, but life is "complex," we tell ourselves, and we have to pick our battles. Of course, when the chips are down, what we really think life means wins out in the end. But in the meantime, we get through life without thinking very hard about what we're doing, and even while esteeming ourselves as highly moral people—even though we are, perhaps unwittingly, cherry-picking which human beings deserve to be treated with respect and which ones we can kick to the curb. A right-wing subhumanist will probably offer treats from Column A to people based on race, religion, nationality, or economic success. A left-wing subhumanist is more likely to pick winners based on age, good health, or their capacity for creativity and enjoyment. Either way, we will ultimately pick people based on how closely they conform to our image of God—that is, how much they remind us of . . . *ourselves.*

How did we get here? Put simply and starkly, Western man tried to pursue a humanist project of understanding and uplifting human life, and in the process he identified God as an obstacle, even an enemy. So we tried to root him out. We tried to create consistent systems that preserved all the good things we take for granted in Western society, while denying God. That is, we tried to build the steeple on the church of humanity with steel ripped from its foundations. Predictably, the whole tower collapsed in the killing fields of the twentieth century. It is clear to honest thinkers that you cannot keep on believing in human dignity without a transcendent reference point. We cannot pull ourselves up out of the animal kingdom by our bootstraps any more than an alcoholic can claw his way back to sobriety without a "higher power." We cannot teach ourselves to see other people as ends rather than means unless we accept some ultimate meaning that is more important than figuring out "what feels good," then doing it. The source of our dignity must lie in God.

The net effect of these moral and intellectual errors is to degrade our common life and make us prone to utter callousness.

Having largely (and sometimes brutally) conquered nature, we face today the much graver and more complex task of controlling ourselves, of using the technological and economic power unleashed by modern science in responsible ways, of preserving the deeper moral truths that come to us through our traditions, in the face of temptations that have never faced man before. Given the mighty technologies we wield, if we fail in our task, we may very well render human beings an endangered species.

The twentieth century for the first time gave us the technological power to exterminate whole ethnic groups, and then the means to wipe out all human life on earth. In recent decades, biotechnology has given us more subtle and targeted ways to work our will. In the United States, doctors and parents acting together have almost wiped out Down syndrome—by aborting more than 90 percent (according to some estimates) of the children diagnosed with it in the womb. Scientists at Harvard and other elite institutions still hope to harness embryos "discarded" from fertility clinics for the medical treatment of adults. Genetic engineering advances by the year toward its consumer-driven goal of "designer" children, whose very DNA will encode the narcissism of one generation in the next and make the dream of eugenicists a living reality. Meanwhile, the U.S. military has developed unmanned drones that are aimed at murderous terrorists but themselves claim hundreds of innocent civilian lives each year. Biological and nuclear weapons are, for the moment, still kept from the hands of terrorists, but at some point they will get hold of them—and use them to slaughter innocents, and avenge any number of grievances, including the "collateral" victims of our drones.

Even as our technological power to kill, harm, or dominate our fellow man increases, our ethics have grown more primitive. If you think of the moral development of a child, you will see the point: We start as absolute solipsists in the cradle, then slowly come to realize that our mothers are separate human beings. Through patient discipline, we overcome the primal selfishness that marks every two-year-old and come to recognize the humanity and the rights of our parents and siblings. The next lesson in altruism comes in the classroom, when we are forced to extend this recognition to strangers in our little tribe of schoolmates. As we mature and expand our experiences, we encounter people who look and act quite alien, and must learn to respect them as well—even (this is the last and highest stage of humanism) to feel solidarity with human beings *as human beings*, though they live in foreign countries and hold opposing views.

The gradual expansion of our human "circle of concern" is one of the great achievements of any civilization—and it is a fragile thing, as we see in every resurgence of nationalism and at the outbreak of every war. The same fragility holds in our moments of personal crisis, when our own most treasured desires are opposed by some intimate obstacle: an inconvenient fetus, a parent who has lingered too long and clings to life, or a stubbornly unresponsive reproductive system. Likewise in political life, when our fellow citizens act in ways we find frustrating or expensive, we are tempted to wish away our common humanity and subject them to treatment we'd consider outrageous if it were applied to us. We stockpile offenders in prisons with cruel conditions and wink at the prevalence of prison rape and violence. We shrug at the many injustices in the application of the death penalty. In economic life, we seek the best product at the lowest price, without regard for the well-being of the people who produced it. That is none of our business. The "invisible hand," we believe, will blindly produce rough justice. Or not. It is someone else's problem.

If we hope to be civilized, at every stage and level of life each one of us must fight against the force of gravity that draws our ethics downward, that drops our standards ever closer to the lowest common denominator of narcissism. But even as we gain greater power to harm each other, our religious creeds—the mightiest forces that have traditionally countered rank selfishness—have begun to go slack and sickly. Dogmatic religions have in large part lost their nerve and trimmed their ethics to suit the prevailing winds. Many churches that still cling to traditional biblical tenets underplay the sacrificial aspects of Christianity in favor of a gospel of self-help or success. As if to compensate, other churches despair of mobilizing souls to aid the needy and instead turn to the mechanism of the government, replacing the Works of Mercy with soulless bureaucracies and "entitlements" that lock the poor into poverty and dependency. It is much easier, and cleaner, to hand a homeless person an EBT card than to buy him a meal and hear his story —much less find him a job.

We hope to lay out here the core principles of a true humanism, one that cuts across political lines and speaks to believers and skeptics alike, offering a set of fundamental insights about the human person and how people live together that can be broadly agreed upon. They reflect the "natural law" that thinkers as widely disparate as Thomas Aquinas, Thomas Jefferson, and Martin Luther King Jr. have appealed to as the criterion by which we must judge any law, policy, or day-to-day decision. With the explosion of human power over other human beings, we need more than ever a common standard of reference, a bare minimum of respect for our fellow mortals, below which we will not go—whatever the personal cost. We are not attempting here to promote a particular creed. We are simply asking for people to raise their moral standards to something worthy of human dignity, to account for the rights and infinite value of every single person—even (and especially) those we find the most inconvenient. In ethics, it is the hard cases that make the best law.

It's a tragic irony that the very part of the world where "human rights" was invented as a concept, where freedom, limited government, and the dignity of the person became fighting creeds—with the power to dethrone tyrants, free slaves, empower workers, offer women equal education and opportunities—has become a place where life is not seen as sacred. Where having large families is seen as an irresponsible act, while euthanasia is viewed as a courageous mission of mercy. You need not be a culture critic, or a Christian, to wonder what went wrong.

How is it that the cultural turn toward humanism that began with the Renaissance's embrace of man's inherent capacity for greatness ended up in the concentration camps and killing fields—and now in the empty cradles of the postmodern, dying West?

Our slide from the godlike glory of Renaissance man to the banality of evil was slow, but it was far from simple. There were many intellectual turnings along the road that carried us from Michelangelo's Florence to Stalin's gulag. But the path we took is clear: By trying to glorify man and free him, we stripped away the reasons to regard human life as sacred and the rules that kept us from mistreating people who got in our way. We learned to dehumanize whole groups of people when it suited us, but as a consequence we were degrading ourselves.

Why we would do such a thing? Don't the most aggressive atheists claim that their reason for rejecting religious faith is that it does not promote "human flourishing"? People who consider themselves "secular" will typically follow that word with "humanist," to underscore that they fight for the claims of man against divine encroachment. We even use the word "humane" to evoke kindness to animals. Why would people who have toppled all the gods for the sake of humanism then go on and shatter the image of man?

Because the old idea of man is demanding, exhausting, and constricting.

Humanism demands that we live up to standards that are difficult. But the long list of virtues specified by classical humanism, which Aristotle catalogued and Aquinas gratefully cribbed, is irrelevant to hapless, featherless bipeds in quest of protein, warmth, entertainment, and pleasure. And that degraded image of man as just another, brainier animal is increasingly popular in our culture—and for a reason. It's an all-purpose excuse for giving up the fight to do what is right, and instead following our instincts and appetites wherever they lead us.

Humanism exhausts our empathy. It insists that we try to feel some solidarity with strangers halfway across the world whose village was swamped by a mudslide, or that we concern ourselves with the physical well-being of the teenaged Asians who sewed our sneakers. If we grant that we ourselves, and every other human being on earth, have an exalted status and the rights that come along with it, we will have to worry about an unending series of other people's problems, when we can barely wrap our heads around our own.

Humanism constricts us and stops us from doing things that would otherwise make sense—like terminating inconvenient pregnancies, then mass-producing embryos in nice clean petri dishes. If scruples arise about bombing thousands of civilians to save our soldiers' lives, it might make us unduly timid about attacking the countries whose policies frustrate us. We might begin to feel guilty about forcing poor countries to sterilize more of their women, as U.S. and U.N. policymakers have routinely insisted as a condition of foreign aid.

Enlightenment thinkers claimed that human freedom of action was overly hemmed in by the dictates of religion, by arbitrary rules plucked from a yellowing Bible or imposed by celibate Italians in cobwebbed scarlet robes. But as things turned out, even those of us who renounced or watered down the specific demands of Christianity found that life didn't become all that much easier. That is because the vast bulk of the moral code that Western believers adhered to did not come from divine revelation or canon law, but instead arose from rational thought about how man should live, given his uniqueness and dignity as the only rational animal. Being secular was not the answer to the problems posed by humanism. In fact, even humanism made far too much of man for our convenience. It became our task to bring the unwieldy creature back down to size so that we could get on with the business of living. Assimilate that insight, and the history of the twentieth century writes itself. Ignore the lessons of the past century, and the next one will be even worse.

Chapter Two

Total War

There is nothing new, advanced, or scientific about the practice of total war. Butchering your enemies—included the wounded, the aged, women, and children—was surely a custom among the cavemen. Ancient civilizations that spared the inhabitants of conquered cities were moved less by moral scruples than by the fact that the defeated were worth more as slaves and subjects than as pyramids of skulls. Empires such as Rome were inconsistent: Sometimes they paid back cities that had resisted them by slaughtering everyone in sight. More often they would enslave and deport whole populations. But in most cases the Romans merely defeated armies, then ruled and exploited conquered nations by replacing their ruling elites.

St. Augustine's "just war" doctrine promoted a higher standard, demanding both a just cause for a given war, and just means in how it was waged. "Just means" meant sparing the unarmed and the helpless, even when it might be militarily advantageous to kill them. Augustine's rules were often ignored. For centuries, Christian rulers started wars on the slightest pretexts. Despite the ideal of chivalry, soldiers frequently punished towns that resisted siege by subjecting them to savage rape and pillage. This practice was taken for granted, so much so that Shakespeare did not fear that he would make his hero King Henry V seem repulsive when he issued this bloodcurdling threat:

> . . . Therefore, you men of Harfleur,
>
> Take pity of your town and of your people,
>
> Whiles yet my soldiers are in my command . . .
>
> If not, why, in a moment look to see
>
> The blind and bloody soldier with foul hand
>
> Defile the locks of your shrill-shrieking daughters;
>
> Your fathers taken by the silver beards,
>
> And their most reverend heads dash'd to the walls,
>
> Your naked infants spitted upon pikes,

Whiles the mad mothers with their howls confused

Do break the clouds, as did the wives of Jewry

At Herod's bloody-hunting slaughtermen.

What say you? will you yield, and this avoid,

Or, guilty in defence, be thus destroy'd? (*Henry V*, 3.3, 1–44)

Both sides in the Crusades were guilty of precisely such behavior. The Spanish and English conquests in the New World were equally ugly, whatever religious motives might have ornamented those land grabs. Nor did the presence of priests among the soldiers do much to restrain the slaughter.

Nevertheless, in the early modern era, there was a concerted attempt to restrain the fury of international conflict in the name of international law and the rights of man—a movement that won over not just statesmen but soldiers, who began to make clean distinctions between combatants and civilians. The effort to protect civilians gained strength in the wake of the Thirty Years' War, in which massacres, disease, and famine claimed between 25 and 40 percent of everyone living in Germany. In the aftermath of that war, European nations strove to professionalize their armies, pay them instead of letting them plunder, and maintain tighter control over their actions, even in victory. The result was that wars after 1648 were significantly less destructive of civilian populations—and hence of the economic value of conquered territories.

A worthy account of this push for effective international laws of war appears in Caleb Carr's *The Lessons of Terror.* Carr shows that the Christian imperative to spare noncombatants only began to be practiced widely when soldiers and their rulers saw the uselessness of attacks on innocents. It became apparent that the very military discipline required to keep soldiers from devastating civilians also produced a much more effective fighting force, while generating far less popular resistance from conquered populations.

Those who reject traditional moral strictures on the conduct of combat and embrace "total war" tend to do so under the rubric of "realism" and pragmatic necessity. Carr defines terror in the moral vocabulary of traditional Western Christian "just war" teaching: He describes terror simply as "warfare waged against civilians, either intentionally or indiscriminately, with the goal of breaking their will to fight." Terrorism is a tactic—not an abstract moral category, nor the monopoly of a particular religion. It is a technique of fighting wars. Whoever targets civilians intentionally as a means of making war engages in a form of terrorism.

The modern concept of total war is in fact nothing new, certainly not the logical or necessary outcome of centuries' experience, much less the result of intellectual "progress." Instead, it is a throwback, an abandonment of the recent moral progress achieved by the West.

Modern total war as we know it began in the savage fighting European colonial powers engaged in against rebellious populations from Africa to India. It came home to Europe in the wake of World War I, in the musings of military strategists in the 1920s, as Williamson Murray documents in his history, *Strategy for Defeat: The Luftwaffe, 1933–1945.* Generals from Germany, France, and England, who had been appalled by the slow, pointless attrition of World War I, tried to imagine ways to break such future deadlocks. The answer they came up with was a cruel one: bombing civilians in cities, until they forced their governments to surrender. Deeply elitist, both fearful and contemptuous of their own nation's working classes, these strategists decided that proletarians were not made of such strong stuff as soldiers. Subjected to protracted assaults from the sky, they theorized, any populace would rise up and demand surrender.

The rapid development of aircraft made it practical to target population centers and test the theory on a grand, destructive scale. More important, from the viewpoint of generals who identified much more closely with their soldiers than with the civilians of either side, strategic bombing promised to spare their troops the grinding slaughter that soldiers had undergone in World War I—at the price of renouncing any scruple of sparing enemy noncombatants.

Most often, this strategy failed. Although most of Germany's victories were accomplished through close air support of combat troops on the ground, instead Hitler threw resources into strategic bombing—leveling cities like Rotterdam and Warsaw, and trying to force a British surrender by targeting its cities. The Allied bombing of Germany weakened but did not cripple German war production, which was mostly moved underground. Murray argues that Allied bombing helped shorten the war by a few months—chiefly by forcing the Germans to use their T-88 guns for antiaircraft instead of antitank warfare. Only in Japan did strategic bombings of cities induce the civilian authority, the emperor, to overrule his generals and surrender. In every other country, Carr documents, civilian morale was left intact or even strengthened by foreign attacks against noncombatants.

The Christian tradition, developed over centuries and through uncounted experiences of slaughter and suffering, and the later philosophy of the Enlightenment taught that civilians must never be justifiably attacked as

13

primary targets. Nor can cities be bombed indiscriminately, either to break the fighting spirit of their inhabitants or to pummel an enemy's infrastructure into oblivion. Applying this standard means that if we wish to hold the Nazis and the Japanese responsible for their vastly greater, more vicious and willful crimes against noncombatants, we must also address the Allied bombing campaigns conducted during the war—air assaults that one of their chief authors, General Curtis LeMay, admitted to his subordinate Robert McNamara, "would get us tried as war criminals if we lost."

Let us remind ourselves what such bombings entailed:

On February 14, 1945, Shrove Tuesday, as the children and parents of Dresden returned in their carnival costumes from the last festival before Lent, British bombers descended upon a city of no military significance, crowded with tens of thousands of civilian refugees who'd fled the onslaught of Russian armies to the east. (Those Russian armies, to avenge the real atrocities committed by the Germans, routinely raped and killed German women in the thousands as they conquered. Our air campaign was meant to speed their advance, ironically—thus ceding to Soviet control larger swathes of postwar Germany.) Using incendiary bombs that ignited thousands of wooden buildings before sucking out oxygen to asphyxiate any survivors, the Anglo-American air forces created a self-sustaining "firestorm" that pulled people into the blaze. In two days, as many as 27,000 people, nearly all of them unarmed civilians, were killed in Dresden—a small portion of the 400,000 noncombatants who died during Allied bombings of Germany. Ash Wednesday dawned on a city of cinders.

By August 1945, with most of its major cities already in ashes from Allied firebombing, Imperial Japan was militarily helpless to do anything but resist a ground invasion of its home islands. Its fleet had been sunk, its air force shot from the sky, its armies evicted from their vast conquests. A nation that could not feed itself was cut off from all trade and entirely surrounded by enemies. American strategists, still smarting from the furious struggle of doomed Japanese on Okinawa, warned of the cost in American soldiers—some put estimates in the high six figures—should the Allies attempt to take the islands. Others wondered if such an invasion was even necessary, since their foe had neither fuel nor food. Still others—perhaps those with the ear of President Truman—thought it wise to showcase the new American weapon, developed at such great cost and in utter secrecy, to send a warning shot to a grasping, ambitious Stalin.

On August 6, 1945, a lone American plane entered the skies over Hiroshima—an industrial town of small military worth—and exploded a single bomb named "Little Boy" at a height of 2,000 feet. The atomic blast that resulted killed some 80,000 people almost instantly and caused the deaths of some 60,000 by radiation poisoning and other causes before year's end. Lingering illnesses would claim many more; according to the city of Hiroshima, the final death toll of the bombing was 237,062.

When the first bombing failed to provoke a Japanese surrender, a second was planned for August 9. After weather conditions forced pilots to avoid the initial target city of Kokura, another American plane descended on the ancient capital of Japanese Christianity, Nagasaki, and again dropped one bomb—this one named "Fat Man." The military targets in the town—major factories—were destroyed that day. So were 75,000 civilians; at least an equal number would die within the year.

Were such Allied air attacks war crimes? Before we decide that question, let us first be fair to the men who made the decisions to launch those attacks in a desperate attempt to end a war that had threatened their nations' existence.

The West was engaged in a total war, one launched by enemies that scoffed at "outmoded" standards of civilized behavior. One of the key factors that drove American leaders such as Roosevelt toward a confrontation with Japan was their real moral outrage at the sickening cruelty Japan practiced in China—routinely raping and slaughtering civilians by the thousands, using Chinese (and later, Allied) prisoners as targets for bayonet practice and as "guinea pigs" on whom to test viruses for biological warfare. The barbarism of Nazi conquests, accompanied by terror bombing, genocides, and the mass execution of hostages, proved a similar goad to our fitful alliance with an embattled and isolated Britain. Our media had not been nearly as zealous in publicizing Stalin's enormous crimes, which predated and exceeded Hitler's; they were covered up by sympathetic leftist journalists, and went nearly unmentioned once he was forced by Hitler's invasion to switch his alliance from Nazi Germany to the West. Some leftist professors and politicians to this day are still Gulag "revisionists." As scholar Paul Gottfried documents in *The Strange Death of Marxism*, in France any mention of communist crimes is treated as prima facie evidence of fascist or even Nazi sympathies.

Most sane observers of history admit that it was an absolute necessity to crush the Axis. As John Lukacs has argued, Nazism was fundamentally more dangerous to the West than communism, if only because the latter was so obviously impossible and insane. The abolition of private property, national independence, organized religion, and the state, and all the other delusions that Marx foisted on intellectuals around the world—none of these could long have stood the reality test. The gap between communist promises and

Soviet reality could only ever have widened over time, leaving a regime as empty and discredited as Brezhnev's sputtering state.

The anti-utopia promised by the Nazis, on the other hand, really was feasible. A dominant "race" really could have enslaved and exploited other peoples on a vast scale, just as Hitler had promised. Whole peoples could have been exterminated, as the Armenians, the Jews, and the Roma ("Gypsies") nearly were. Hitler, who organized the murder of at least 20,946,000 civilians[1] in the course of losing the war, had explicit plans to double or triple that number if he had won.[2] Entire nations could have been consigned to slavery for centuries. The Mongols managed it. So did the Arabs and the Ottomans. Hitler's "promises" were indeed possible, and his degraded ethics were all too well suited to modern man.

With these atrocities in mind, we can begin to understand why Allied leaders insisted on unconditional surrender—a policy that prolonged the war into 1945, by far its bloodiest year, and guaranteed that the Axis governments would resist to their last iota of strength—arming twelve-year-old boys in Germany with rifles they couldn't lift, and preparing old men and peasant mothers in Japan to fight with rocks and sticks. Our two most dangerous enemies fought to the bitter end before submitting. It took five days after the second atomic bomb for the Japanese at last to accept surrender.

It is true that Americans were subject, as all men are subject, to the blind ferocity of war, and tempted to answer enemy ruthlessness tit-for-tat. Niall Ferguson, in *The War of the World*, documents the fact that frequently Allied soldiers simply shot German or Japanese soldiers attempting to surrender. Other soldiers collected the severed ears, or boiled skulls, of their enemies; a chilling photo in Ferguson's book shows a wartime photo of an American girl reading her soldier boyfriend's letter from the front, perched beside the "Jap skull" he proudly sent her. Such ugly facts, along with the savagery of our bombing campaigns, led the great Catholic philosopher Elizabeth Anscombe to describe the insistence on unconditional surrender, instead of a

---

1 "Democide" scholar R. J. Rummel's estimate of the most likely death toll, in *Death by Government* (Brunswick, NJ: Transaction Publishers, 1994), 111.

2 As Timothy Snyder documents in *Bloodlands* (New York: Basic Books, 2012), the Nazi policy for expansion to the Urals, made explicit in its "Generalplan Ost," included the direct killing or forced starvation of tens of millions of Slavs, and the forced expulsion of even more millions to uncertain fates beyond the Urals. Jews, while the first and most helpless of Nazi victims, were far from the only racial groups they targeted in their quest for a vast, continental empire.

negotiated peace with the Axis governments, as "visibly wicked" and driven by "villainous hatred."

But that is unfair, for several important reasons. The atrocities committed by the German and Japanese regimes against civilians outside the course of combat had genuinely shocked and disgusted the leaders of Great Britain and America. The vicious irrationalism espoused by the leaders of both enemy countries, the proudly Machiavellian dishonesty of their diplomacy leading up to the war, the blatant immorality of their war aims—all these factors made it unthinkable for Allied leaders to negotiate with the existing governments of Germany or Japan and work out peace arrangements that would leave those nations' ruling elites in power. Neither the Germans nor the Japanese had shown the slightest inclination to bargain in good faith or to respect the rights of the peoples they had conquered. Why should the nations they had tried and failed to conquer offer them any quarter? A negotiated peace, it should be obvious, would have made trials such as were held at Nuremberg impossible. Indeed, any truce that avoided Allied occupation would have permitted the guilty powers to erase most of the evidence of their war crimes.

But the starkest goad that drove the Allies to demand unconditional surrender in World War II was the vivid memory of how World War I had ended. At the moment the Kaiser's government gave up the fight on November 11, 1918, not a single foreign soldier stood on German soil; in fact, German armies still held large swathes of Belgium and France in the west and vast chunks of former Russian territory that had been captured during the war. The harshly punitive victors' peace imposed on Germany, which helped guarantee future conflicts over territory and reparations, could be blamed on the Social Democratic politicians who had come to power just in time to sign the one-sided Treaty of Versailles. What is more, the German military that had lost the war could foster the myth that Germany had been "stabbed in the back" on the verge of final victory. That blatantly baseless narrative was deliberately fostered by German officers after the war—for instance, by hiring propagandists to spread it among the ranks of unemployed army veterans. One of the most gifted speakers they employed was a failed Austrian art student named Adolf Hitler.

Allied leaders were not about to make that same mistake again. They could not negotiate a peace while German armies still held France and other conquered nations and still operated extermination camps such as Auschwitz—a peace that would leave in power some slightly watered-down version of Nazi militarism, which might in ten or twenty years be denounced

17

as yet another "stab in the back." Germany would have to be conquered, occupied, and purged. So would the murderous, almost psychotically militaristic Japan. It is impossible to blame Franklin Roosevelt, Harry Truman, or Winston Churchill for insisting on this point. Anything less would have amounted to masochistic appeasement.

Could we have used the atomic weapons we had developed in a less inhuman way, one that better respected Western moral norms—for instance, by preparing for an invasion of Japan and "telegraphing" where it would occur, then using our atomic bombs primarily on Japanese soldiers instead of civilians? This is not an alternative history book, nor are we qualified to play armchair general at the safe distance of seventy years. But we are forced by the plain implications of the moral norms that let us condemn the Axis slaughter of civilians to say that the massive bombings used by the Allies were also immoral. Limiting civilian casualties should have been at least one of the factors in choosing bomb targets, yet there is little evidence that Allied leaders even worried about the ethics of liquidating enemy citizens from the air; indeed, it appears that on this point the Allies permitted their enemies to drag them down to their level. It was a level, of course, that Stalin had reached long before.

This moral slide into subhumanism on the part of the only powerful countries on earth with a moral compass had real and lasting consequences. Because we had ended the war with Japan by using atomic weapons on cities, and thereby saved hundreds of thousands of Allied soldiers' lives, we adopted Hiroshima and Nagasaki's fate as a model for future wars. When the Soviet Union continued its military buildup even after the war was over and savagely imposed totalitarian governments on Eastern Europe, we relied for defense on our air superiority—particularly our greater supply of atomic weapons. Rather than try to match the ever-increasing Soviet advantage in conventional forces, we let it be known that we would meet any Russian attack on Western Europe with massive nuclear attacks on Russian cities—which would, we knew, be met by almost equal attacks on the United States and Western Europe. We adopted a "first-use" policy and held to it through most of the Cold War; we developed ever larger and more devastating bombs, and trembled when the Soviets did the same. Every "small" conflict, from Korea to Cuba, thereby became a crisis in which our leaders had to weigh the option of mutual extermination. As we have learned, there were several occasions when miscommunication, or weakness and folly followed by bluster, brought the world within a hair's breadth of launching such a war of human extinction. It was luck, or perhaps Providence, that kept us from the brink long enough for the Soviet system to undergo its unavoidable economic implosion—an outcome predicted as early as 1920 by Ludwig von Mises.

Our acceptance of the "doctrine" of mutually assured destruction also coarsened us morally. Then-Monsignor Fulton J. Sheen expressed this insight in a 1974 talk that, tellingly, was never broadcast in the United States:

> When, I wonder, did we in America ever get into this idea that freedom means having no boundaries and no limits? You know I think it began on the sixth of August 1945 at 8:15 am when we dropped the bomb on Hiroshima. That blotted out boundaries. The boundary of America that was the aid of nations, and the nations that were helped. It blotted out the boundary between life and death for the victims of nuclear incineration. Among them even the living were dead. It blotted out the boundary between the civilian and the military. And somehow or other, from that day on in our American life, we say we want no limits and no boundaries.[3]

It is significant that Sheen made these remarks not long after the decision in *Roe v. Wade* removed any boundaries to what Americans could do to the innocent in the womb, in defense of their own notion of freedom. But Sheen had taken a similar stand much earlier, in the immediate wake of the bombings and the jubilation of peace. As the *Bulletin of Atomic Scientists* reported in May 1946:

> Msgr. Fulton J. Sheen of Catholic University in a sermon on April 7 in St. Patrick's Cathedral in New York scored our use of the bomb on Hiroshima as an act contrary to the moral law and said, "We have invited retaliation for that particular form of violence." Both obliteration bombing and use of the atomic bomb are immoral, Msgr. Sheen said, because "they do away with the moral distinction that must be made in every war—a distinction between civilians and the military." . . .
> Discussing arguments that use of the atomic bomb shortened the war and saved the lives of American fighting men, Msgr. Sheen declared: "That was precisely the argument Hitler used in bombing Holland."[4]

---

3 Quoted by Zac Alstin in "What Did Sheen Know?" *Bioethics Research Notes*, Vol. 22, no. 4, 59.
4 Ibid., 59–60.

A decent regard for civilian lives does not imply that we should be willing to sacrifice indefinite numbers of our soldiers to avoid any innocent deaths. Commanders must balance their first concern—winning the war, with minimal losses—against the solemn duty to spare civilians wherever possible. We can never target civilians directly or intentionally, nor totally disregard the cost in civilian lives of a military victory. To do so is to let our enemies' worst instincts infect our own morality—with consequences that may well outlive the peace, as Sheen observed. Our conduct of World War II was not determined entirely by the desire to spare our soldiers' lives. Had that been our main concern, we could have refused to invade Continental Europe at all, and spared our men such slaughters as happened at Anzio and Normandy—leaving the conquest of Hitler to Stalin's advancing armies. Our leaders knew that a communist-occupied Western Europe was not in America's interest, and so were willing to spend the lives of hundreds of thousands of men to avoid it. Restricting our use of massive urban bombing in the war would also have cost soldiers' lives. Our statesmen could have decided that such a grim sacrifice was worthwhile, to avoid the degrading moral effects of fighting ruthlessly against civilian populations.

Broadcasting our willingness to obliterate enemy civilians in the course of self-defense would become an ugly necessity during the Cold War. But its legacy continued well beyond the removal of the Soviet Union and China as likely adversaries. We and those countries still target each other's cities with massive nuclear weapons to this day.

In the wake of the attacks on September 11, 2001, editors at the leading conservative publication *National Review Online* famously mused about whether we ought to "nuke Mecca." Conservative journalists would not, we think, have quipped back and forth about whether to level every building, gas all the schoolchildren, and incinerate all the old people and women of Mecca. But the quick, decisive nature of a nuclear attack helps us ignore the blood-soaked realities. We can skip over the details of the slaughter, which we neatly hide in two bumper-sticker syllables: "Nuke 'em!"

A similar callousness can accompany our use of other, less obviously indiscriminate technologies designed to spare our soldiers, if need be at the cost of enemy civilians, such as pilotless drones directed by computer algorithms to target regions where terrorists are suspected of hiding, and then to incinerate any group of men of military age, with no further evidence of terrorist guilt needed. As our citizens increasingly spurn the sacrifices of military service, while hoping to retain the advantages of inhabiting a military superpower, we can only expect that the impetus will increase for America to use pilotless machines of death against its enemies, further insulating us from the consequences of our actions. Conscience is a muscle. You use it or lose it.

One answer to modern, subhumanist ruthlessness is an attractive but toxic temptation: radical pacifism. It has the same clean, simple logic, and it offers a subtler opening for asserting the will to power—via the service entrance. Pacifism affords its adherents the privilege of looking down on the actions of every man and woman throughout the whole of human history and on the instincts of every human being who has ever lived. There is no drive more rootedly human than the will to preserve yourself and to protect your loved ones, but this is an instinct pacifism condemns, either openly or secretly. Any position that asks that you passively watch your spouse or children be raped, enslaved, or killed is intrinsically antihuman. (Inconsistent pacifists, who would protect themselves and their families, but won't take part in protecting their neighbors and fellow citizens, are simply and radically selfish.) Pacifism can also slide into subhumanism, since it devalues the lives and liberty of every human being, which are simply not worth fighting for.

The wholesome and healthy impulse of self-preservation can be perverted, of course, if it is not tempered by solidarity and a keen sense of the intrinsic moral worth of strangers. But anyone who condemns the self-protective drive in itself is saying that human nature is intrinsically perverse and fundamentally evil—the product of a depraved or incompetent god (as the ancient Gnostics taught), or the ugly outcome of unfortunate evolution. Perhaps we inherited too many genes from those killer chimps.

Such a person, whether or not he knows it, is also feeding into the worst and most warlike impulses in the tangled-up human heart. How so? The obvious part of the answer is that when the leadership classes in free countries like England declare—as the Oxford Union did in 1933—that they "will not fight for king and country," they are sending a clear message to the leaders of other countries, such as the Germany that had just welcomed Hitler as its chancellor. Their message of war-weariness, cynicism, and self-congratulation was not lost on those millions of Germans who were outraged by the unfairness of the Treaty of Versailles, whose takeaway from World War I was not "never again," but "next time we won't be such sentimental milksops."

The less obvious and more important part of the answer can be found in Elizabeth Anscombe's classic essay, "War and Murder," in which she demolished the biblical and the philosophical case for pacifism. But more importantly, she points out how it enables and advances the cause of total war. As she wrote:

Now pacifism teaches people to make no distinction between the shedding of innocent blood and the shedding of any human blood. And in this way pacifism has corrupted enormous numbers of people who will not act according to its tenets. They become convinced that a number of things are wicked which are not; hence seeing no way of avoiding wickedness, they set no limits to it. How endlessly pacifists argue that all war must be *a outrance*! that those who wage war must go as far as technological advance permits in the destruction of the enemy's people. . . .

Pacifism and the respect for pacifism is not the only thing that has led to a universal forgetfulness of the law against killing the innocent; but it has had a share in it.[5]

Pacifism presents people with a choice between absolute, utter ruthlessness, and passivity and surrender. With no other alternative, healthy people will pick ruthlessness every time. But this is an utterly false choice, one that emerges because our morality has been blunted and dulled by our bad metaphysics.

In *To End All Wars*, the gifted writer and moralist Adam Hochschild presents a vivid and deeply humane portrait of a small band of principled people in England who spoke out against World War I. It's impossible not to admire these men and women who braved contempt and ostracism, poverty and prison, to oppose that useless and futile slaughter. Apart from moral uplift, however, another thing one takes away from their story is the sense that their efforts were also futile. And you are led to wonder why. With Anscombe's remarks in mind, the answer emerges: Instead of making a principled case that this war was needless and wasteful, and offering reasons that drew on the shared, Christian/liberal consensus, these activists urged against the war on grounds of absolute pacifism. In some cases they also invoked socialism, arguing that the working class of every nation ought to unite against their rulers, not fight among themselves. Grounded as their actions were on two false (and more important, unpersuasive) premises, it is no surprise that their slogans were easily drowned out by patriotism that was morphing into jingoism and bloodlust.

What might have been more effective was a concerted effort by Christians and conservatives on both sides of the conflict to argue that *this*

---

5 Elizabeth Anscombe, "War and Murder," reprinted in *Absolutism and Its Consequentialist Critics*, ed., Joram Graf Haber (Lanham, MD: Rowman and Littlefield, 1994), 36–37.

war was neither just nor necessary. A few such voices emerged, but too few to matter. Pope Benedict XV made just such arguments, but he was ignored. The troops on both sides who forged a spontaneous "Christmas truce" in 1914 were acting in the same spirit. They were threatened with punishment for "mutiny" by military leaders who still imagined that a quick victory was possible. The newly crowned Austro-Hungarian ruler Karl I attempted in 1917 to broker a peace without annexation, even as his German allies schemed to infect Russia with the plague bacillus of Bolshevism. But by that point the combatant nations were too far gone—they had spent too much wealth and too many lives to settle for anything less than triumph. The very type of men who should have been fighting for a negotiated peace had gotten caught up in the frenzy: G. K. Chesterton and Hilaire Belloc on the one side and Thomas Mann on the other each proclaimed this war a "crusade" for civilization. The poet Charles Péguy had joined the army and died in one of its first battles. The American Catholic bishops, eager to prove their patriotism, flouted the Vatican's call for peace and urged their congregants to enlist. And so on. The complicity of Christians in furthering this war of unprecedented destruction and futility did more to discredit the churches in the long run than any atheist tract ever published. As Hochschild reported:

> Ferocity about the war could be heard everywhere. "Kill Germans! Kill them!" raged one clergyman in a 1915 sermon. ". . . Not for the sake of killing, but to save the world. . . . Kill the good as well as the bad. . . . Kill the young men as well as the old. . . . Kill those who have shown kindness to our wounded as well as those fiends who crucified the Canadian sergeant [a story then circulating]. . . . I look upon it as a war for purity. I look upon everybody who dies in it as a martyr." The speaker was Arthur Winnington-Ingram, the Anglican bishop of London.[6]

We would be shocked today to hear such sentiments coming from any clergyman. Pacifism has displaced militarism as the bad idea of choice among many prominent Christians. But today our military policies are much less influenced by even residual Christianity than they were in 1915, and we are still tempted to adopt a callous disregard for the lives of civilians among our enemies. How much discussion is there among Americans of

---

6 Hochschild, 151.

the 123,989[7] noncombatant deaths that occurred in our war in Iraq? How seriously do Americans take the growing civilian casualties of the decade-long drone campaign we are stilling conducting against Islamic terrorists? When our pundits demand that we confront the aggressive actions of this or that dictator, how often does anyone trouble to point out the huge civilian death toll that would accompany any military intervention to preserve the West's prestige and assert its influence? These must be weighed in the balance against the uncertain benefits of our proposed interventions. Until and unless civilian deaths take center stage in our discussions of prospective wars, we will go on making the callous decisions inspired by militarism. Unless the leaders of nuclear-armed states take seriously the duty to dismantle strategic weapons aimed at civilians, we will go on living under the shadow of the twentieth century's darkest discovery, total war.

For Further Reading:

Elizabeth Anscombe, "War and Murder," reprinted in *Absolutism and Its Consequentialist Critics*, ed., Joram Graf Haber (Lanham, MD: Rowman and Littlefield, 1994).

Patrick J. Buchanan, *Churchill, Hitler, and the Unnecessary War* (New York: Three Rivers Press, 2009).

Caleb Carr, *The Lessons of Terror* (New York: Random House, 2002).

Niall Ferguson, *The War of the World* (New York: Penguin, 2007).

Paul Glynn, *A Song for Nagasaki* (San Francisco: Ignatius Press, 2009).

John Hersey, *Hiroshima* (New York: Vintage, 1989).

Adam Hochschild, *To End All Wars* (New York: Houghton Mifflin Harcourt, 2011).

Williamson Murray, *Strategy for Defeat: The Luftwaffe, 1933–1945* (Dulles, VA: Brassey's, 1996).

Timothy Snyder, *Bloodlands* (New York: Basic Books, 2012).

Craig M. White, *Iraq: The Moral Reckoning* (Lanham, MD: Rowman & Littlefield, 2010).

---

7 The low estimate given by Iraqbodycount.org, which offers a maximum count of 138,125.

Chapter Three

Racism and Nationalism

In one sense, racism and nationalism are as old as the human family. Empathy is a challenge for each of us, and we spontaneously feel it more intensely and automatically toward those who are closely related to us— first, our close relatives, then those who look and talk most like us. Insofar as racial and ethnic groups can be experienced as a vast, extended family, outsiders are sometimes easier to exclude from the circle of empathy. Some American Indian tribes refer to their members as "humans," using other epithets for nonmembers; Greeks scorned "barbarians" (non-Greeks) as much for their odd appearance as their uncouth-sounding speech and alien customs. We could multiply such examples of spontaneous xenophobia by looking at cultures on every continent and in every century.

Of course, modern biology shows us that by any definition, human beings are a single family, with roughly comparable qualities and a fixed, common nature. Just a few morally insignificant biological adaptations separate black from white from brown, and every human being who walks the earth is descended from common parents—as the Book of Genesis tells us. The truth of human brotherhood, which the Christian Church asserted dogmatically in the wake of Europe's discovery of America, was widely disseminated and authoritatively taught for hundreds of years from pulpits and podiums alike. It was vindicated by the fact that non-Europeans from "primitive" lands proved quite capable of learning European languages and absorbing its highest culture—as Europeans could learn from the ancient civilizations of India and China.

But this common knowledge of human equality cuts against the grain of our inborn narcissism, and it was almost lost in the course of the nineteenth and twentieth centuries in the most educated countries on earth—to be replaced in the minds of millions by a much more primitive, atavistic denial of the humanity of the Other. The most extreme and appalling instance of neotribalism, which is so widely known that it hardly requires elaboration, took place in Nazi Germany, where political ideologues invented a new, brutal religion to serve the invented god of race, and crafted an elaborate pseudoscientific theory that scapegoated Jews for every social problem and for the crises facing Germany.

25

However modern, "scientific" racist theory did not begin in Germany, but in England. Nor were its proponents content with asserting a hierarchy of the races. Science since Descartes had been redefined as a practical venture, aimed at increasing human mastery over nature. So any racial science worthy of the name must have a pragmatic action agenda. And modern racism did, in the form of eugenics.

This discipline began with the man who named it—Francis Galton, cousin and early disciple of Charles Darwin. The first book of scientific eugenics was Galton's *Hereditary Genius,* published in 1869. Drawing careless inferences from the work of his more rigorous relative, Galton theorized that the process of natural selection could be speeded up and made less painful (fewer "unfit" would be born and need to die off) by "scientific management" of the human breeding stock. Here, science was pressed into the service of upper-class prejudice, and soon academic conferences in Britain, Germany, and the United States were being convened to explore how the human race could be better bred on the model of pedigree cattle. Academic chairs of eugenics were established at first-rate research sites like the Kaiser Wilhelm Institute and (in the United States) at the Eugenics Records office, hosted from 1910 to 1940 at the Cold Spring Harbor Laboratory, and lawmakers took note of the burgeoning "consensus" among scientists. In cold fact, the science underpinning the whole eugenic enterprise was careless, hopelessly biased to reproduce the prejudices of the researchers, and wholly insufficient to support such a radical enterprise as remaking the human race.

By the 1920s, with the support of Margaret Sanger's Planned Parenthood and funding from health crank and cereal magnate Harvey Kellogg, more than a dozen U.S. states had enacted laws requiring the sterilization of "idiots" and "imbeciles," which in practice meant that American citizens were castrated for failing an I.Q. test.

In 1934, Sanger sought to take advantage of the New Deal's push to regulate ever more aspects of American economic and social life, to obtain passage of a "baby code" that would restrict parenthood to those who could obtain a one-time, renewable "parenthood license." She laid out her proposal for social control in the *American Weekly*:

Article 1. The purpose of the American Baby Code shall be to provide for a better distribution of babies, to assist couples who wish to prevent overproduction of offspring and thus to reduce the burdens of charity and taxation for public relief, and to protect society against the propagation and increase of the unfit. . . .

Article 2. Birth control clinics shall be permitted to function as services of city, county, or state health departments, or under the support of charity, or as non-profit self-sustaining agencies, subject to inspection and control by public authorities. . . .

Article 3. A marriage license shall in itself give husband and wife only the right to a common household and not the right to parenthood.

Article 4. No woman shall have the legal right to bear a child, and no man shall have the right to become a father, without a permit for parenthood.

Article 5. Permits for parenthood shall be issued upon application by city, county, or state authorities to married couples, providing they are financially able to support the expected child, have the qualifications needed for proper rearing of the child, have no transmissible diseases, and, on the woman's part, no medical indication that maternity is likely to result in death or permanent injury to health.

Article 6. No permit for parenthood shall be valid for more than one birth.

Article 7. Every country shall be assisted administratively by the state in the effort to maintain a direct ratio between the county birth rate and its index of child welfare. Whenever the county records for any given year show an unfavorable variation from this ratio the county concerned shall be taxed by the state according to the degree of the variation. The revenues thus obtained shall be expended by the state within the given county either in giving financial support to birth control clinics or in other ways calculated to improve the situation involved.

Article 8. Feeble-minded persons, habitual congenital criminals, those afflicted with inheritable disease, and others found biologically unfit by authorities qualified judge should be sterilized or, in cases of doubt, should be so isolated as to prevent the perpetuation of their afflictions by breeding.[1]

---

1 Margaret Sanger, "America Needs a Code for Babies," March 27, 1934, archived in the Public Writings and Speeches of Margaret Sanger, http://www.nyu.edu/projects/sanger/webedition/app/documents/show.php?sangerDoc=101807.xml.

The rise of eugenic pseudoscience in America was aided by the widespread acceptance of racist institutions throughout the country—the systematic segregation and political disenfranchisement of African Americans, the confinement of Indian tribes to reservations, the explicitly racist bans on Asian immigration into America, and the implicitly racist provisions of other immigration laws designed to maintain a "Nordic" majority in America. Eugenics had quite a future in the land of the free. It may only have been the savage extremes to which this doctrine would be taken in war-ravaged Europe that prevented a much more extensive and horrifying application of eugenic principles in the United States.

With the 1933 Nazi takeover in Germany, the most literate country in human history was remade to fit a murderous "science of race." With very few exceptions, as John Cornwell's grim study *Hitler's Scientists* documents, the scientific establishment fell in line with the new political creed. Nazi authorities pointed to American laws as models for their own, unspeakably more aggressive racial regime, a full decade before the Final Solution was even decided upon. Although the defeat of the Nazi regime helped to expose and discredit scientific racism, eugenic ideas persisted in America for decades, and the last compulsory sterilization law was not repealed until 1974, in Virginia.

Why was a false and arbitrary scientific theory able to survive and spread for decades? How did "civilized" nations justify liquidating not only conquered foreigners, but their own citizens, based on hazy, poorly defined, and empirically falsifiable claims of fundamental racial differences between groups as closely related (for instance) as Slavs and Germans? How could Nazis march into Polish cities full of baroque architecture, with medieval universities that had housed Poles such as Copernicus, and convince themselves that they were subjugating "primitive subhumans"? How could millions of people who had been educated on Kant and Schiller adopt the bizarre Nazi theory that Jews were biologically driven to tear down "Aryan" cultures? Or that Jews could be blamed for both finance capitalism and international communism? The political brilliance of the Nazis belies any attempt to dismiss them as stupid or foolish. It took political philosopher Peter Viereck some six hundred pages in his masterwork *Metapolitics* to explore the deep, branching roots of Nazi ideology in misguided romanticism and perverted science. And his reflections do not even attempt to explain the popularity of eugenics outside of Germany.

The rise of eugenic racism was offered its best provisional explanation by a thinker we will consider later in greater depth—the social philosopher and economist Wilhelm Röpke (see Chapter Eleven). A brilliant analyst of technical economics trained in the Austrian School by his mentor Ludwig von Mises, Röpke surpassed his colleagues in his depth of social analysis and understanding of history. In *The Social Crisis of Our Time*, Röpke explains that all of Europe had been rendered vulnerable to radical ideologies by the sudden and unsettling social changes imposed by rapidly growing industry and technology. Men whose families might have worked in the same trade for centuries in the same historic village with the same churches where their ancestors had been baptized, married, and buried were suddenly uprooted by complex economic forces and driven by the falling price of crops and rising industrial wages to move to vast, anonymous cities. In Germany, where the Industrial Revolution was delayed until the mid- or late-nineteenth century, the wounds from all these changes were still fresh.

There men and women were starkly cut off from the networks that had linked them to their neighbors in patterns of solidarity and cooperation, and that helped resolve their conflicts peaceably. As the schools they attended were secularized, their links with the faiths of their fathers were slowly eroded, and they were soon reduced to solitary individuals facing the consequences of choices made by wealthy investors or faraway consumers. Unable to control their economic or even geographic destinies, such men looked for new ways to find friends and allies, new sources of identity, and new ways to advance or defend their interests. Cut off from their ancestral villages, extended families, churches, and other social networks, these "proletarianized" workers had only two lively choices: the rapidly growing web of socialist labor unions, clubs, and political parties, or the radical nationalists, their more militaristic competitors.

Put simply, men were offered the choice of forging a new sense of self and belonging according to class or according to race. To put a face on the forces that held them back and frustrated them, they could designate as enemies either their landlords and employers, or the menacing foreigners in neighboring countries and untrustworthy "aliens" who lived in their midst. The particular evil genius of National Socialism, as Röpke noted, was that it combined the most potent negative elements of both movements in the figure of the grasping, alien, capitalistic Jew—who secretly, they asserted, worked to bring about a Red dictatorship. (This case was easier to make because of the early prominence of Jews in many communist movements and regimes— from which they were later purged, as happened in Stalin's Terror, and again in postwar Poland and Hungary.)

But we cannot blame Adolf Hitler for the vast majority of the race-based slaughters the past century had to witness. R. J. Rummel, the great statistician of "democide," documents in *Death by Government* some 133.1 million intentional killings of civilians by governments in the twentieth century. It is probably impossible to sort out how many of the 61.9 million killed in the Soviet Union were singled out for extermination because they belonged to ethnic groups considered "suspect" by Stalin. (As Niall Ferguson shows in *The War of the World*, the Soviet regime was engaged in the murderous mass removal of ethnic groups such as Poles and Ukrainians a full decade before the Nazi regime opened its first concentration camp.) But mass murders in which ethnic differences were decisive included the Japanese butchery of some 5.9 million Chinese, the Turkish killing of almost 1.9 million Armenians, and Pakistan's murder of 1.5 million residents of what is now Bangladesh during that country's war of independence. Lesser but still appalling totals were racked up in Rwanda, in Sri Lanka, and in the bloodthirsty, three-way war among Serbs, Croats, and Bosnians during the 1990s, which featured the revival of an age-old tactic of racial revenge that also marked the Soviet conquest of Nazi Germany: organized rape. The conflict between the government of Sri Lanka and the minority Tamil Tigers claimed some 100,000, mostly civilian, lives—and also produced the innovative terrorist technique of suicide bombing.

Ethnic cleansing and intra-ethnic warfare continue to this day. Even as the West agonized about the slaughters in the Balkans, an organized program of genocide was being carried out in Africa in the full view of the world—which took little notice:

> The Nuba peoples of the central Sudanese region of South Kordofan were faced with complete annihilation by a genocidal campaign waged by the Government of Sudan from 1985 until roughly 1993, although the violence persisted until a ceasefire was agreed upon in January 2002. The conflict was more or less resolved as part of the January 2005 Comprehensive Peace Agreement that settled the long-standing North-South Civil War. Indeed, genocide in the Nuba Mountains was committed in the context of this war, as the (Northern) Government of Sudan's brutal counterinsurgency campaign against the (Southern) Sudan People's Liberation Army (SPLA) caught the Nuba peoples in the middle. The government aimed to depopulate the area and completely destroy all vestiges of Nuba society.[2]

---

2 Techshon Racine, Anthony Nath, and Jeff Benvenuto, "Anatomy of the Nuba Genocide," http://nubagenocide.webs.com/anatomyofthegenocide.htm.

Thousands of Nuba people still reside in refugee camps, and human rights observers fear that the next grave disorder in Sudan could result in a resumption of the genocide against them.[3]

The civil war in Syria, which has nearly destroyed urban life in that country and claimed up to 150,000 lives as of this writing, is fueled in part by the fear that a victorious Sunni majority dominated by jihadist elements might impose ethnic and religious cleansing.

If we look back at the massacres of previous centuries, we might begin to see the explosion of racist violence in the twentieth century less as a hideous innovation than as the resurgence of a profoundly human temptation. Our dark impulse to exclude and victimize the Other can only be kept at bay by consciously cultivating a sense of our common humanity.

It may be that what is unusual is not tribalism but its opposite: universalism, the acceptance of a human dignity uniting the whole human family. The effort of empathy is a costly one, and the task of reviving and reasserting the universal rights of man is one that falls to each generation in turn. It is made no easier when the leading sectors of society in the most powerful nations on earth are morally crippled by a subhumanist view of man, which undermines any argument for self-sacrifice and dissolves transcendent moral norms in the acid of relativism.

It may be true that white Westerners feel too guilty or socially constrained to express racial animus, but as Western societies become ever more diverse, that taboo is eroding. Xenophobic parties are growing in strength across Europe, in response to the reckless embrace by European elites of forced multiculturalism and unchecked mass immigration. Furthermore, the new groups migrating to Western lands are entirely free of white guilt, and bring their own bigotries with them. In the absence of a vital moral discourse that reinforces common humanity and human rights, there is no reason to expect these new residents to be magically immune to the historic human temptation of racial groupthink and violence. The violence that marks racial conflict between native-born African Americans and Mexican immigrants in cities like Los Angeles may offer a window into the broader, pan-Western future. What is more, it is clear that the lessons the West learned from the racist excesses of the twentieth century were woefully incomplete, amounting to little more than:

---

3 Eric Reeves, "Genocide in the Nuba Mountains," http://sudanreeves.org/2013/10/11/genocide-in-the-nuba-mountains-a-retrospective-on-what-we-knew-june-2011-2013/.

1. It is wrong for white people to discriminate against others.

2. It is wrong for European nations to conquer and colonize non-European nations.

3. Because Hitler used ethnic identity as a pretext for murdering people, Western nations must abandon any ethnic or historical basis for their identities—even nations that were conquered and terrorized by Hitler, such as Poland and Ukraine.

4. None of these lessons apply to non-Western nations or nonwhite people living in them.

Generals always blunder by planning for and refighting the last war. In the battle against racism, our culture certainly seems preoccupied with preventing such unlikely occurrences as the rise of National Socialism in Germany, while ignoring or excusing the real and lively threats to human dignity that are arising across the world, even in Europe. Watchdogs who track anti-Semitism in Europe focus much of their attention on tiny, contemptible fringe groups of nationalistic thugs instead of the groups that actually perpetrate most of the anti-Jewish violence across Europe—radicalized Muslims.

Indeed, if we use a more realistic definition of nationalism, we will find that Islamist movements today ought to be included in it. They constitute a grave and growing threat to the safety and liberty of hundreds of millions of people—including both non-Muslims and those Muslims who reject the revival of sharia law. Religious and ethnic identities often blend and fuse, particularly in the minds of persecutors. So it makes perfect sense to include the worldwide epidemic of religious persecution, most of it perpetrated by radical Muslims, under the heading of racism and nationalism. For these Muslims, there is only one nation: the House of Islam. Everything outside it is the House of War, which they are called to convert, or to conquer and control. Non-Muslims in such societies must either convert or accept a kind of Jim Crow status as inferior, humbled, third-class citizens (*dhimmis*) who are forbidden to take part in politics and expected to give way to Muslims in every sphere of life. This is the goal pursued by Islamists who target Christians in a long list of countries from Nigeria and Sudan to Pakistan, and treasured by radical Muslims who dream of breeding and bombing their way to power in England and France. Ancient Christian communities have already been ethnically cleansed from Iraq in the wake of the U.S. invasion, and Christians (among other religious minorities) fear that a similar fate faces them in Syria, should the al Qaeda–linked rebels in that country overcome its brutal, but religiously neutral, Ba'athist regime. Christians in Egypt face mounting violence as they are made the scapegoats of Islamist frustration in the wake of the military's crackdown on the Muslim Brotherhood.

We must admit to ourselves the ugly fact that Islamism is an ideology and that its hoped-for Caliphate is a virtual nation (like the Greater Germany Hitler dreamed of). Radical, nationalistic, anti-Semitic, and anti-Christian radicals number in the millions and seek to control whole countries through groups like the Muslim Brotherhood, which was only dislodged from Egypt in 2013 through a brutal military coup. Such groups' explicit agendas are both expansionist and totalitarian—openly calling for conquest, and for the domination of every sphere of life by their rigid ideology. Such groups are leading what journalist John L. Allen has called *The Global War on Christians*, although Hindus, Jews, Alawites, secular Muslims, and other would-be victims also number on their list. In certain ways and for certain groups, it really is 1933 all over again.

For Further Reading:

John Allen, *The Global War on Christians* (New York: Image, 2013).

Edwin Black, *The War Against the Weak* (Westport, CT: Dialog Press, 2010).

John Cornwell, *Hitler's Scientists* (New York: Penguin, 2004).

Paul Marshall et al., *Persecuted: The Global Assault on Christians* (Nashville, TN: Thomas Nelson, 2013).

Wilhelm Röpke, *The Social Crisis of Our Time* (New Brunswick, NJ: Transaction, 1991).

R. J. Rummel, *Death by Government* (New Brunswick, NJ: Transaction, 1997).

Peter Viereck, *Metapolitics* (New Brunswick, NJ: Transaction, 2003).

Chapter Four

Utopian Collectivism

It is easy for those of us who grew up during the Cold War to imagine that the impulse to reshape society by force and compel its members to follow a top-down, rationalist plan imposed by intellectuals was born with Karl Marx and died when the Berlin Wall fell. Our own experience of the radical violence that collectivism commits against human nature will always be connected with historical communism, which really did begin in the West in 1917 and largely end there in 1989. (This leaves aside, of course, hellish holdouts like North Korea and Cuba.) Historical communism was simply the most successful example of this abstract rage for order.

Certain ancient tyrannies foreshadowed modern totalitarianism. The governing class of Sparta sacrificed any trace of privacy or liberty; the Mongols committed genocides that would do a modern dictator proud. But we need not review the long, dark history of unjust societies that failed to respect what we now call human rights.

What proved uniquely powerful in the twentieth century was the merger of absolute, unaccountable power and utopian idealism. In Tsarist Russia, a creaky autocracy used bands of Cossacks to suppress dissent and repress its resident Jews, but this use of force was employed in defense of a deeply imperfect and uninspiring regime. The use of force was meant to keep the Romanovs in power—not to effect a fundamental transformation in human nature and usher in a secular messianic age. The very fact that the reactionaries' promises were so modest profoundly limited their appeal to intellectuals, and shrank the pool of talent on which the regime could draw. It is also harder for educated people to justify escalations of violence and disruption wielded in the name of stability and continuity, than comparable excesses conducted in the service of an "ideal." Intellectuals throughout the twentieth century have reflected this unconscious double standard, judging the crimes of monarchs and churchmen by a stern criterion of humanism, while cutting enormous slack to (or actively helping to obfuscate) the much greater violence committed in the name of "progress," "revolution," or "the people." To give just one truly egregious example: that heroic witness to the Gulag, Aleksandr Solzhenitsyn, saw his reputation tarnished almost irretrievably by some ambiguous remarks he made that (some said) favored a restored Russian monarchy in place of communism. At the very same universities where Solzhenitsyn was being flayed, thinkers held up for emulation included unrepentant Stalinists like Sartre and Western Maoists who defended the Cultural Revolution—while it was under way—such as Julia Kristeva and Michel Foucault. Thinkers who would rightly be repelled by the brutalities of a simple, self-serving dictator such as Francisco Franco saw their vision fog over when it came to the prisons of Fidel Castro or the murders ordered by Che Guevara. For a bitterly ironic testament to the gullibility of intellectuals when it comes to assessing the crimes committed along the road to utopia, see Paul Kengor's massively documented study *Dupes* and Paul Hollander's *Political Pilgrims*.

Enlightenment thinkers did a yeoman's job of exposing the brutality and will to power that can hide behind, or infiltrate and corrupt, religious zeal. Outside of Putin's Russia, where a church long battered by the state looks now for some recompense and support—albeit at the price of supporting a corrupt autocratic government—there are few places where Christians would ever envision employing coercive power to Christianize the state. Even at its high-water mark in the 1980s, the Christian Right in America sought only to restore moral norms that were shared by many nonbelievers and could be supported by secular, natural law arguments—norms such as respect for the life of the preborn and a traditional definition of marriage. There is no constituency anywhere in the West, outside of radical mosques, for state-imposed religion. And yet the discussion of church and state is conducted in liberal circles as if the Inquisition were camped out in church basements, preparing to torture "heretics."

But the will to power never sleeps. The urge to dominate one's fellow man and reshape him like clay to match some mental ideal is a strong one, especially for intellectuals. Frederic Bastiat pointed to this impulse in classical thinkers, especially Plato. It is probably true that the rise of Christianity, with its tantalizing hints of a "New Jerusalem" on earth, encouraged the tendency of the truly oppressed (and the merely ambitious) to imagine a perfected world, to be achieved through the force of arms. Millenarian movements that emerged throughout the Middle Ages and erupted with enormous force in the Reformation bear witness to the recurrent, addictive attractions of utopia. The cruel attempts at social engineering undertaken by French revolutionaries prove that religious faith need not play a part in any such schemes; the loss of faith serves only to remove the last few scruples once imposed by Christian morality. Without a belief in the afterlife, and its promise of all tears wiped away and original justice restored, secularized utopias are more prone to frenzied, desperate efforts to force their success in this, the only go-round that any of us will get.

It requires an imaginative effort to reach back behind the rusted, blood-spattered hulk that Marxism became wherever it was put into practice and see how for millions of people it was a real and vital faith—for which they were willing to work for decades secretly or openly organizing, to conspire in backrooms, to betray their countries as spies, to kill for and to die for as terrorists. To understand all is not to forgive all, but it does play a vital role in defusing and redirecting such dangerous zeal. It is worthwhile for today's social reformers to make the effort of empathy with these political soldiers by delving into some of the greatest works that chronicle how utopian collectivism reshapes the human soul.

Man's Fate (1933), by the French novelist André Malraux, shows Chinese communists enduring horrific suffering at the hands of corrupt, oppressive warlords in the 1930s. In their shared struggles and even in the crimes they jointly commit, they forge a passionate connection to each other, a sense of profound purpose and belonging that perversely replicates the bond that linked the Apostles after Pentecost. With bracing honesty, Malraux explores the spiritual effects on underground communists of involvement in acts of assassination and terror, committed on the orders of revolutionary leaders in the service of the distant, gleaming prospect of a transfigured human world. These figures steel themselves to acts of ruthless violence, and some are themselves remade into "new men"—but not the new men promised by Marx in his wistful fantasy of mankind freed from necessity to become a race of happy dilettantes. No, these revolutionaries made of themselves what so many Russian dissenters became after moving in nihilist circles and schooling each other in the tsar's lax prisons and exile camps: doctrinaire, cold, and loveless, an unnatural hybrid of mystic and inquisitor, of the sort Dostoevsky had warned against in *The Possessed*. (For a much fuller exploration of the psychology of revolutionary terrorists, see Joseph Conrad's *The Secret Agent* and Michael Burleigh's magisterial study *Blood and Rage: A Cultural History of Terrorism*.)

In the martyrdom that some of them embrace, these revolutionaries attempt their own redemption, becoming their own Christ-figures, selflessly winning for future generations a paradise on earth. Or so they convinced themselves. This passionate work was written by Malraux while he still believed in the Marxist vision, and so it offers a unique window (of real literary value) into the soul of the true believer. Its author later became the most respected literary supporter of the great conservative statesman Charles de Gaulle.

Witness (1952), by Whittaker Chambers, is a spiritual memoir by the former spy for Stalinist Russia who later testified against his fellow communists, exposing a ring that had infiltrated the highest echelons of the U.S. government before World War II. It potently shows the shape of the void in the soul that utopian faith can flood in to fill. Raised a conventional Christian in a family scarred by economic failure and his parents' loveless marriage, Chambers benefited from the impressive social mobility offered in America—leaving his bankrupt parents to join the best and brightest at Columbia University. It was there that he encountered among his teachers and fellow students the blasé dismissal of Christian claims that even today exerts such a strong pressure on poorly formed young believers. Unable to defend his patchy, inherited faith, but still possessed of a youthful idealism, Chambers searched for an alternative worldview that would comprehensively answer the riddle of human suffering. Chambers found in Marxism a redemptive myth that explained the persistence of injustice in "scientific" terms and promised that the laws of history themselves dictated that injustice must end—in a bloody but brief revolution, which would be followed by a classless and then a stateless utopia. He saw in Lenin's and Stalin's Soviet Union a church that was making this gospel real, struggling fiercely against the forces of organized selfishness and exploitation. In other words, Marxism was the crowning glory of the entire Enlightenment project, aimed at dismantling archaic and superstitious hierarchies to make way for human greatness and happiness. Compared to that shining vision, what were the property rights of a few "greedy" Ukrainian farmers, or the free-speech claims of "parasitical" Russian priests?

And so Chambers followed the logic of his new beliefs into the secret service of the American Communist Party, which recruited him as an agent of espionage against the "bourgeois" government of the United States. In the service of the Party, Chambers was ordered to commit many crimes; when his wife, Esther, became pregnant, the diktat came down that the Party would be best served by an abortion. And that proved to be a turning point. Chambers wrote:

> As an underground Communist, I took it for granted that children were out of the question. . . . Abortion, which now fills me with physical horror, I then regarded, like all Communists, as a mere physical manipulation.
>
> One day, early in 1933, my wife told me she believed she had conceived. No man can hear from his wife, especially for the first time, that she

is carrying his child, without a physical jolt of joy and pride. I felt it. But so sunk were we in that life that it was only a passing joy, and was succeeded by a merely momentary sadness that we would not have the child. We discussed the matter, and my wife said that she must go at once for a physical check and to arrange for the abortion.

When my wife came back . . . she was quiet and noncommittal. The doctor had said there was a child. My wife went about preparing supper. "What else did she say?" I asked. "She said that I am in good physical shape to have a baby." My wife went on silently working. Very slowly, the truth dawned on me. "Do you mean," I asked, "that you want to have the child?"

My wife came over to me, took my hands and burst into tears. "Dear heart," she said in a pleading voice, "we couldn't do that awful thing to a little baby, not to a little baby, dear heart." A wild joy swept me. Reason, the agony of my family, the Communist Party and its theories, the wars and revolutions of the 20th century, crumbled at the touch of the child. Both of us simply wanted a child. If the points on the long course of my break with Communism could be retraced, that is probably one of them—not at the level of the conscious mind, but at the level of unconscious life. . . .[1]

After his daughter, Ellen, was born, as Chambers was feeding her, he found himself contemplating the baroque design of her ear—and finding it a mystery that eluded explanation. His fiercely held subhumanist faith taught that this, his little child, was purely disposable, and that her ear was the product of blind and meaningless chance. Could he really, holding his child, still believe that? And if not, what then—what of the children who even then were starving because the Party in Russia had taken their parents' land or shipped their family to Gulag camps? This moment of epiphany worked inside Chambers's heart like sand in an oyster. He was already on the road home.

Darkness at Noon (1940), by ex-communist Arthur Koestler, is a searing look inside the soul of a zealot at a time when his faith is tested. The protagonist of the novel, Nicholas Rubashov, spends most of the story in an unnamed prison in a city that is clearly Moscow in 1938. This was the height

---

1 Whittaker Chambers, *Witness* (New York: Random House, 1987), 325–27.

of Stalin's Terror, the purge during which his regime arrested, interrogated, and often tortured more than 1.5 million Soviet citizens on trumped-up charges of espionage, sabotage, and "counter-revolution," killing anywhere between 600,000 and 1.2 million people.

The dictator's motives for these extreme actions have never been fully explained. It seems clear that he wished to obliterate any alternatives to his leadership by wiping out colleagues in the Party who might serve as (or support) internal opponents, so he first targeted the most loyal and dedicated communists, the "Old Bolsheviks" who had helped Lenin make his Revolution in 1917. Soviets of Jewish extraction, who had been overrepresented in the ranks of the Bolsheviks and other revolutionary parties, were also particular targets of the purge. In a peculiar refinement of cruelty, Stalin insisted that the most high-profile defendants be forced to sign confessions, admitting to elaborate, implausible lists of impossible crimes—sometimes, for instance, to spying on Soviet Russia simultaneously on behalf of Nazi Germany, Great Britain, and the Vatican, or to committing acts of industrial "wrecking" on a massive scale. Refined methods of interrogation and torture were used to wring confessions out of Stalin's former rivals for power such as Grigory Zinoviev, Lev Kamenev, and Nikolai Bukharin. The family members of the "guilty" were also routinely sent off to lethal exile in the Gulag, and the effect of the Terror on Soviet life was to turn the entire country into a paranoid nest of informers, spies, policemen, and terrorized serfs—perhaps the worst, most toxic environment in which large numbers of human beings had ever had to live, a vast national concentration camp. It would serve as the direct inspiration for the society depicted in George Orwell's *1984*.

This purge was the event that drove Koestler and many other longtime communists to question and finally renounce their faith in Marxism. However, what interested him as a novelist was the fact that so many continued to believe—including some of the men Stalin indicted and brought to trial. Drawing on the perplexed, tortured writings that emerged from such purge targets as Bukharin, Koestler creates in Rubashov a character whose dedication to communism is impossible to shake. He has accepted, intellectually, all the propositions of Marxism. He has had it "proven" to him that the laws of history dictate a glorious communist victory, and that along the way to the promised utopia of humanism there must be a stage of struggle, during which the "dictatorship of the proletariat" has the duty to be ruthless against the forces of reaction and inequality. Rubashov himself, as the novel reveals in flashbacks, has repeatedly had to display that kind of ruthlessness, even against his fellow communists when their actions or opinions were "objectively" counterproductive to the Revolution's goals. In the course of his conversations with his fellow prisoners and interrogators, Rubashov accedes to the subsequent lethal links in the chain of Marxist logic: Since the voice of the laws of history is the proletariat, and the voice of the proletariat is the leadership of the Communist Party, then whatever line the Party takes at a given moment is infallibly correct. Hence any dissent from the Party, whether intentional or accidental, is not only mistaken, but "objectively" criminal. Furthermore, the only judge who is competent to decide if one has dissented is the Party itself. So however false its indictments might seem to be—Rubashov knows that he has never spied or committed sabotage—its verdicts are always just. The duty of a loyal communist whom the Party has deemed a threat to the Revolution is to sign whatever confession is put before him. Going meekly to his own execution is the final service he can offer the Party. If he refused to do it, he would only be proving himself the worst kind of traitor, an "individualist" who elevated his own solitary conscience against the overwhelming verdict of history and "science."

Beyond what it tells of the power wielded by "heroic" strains of subhumanism, *Darkness at Noon* gives unique insight into how the human will to believe can suppress the mind's stubborn drive to think. Anyone who has escaped from a situation in which he subscribed to religious or ideological groupthink, or from an abusive cult of personality, will recognize the mental gambits and cognitive evasions that "true believers" use to insulate their creeds from the corrosive force of facts.

Lenin in Zurich (1976), by Aleksandr Solzhenitsyn, was published as a stand-alone novel, even though its narrative, broken up into parts, also appears in the author's epic series of history novels, *The Red Wheel*. It is made up of the sections written from the point of view of Nikolai Lenin, and its closest literary analogue is probably *The Screwtape Letters*. As C. S. Lewis admitted in the prefatory remarks to his book, it can be profoundly disturbing, even debilitating for an author to set himself the task of examining evil from the inside. Like an autopsy, it's an ugly but sometimes necessary task. What drove Solzhenitsyn to shrink his vast, capacious spirit so that it could fit into the nasty little tin box that was the mind of an ideologue was the necessity to explain. In fact, his *The Red Wheel* is an attempt to construct a counter-narrative of the history of his country, one meant to stand against the accounts produced by Western historians sympathetic to socialism, who have insisted over the decades on propagating a long list of myths about what happened to Russia in the twentieth century. The most popular fantasy, which endured the longest despite the inexorable release of evidence to the contrary, pictures Lenin as a fundamentally progressive revolutionary, whose attempt to liberate Russia was tragically hijacked by the thuggish Stalin—whom true believers will try to insist was not even really a Marxist, but merely a bandit who adopted an ideology to cover his hunger for power. No one can innocently accept this myth who reads of the massive repressions ordered by Lenin, or peruses the letters in which he greets with glee the news of peasants executed for "hoarding" their own grain or of helpless clergymen starved to death. Indeed, a single telegram sent by Lenin in 1918, long available to the public, should have sufficed to put to rest the myth that he was merely a "liberal in a hurry." As he wrote his subordinates on August 11 of that year:

> Comrades! The uprising by the five kulak *volosts* [regions] must be mercilessly suppressed. The interest of the entire revolution demands this, for we are now facing everywhere the "final decisive battle" with the kulaks. We need to set an example.
>
> 1. You need to hang (hang without fail, so that the people see) no fewer than 100 of the notorious kulaks, the rich and the bloodsuckers.
>
> 2. Publish their names.
>
> 3. Take all their grain from them.
>
> 4. Appoint the hostages—in accordance with yesterday's telegram.
>
> This needs to be done in such a way that the people for hundreds of *versts* around will see, tremble, know and shout: they are throttling and will throttle the bloodsucking kulaks.
>
> Telegraph us concerning receipt and implementation.
>
> Yours, Lenin.
>
> PS. Find tougher people.[2]

Solzhenitsyn does much more than document statements like this one; in *Lenin in Zurich*, he goes back before Lenin's sudden rise to power—as a

---

2 "Telegram to Comrades Kuraev, Bosh, Minkin, and other Penza communists," www.marxists.org/archive/lenin/works/1918/aug/11c.htm.

cat's paw of the Kaiser's Germany, which was desperate to knock Imperial Russia out of the war—to explore how a highly talented intellectual, whose politics were impeccably "progressive," could at the same time be such a narrow, bitter dogmatist who was coldly willing to murder unarmed civilians by the thousands and deport countless more to internment camps to freeze or starve. In the novel, Solzhenitsyn depicts Lenin's conflicts with rival socialists in exile, whom he attempted to lead by turns through bullying or flattery. Having convinced himself that he had arrived at the only plausible action plan for putting Marxism into practice, he regarded anyone who differed even on tactics as, in effect (and perhaps in intention), a saboteur. Lenin's tactic, as he repeated over and over again, was to "split the Party!" until he had pared away anyone who was not completely docile. What remained was a rump of a rump of a faction, which in 1917 skulked in Swiss exile with few connections left back in Russia. As the narrative progresses, Lenin appears more and more like some crank conspiracy theorist who spends his days uselessly hectoring a shrinking band of fanatics and servile followers. Indeed, it seems implausible that such a man could come to manage a chicken coop, and the terrible knowledge that he will soon gain absolute, life-and-death power over a vast continental empire imbues the novel with an almost unbearable irony. Reading it is like watching a bus full of innocent refugees head off a cliff in excruciating slow motion.

So what explains Lenin's rise as dictator? It is, Solzhenitsyn suggests, precisely his dogmatism, his unshakeable certainty of the righteousness of his actions. In a Russia whose liberal intelligentsia knew only one thing for certain—there are no enemies to the left—there was no coherent party representing moderate reform. The sane and prudent modernizing minister Pyotr Stolypin, who serves as the tragic hero of Solzhenitsyn's entire epic, had years before been murdered and his supporters ousted from power. The tsar's regime was defended only by the bigoted, timid, or venal, while those who demanded reform were so insatiable to dethrone him and wipe clean the slate of Russian history that no radical on the left could ever seem dangerous. So Alexander Kerensky, who formed the Provisional Government after the abdication of Nicholas II, did little to hamper Lenin's obvious moves toward seizing military power. When less radical socialists looked at their more fanatical colleagues, what they felt was not prudent fear, but a kind of bad conscience—almost as if their moderation were proof of cowardice. Readers of Tom Wolfe's *Radical Chic* will recognize this psychological pattern, remembering Leonard Bernstein hosting murderous, anti-Semitic Black Panthers at his posh New York apartment. Throughout the 1970s, left-wing European elites would show the same indulgence toward the Red Brigades, the PLO, and the Baader-Meinhof Gang, as Michael Burleigh documents in *Blood and Rage*.

In a time of roiling confusion, power fell to the man with a plan and a cult possessed of absolute, dogmatic certainty—a man whose vision of transformation was so absolute and simplistic that it could be squeezed into vulgar pamphlets, regurgitated as war chants, ingested like a stimulant, in much the same way that Hitler's fathomless radicalism would trump the lesser passion of other, more rational German nationalists. To use a visual metaphor: the hammer and sickle or the swastika are much simpler for the untalented to scrawl in slum graffiti than more traditional emblems of more complex political systems, such as the Prussian or Austrian eagle. Ideologies crafted by bitter sectarian intellectuals to appeal to the street toughs and envious layabouts would actually displace political philosophy throughout the West in the wake of World War I.

The numberless crimes and final collapse of the Soviet Union did not, alas, entirely discredit the political philosophy that it faithfully put into practice. Few today still believe in Marx's utopia. But debates about rising inequality in the West have reignited interest in Marxist analysis and encouraged the revival of the language of class warfare among certain intellectuals and activists. Because of the rise of "new Marxism," it is essential to remind people of the historical record and recall what Marxist movements produce when they come into power: a statist, bureaucratic behemoth that manipulates the masses it keeps ignorant, and grants wealth to those with power. The regimes that result from applied Marxism bear no resemblance to his classless, stateless utopia, but look much more like Castro's Cuba, Chavez's Venezuela, or Jong-Un's North Korea. What Marx called dialectical materialism, put into practice, devolves into a system that in *1984* Orwell called oligarchical collectivism—the concentration of money and power in the same hands, which are thus insulated from competition in the marketplace or the public square. This is what Marxism generates, as surely as fascism generates racial hatred and war.

For Further Reading:
Frederic Bastiat, *The Law*, bastiat.org/en/the_law.html.
Michael Burleigh, *Blood and Rage* (New York: Harper Perennial, 2010).
Whittaker Chambers, *Witness* (Washington, DC: Regnery, 1987).

Stephane Courtois et al., *The Black Book of Communism* (Cambridge, MA: Harvard University Press, 1999).

Paul Kengor, *Dupes* (Wilmington, DE: Intercollegiate Studies Institute Press, 2010).

Arthur Koestler, *Darkness at Noon* (New York: Scribner, 2006).

Erik von Kuehnelt-Leddihn, *Leftism Revisited* (Washington, DC: Regnery Publishing, 1991).

Mark Levin, *Ameritopia* (New York: Threshold, 2012).

James F. Pontuso, *Assault on Ideology* (New York: Lexington Books, 2004).

Aleksandr Solzhenitsyn, *Lenin in Zurich* (New York: Farrar, Straus, & Giroux, 1990).

Kurt Vonnegut, "Harrison Bergeron," in *Welcome to the Monkey House* (New York: Dial Publishing, 1998).

Chapter Five

Radical Individualism

On the face of it, radical individualism is far less repulsive than the other ideologies we've covered so far. It is much more truthful and principled than racism, and makes more modest claims than utopian collectivism. Its "body count" of innocents seems much lower than its competitors. Much of what is healthy in American culture and politics can be traced to a rugged individualism based on people fiercely defending their rights. Individualism is a medicine that Europe desperately needed to burn out the tangled mass of privileges, unjust social hierarchies, and economic absurdities that it had inherited from feudalism.

The evils of feudalism should not be sanitized, as certain nostalgic and paternalistic Catholic thinkers are prone to do—especially those who damn Enlightenment liberalism, and many of those who fancy themselves Distributists. Alexis de Tocqueville, no fan of social revolution, painted this picture of feudalism during the presidency of George Washington:

> In the majority of states in Germany in 1788 the peasant could not leave the manor, and if he left it he could be pursued wherever he went and returned to it by force. He was subject to manorial justice, which watched over his private life and punished his intemperance and his laziness. He could not rise in rank, nor change his profession, nor marry without his master's consent. A great part of his time had to be given to the master's service. Several years of his youth had to be spent in the domestic service of the manor. The seigneurial *corvée* [forced, unpaid labor] existed in full strength, and could extend, in certain countries, up to three days a week. It was the peasant who rebuilt and maintained the lord's buildings, brought his produce to market and sold it, and was charged with carrying the lord's messages. The serf, could, however, own land, but his title was always very insecure. He was required to cultivate his field in a certain way, under his lord's supervision, and he could neither sell it nor mortgage it at will. In certain cases he was required to sell its produce; in others he was forbidden to sell it: he was

always required to farm his land. Even his children's inheritance did not go to them intact: a portion was ordinarily kept by the manor.[1]

Imagine being born into such conditions, with no way out. Imagine that your entire family had lived this way for centuries, looking with longing at the freedom enjoyed by your countrymen who happened to be born in the upper classes, or born in a city where serfdom was banned. Now you understand the appeal of classical liberalism.

By the eighteenth century, serfdom had been rolled back from large parts of Europe, but the subjugation to arbitrary and paternalistic authority described above depicts the lives of millions of people in Europe from the fall of Rome until the Enlightenment. For hundreds of years between the first barbarian invasions and the widespread establishment of order, such a social system was no doubt the best men could do, but it had far outworn its necessity by the end of the Middle Ages; the survival of feudal privilege after that can be traced to inertia and upper-class self-interest. The rise of early capitalism beginning in the twelfth and thirteenth centuries began to undermine the hereditary order of society and free up the productive energies of the West—in part by dismantling the suffocating monopolies enjoyed by members of guilds, who had the legal power to fix prices and quash competition.

Although clergymen often defended feudal arrangements—indeed, many themselves were feudal lords and benefited from them—they are clearly incompatible with the Christian idea of the person. Insofar as the Enlightenment and its individualism were committed to clearing away such residual evils from Europe's oligarchical past, they were indeed putting Christian ethics at long last into action—as Pope John Paul II observed in *Memory and Identity*.

But man cannot live on medicine. And if feudal survivals can be seen as a kind of cancer, the individualism that cured it contained its own toxins, whose dangers only really began to manifest themselves in the nineteenth and twentieth centuries. Individualism freed the serfs and helped free the slaves; in its contemporary, radicalized form, it also provided the logic for legal abortion. Add up all the preborn victims of abortion in the West and radical individualism begins to rack up its own body count. Drive the devil out the door and he will creep back in through the window. Now let us look at the shadow side of

---

1 Alexis de Tocqueville, *The Old Regime and the Revolution* (Chicago: University of Chicago Press, 1998), 111.

individualism, the aspects of human nature its proponents suppressed and the side effects that resulted.

The notion of man as an antisocial animal first arose in the Enlightenment, as a side effect of Thomas Hobbes's attempt to sideline the power and constrict the freedom of the churches. In the wake of the brutal English Civil War, which pitted radically Protestant Puritans against conservative Anglicans and England's surviving Catholics, Hobbes decided that faith was a profoundly disruptive force, an acid that could eat away the loyalty of a subject toward his ruler and divide a country against itself. Although a tame church could swing incense before a throne whose authority was guaranteed by God, religion could do the opposite: If a king departed from the established creed, faith could make men rebels. It could goad terrorists like Guy Fawkes to plant bombs in Parliament and preachers like John Knox to cause the overthrow of a queen. In Hobbes's time, faith had helped drive the partisans of Cromwell to execute a monarch and replace his regime with a republic. Religious wars still raged in France and the Netherlands between Catholic and Protestant, and dissidents from the state-run Church of England (both Catholic and Puritan) were a simmering threat to uniformity and public order. Men might kill for a political cause; they would placidly die for God. And a monarch's temporal punishments could always be trumped by the hope of eternal reward.

So Hobbes conceived of a different origin of power, which did not rely on God and hence was immune to religious objections: Primitive man, he claimed, was born in a chaotic and brutal "state of nature." Each man was absolutely free—free to die of hunger, or in fights over food and the choice of a mate. In order to postpone the greatest evil, his own death, he willingly renounced this primal freedom, and in forming the "social contract" subjected himself to the state. Only the state could harness the wild energies of the mass of men and protect them from each other and themselves. The state was not a servant that some unearthly authority had imposed on man to preserve an abstraction such as "justice." It was more like a feudal lord, to whom the human race had bound itself for life in return for protection from death. Because it was absolutely necessary, the state must be perfectly free—free to pursue what the ruler perceived as the common good without rebellion or even resistance from its subjects, who if they attempted to push back against it were simply summoning back from man's dark, primitive past the specter of total chaos.

The absolutist consequences that Hobbes drew—dismissing any claim to individual liberty as the seed of civil war—would not find favor in the English-speaking world, but his premises fared much better. Later thinkers would soak in his assumption that man is fundamentally selfish. We contract with the state to suit our own self-interested purposes, which cannot be judged by any external standard—although they can bounce up against the wishes of someone else, a conflict that must be accommodated. Individual human beings ought to be seen on the model of atoms careening against each other in the void. Hence the law is a system of forces that helps to arrange the particles that make up a society into patterns, patterns that more effectively permit these atoms to remain in existence and exert their native force. In other words, individuals were free to maximize their pursuit of what they wanted, disregarding any moral law, subject only to the overweening power of the state.

John Locke took this radical premise and infused it with some of the moral content we recognize from the humanist view of man. Here is a clear, useful summary of what Locke built out of Hobbes's materials:

> According to Locke, the State of Nature, the natural condition of mankind, is a state of perfect and complete liberty to conduct one's life as one best sees fit, free from the interference of others. This does not mean, however, that it is a state of license: one is not free to do anything at all one pleases, or even anything that one judges to be in one's interest. The State of Nature, although a state wherein there is no civil authority or government to punish people for transgressions against laws, is not a state without morality. The State of Nature is pre-political, but it is not pre-moral. Persons are assumed to be equal to one another in such a state, and therefore equally capable of discovering and being bound by the Law of Nature. The Law of Nature, which is on Locke's view the basis of all morality, and given to us by God, commands that we not harm others with regards to their "life, health, liberty, or possessions" (par. 6). Because we all belong equally to God, and because we cannot take away that which is rightfully His, we are prohibited from harming one another. So, the State of Nature is a state of liberty where persons are free to pursue their own interests and plans, free from interference, and, because of the Law of Nature and the restrictions that it imposes upon persons, it is relatively peaceful.

> The State of Nature, therefore, is not the same as the state of war, as it is according to Hobbes. It can, however, devolve into a state of war, in particular, a state of war over property disputes. Whereas the State of Nature is the state of liberty where persons recognize the Law of

Nature and therefore do not harm one another, the state of war begins between two or more men once one man declares war on another, by stealing from him, or by trying to make him his slave. Since in the State of Nature there is no civil power to whom men can appeal, and since the Law of Nature allows them to defend their own lives, they may then kill those who would bring force against them. Since the State of Nature lacks civil authority, once war begins it is likely to continue. And this is one of the strongest reasons that men have to abandon the State of Nature by contracting together to form civil government.[2]

As Scott Hahn and Benjamin Wiker document in *Politicizing the Bible*,[3] Locke was a philosophical radical who schooled himself to caution. In private correspondence, he hinted that he rejected the claims of Christianity, but in his political writing he sought only to moderate them, to make a place for the churches as moral advisors in a society oriented toward maximizing wealth and technical progress. Christianity could be tolerated, so long as it was tolerant.

Likewise, in discussing basic, secular ethics, Locke poured a new, thinner wine into medieval wineskins. Unlike the willfully provocative Thomas Hobbes, who earned himself public infamy alongside Machiavelli, Locke spoke the older language of the humanist tradition. But he meant different things by the words.

The concept of natural law (or the "law of nature") was an ancient one, derived from Aristotle and the Stoics, and Christianized by Aquinas. It traditionally meant the entire body of what can be known by reason alone, including what can be known about morality, without divine revelation. By reason, thinkers did not mean merely "experimental science" or mathematical deduction, but also included the results of philosophical argument. In this pre-Darwinian world, the notion that objects and processes in nature could be said to have a purpose (a "*telos*") was taken for granted. Hence reason tells us that the sex organs are clearly "intended" first for reproduction, and that marriage is a contract designed to regulate the bearing and raising of children. In what is now called "classical natural law," thinkers argued that we could know by reason that God exists and that the soul is immortal, plus a great deal more. Aquinas even asserted that the Ten Commandments

---

2 Celeste Friend, "Social Contract Theory," *The Internet Encyclopedia of Philosophy*, www.iep.utm.edu/soc-cont/#SH2a.

3 Hahn and Wiker, 440ff.

largely restated and gave revealed authority to moral truths that reason could turn up unaided. That robust tradition of natural law, though already under attack by Descartes, had been passed along in England by thinkers such as the Thomistic Anglican Thomas Hooker.

When Locke wrote his *First Treatise of Government* and *Second Treatise of Government*, he consciously used the older terms, like "law of nature," when arguing for a distinctly new view of politics. But Locke did not mean what Aristotle, Aquinas, or Hooker would have meant by those terms. Instead, he trimmed back the whole of what man can know about morality by reason to a truncated form of the Golden Rule: Because God made us, and we are ultimately his property, we cannot harm other individuals in their "life, health, liberty, or possessions." This phrase sounds familiar, of course; the Declaration of Independence defines as "inalienable rights" the rights to "life, liberty, and the pursuit of happiness," a thoroughly Lockean list. Natural law, which for Aristotle, Aquinas, and most of the thinkers in the English legal tradition had described a long list of virtues required for man to flourish, had been reduced to a safeguard for individual rights—and nothing more.

These rights make an excellent starting point, a non-negotiable bottom line of what the state exists to protect. A philosopher would call them "necessary but not sufficient" because they state essential elements of the common good, but do not go far enough. The fact is that few of the Founding Fathers who signed the Declaration of Independence thought that defending Lockean rights was the only legitimate goal for government. Most of the signers were not Enlightenment Deists, who rejected both biblical revelation and traditional notions of natural law, but rock-solid Protestants who were deeply convinced of original sin and considered religious faith indispensible for a free society to survive. As Samuel Gregg writes:

> The Founders had little doubt that a virtuous citizenry was a prerequisite to the stability of a free republic. No one can seriously doubt that most of them would have regarded modern hedonistic accounts of liberty as not only intellectually shallow but also deeply corrosive of a society's capacity to remain free. James Madison, for example, informed the Virginia Assembly that limited republican government without a virtuous society was "chimerical."

> Likewise Jefferson insisted without equivocation in his *Notes on the State of Virginia* that virtue "is the manners and spirit of a people

which preserve a republic in vigor." Inspired in many cases by reflection on the writings of Romans such as Cicero and eighteenth-century philosophers such as Montesquieu, they spoke of virtues such as honesty, trust, and industriousness, but also of marriage and religion.

Regarding the latter, they had few doubts about its centrality to free societies that took virtue seriously. In the year the American colonies declared independence, John Adams stressed in his correspondence that "Statesmen, my dear Sir, may plan and speculate for liberty, but it is religion and morality alone, which can establish the principles upon which freedom can securely stand." Washington was thus hardly alone among the Founders when he proclaimed in his 1796 Farewell Address that public happiness could not be attained without religion or private morality.[4]

Most Americans, including those who founded the nation, expected the government to be guided by principles that exceeded Locke's narrow account of the natural law, and to inform its understanding of natural rights with the wider and deeper wisdom gained from tradition, philosophy, and even religion. This explains why there was never any prospect in 1800, for instance, of extending marriage rights to same-sex couples—a proposal nowadays popular because it is seen as a logical extension of Locke's single-minded preoccupation with defending the autonomy of the individual. Obscenity laws were widespread and strictly enforced—although it is hard to make a consistent Lockean case for them. Polygamy was and still is (as of this writing) banned in every state, even though it restricted the "liberty" of individuals to make their free sexual choices. The same logic applies to restrictions on prostitution, the sale of human organs, and suicide.

From the founding well into the 1950s, marriage law reflected the interest of society in the protection of the family as a unit and the welfare of children, which stood in clear tension with the liberty of individual citizens to act however they wished. Then "no-fault" divorce laws applied Lockean logic (more consistently than Locke ever had) to the institution of marriage. The devastating impact of the collapse of stable marriage on the well-being of children throughout the West has been documented exhaustively by social scientists in subsequent decades. The children of divorce are much more likely to get pregnant out of wedlock, commit crimes, go to prison, earn

---

4 Samuel Gregg, *Tea Party Catholic* (New York: Crossroad, 2012), 52–53.

lower incomes, suffer depression, be afraid to commit to relationships, and use illegal drugs.[5] Radical individualism did for the Western family what Marxism did for Soviet agriculture. That alone should be enough to prove that Locke is not enough—and that in chemically pure form he can be poisonous.

But the most destructive application of radical individualism applies to a relationship even more intimate than marriage—the primal bond between a mother and child. Beginning with *Roe v. Wade* in 1973, but culminating in the much more logical, and hence more destructive, decision, *Planned Parenthood v. Casey* in 1992, the U.S. Supreme Court adopted radical individualism as the sole criterion by which to judge laws governing abortion. As the court ruled:

> Our law affords constitutional protection to personal decisions relating to marriage, procreation, contraception, family relationships, child rearing, and education. . . . Our cases recognize the right of the individual, married or single, to be free from unwarranted governmental intrusion into matters so fundamentally affecting a person as the decision whether to bear or beget a child. . . . Our precedents "have respected the private realm of family life which the state cannot enter.". . . These matters, involving the most intimate and personal choices a person may make in a lifetime, choices central to personal dignity and autonomy, are central to the liberty protected by the Fourteenth Amendment. *At the heart of liberty is the right to define one's own concept of existence, of meaning, of the universe, and of the mystery of human life* [emphasis added].[6]

The implications of this decision were extraordinarily radical—particularly those of the last sentence quoted above, which empties out every trace of the humanist content that Locke had added to render Hobbes's atomism palatable. The key words of the Declaration fall apart. "Life" loses its sacredness and becomes mere "survival." "Liberty" ceases to be the freedom to do what is right and turns into empty willfulness. The "happiness" we are free to pursue sheds its original meaning (the joy that comes from a life

---

5 For a brief survey of the massive scholarship documenting these and other impacts of divorce, see Amy Desai, "How Could Divorce Affect My Kids?" at www.focusonthefamily.com/marriage/divorce_and_infidelity/should_i_get_a_divorce/how_could_divorce_affect_my_kids.

6 *Planned Parenthood of Southeastern Pa. v. Casey*, 505 U.S. 833 (1992).

well-lived), and instead becomes the empty pursuit of transitory, pleasurable moments (see Chapter Six). The "law of nature" and of "nature's God" lose what substance Locke had left them when every person has the fundamental right to act as an absolute solipsist, arbitrarily defining for himself the basic terms of rational discourse. It is hard to see how any communal life would be possible in a society where such a radical freedom was in fact taken seriously—except if an all-powerful Leviathan were to impose its own equally arbitrary order from above.

A rigorously libertarian society that allowed abortion and deregulated marriage should also, logically, remove the state from every economic transaction among adults. No minimum wage or workplace safety laws could morally be imposed to block the pure autonomy of workers and employers; racial discrimination and every other form of bias would have to be protected as part of the absolute freedom of contract. People would be free to enter into slave contracts and gladiatorial games. No unemployment insurance, welfare, or other paternalistic programs would be funded by the taxpayer, who would pay a flat rate for basic services such as police protection—that is, if the anarcho-capitalists now dominant in libertarian circles had not convinced the citizens to disband the state itself, in favor of competing private enforcement agencies. Surely the absolute liberty to redefine existence also implies the right to reject the state structure that currently exists and start up an independent alternative mode of protecting one's rights. Why should the state we have inherited from our parents enjoy an arbitrary monopoly of deadly force?

Here is where irony grabs the steering wheel. No society has ever even tried to apply radical individualism consistently throughout every realm of life. Indeed, even as the West has become more morally atomistic, the role of the state in directing economic and social life has vastly increased—in part because the pathologies that arise from the breakdown of the family and other natural units of social order cause so much harm that worried citizens invoke the state to repair the damage. The troubled children of broken homes are placed in state-sponsored after-school programs and kindergartens in an effort to make them more productive citizens. The unemployable teens who drop out of school find themselves on the public dole, or else end up as part of America's ever-burgeoning prison population. Single mothers whose "baby daddies" have abandoned them find in the government a generous absentee father. Even as the rhetoric of freedom (wrongly defined) is used to break down nongovernmental sources of authority—such as churches or families—the power and price of coercive authority grows. Modern

Westerners have seen the grave deficiencies of radical individualism, and instead of rectifying them by reasserting what natural law actually means, they have chosen to fill in the void by inventing an equally radical notion of equality. Citizens, then, must be free to live as solipsistic and self-destructive hedonists, but not all of them have the talent, wealth, or wit to pursue such a life. Some of them will founder and fail. So it is our job as taxpayers to underwrite their lifestyles, to fund their lives and pursuit of happiness by surrendering some of our liberty—but only in economic matters. We are still free in the bedroom, which is where the "intimate and personal choices" all take place (according to the Supreme Court), and that is what really matters.

Radical individualism would do less damage, of course, if the welfare state were to be abolished, and people were forced to sink or swim based on the outcomes of their own decisions. In such a starkly Darwinian order, people who used drugs, got pregnant out of wedlock, or otherwise failed to develop the basic civilized virtues would simply go hungry. A rough, reality-based code of self-reliance would emerge, while any charity offered would come from voluntary agencies such as churches—which would be free to demand that the people who took its benefits hew to a higher standard of conduct, make better choices, and develop the skills required for self-reliance. That is exactly what private Christian charities used to demand, with results that were far more transformative and respectful of the needy as fully human beings than today's value-neutral government handouts (see Chapter Nine).

What the welfare state offers instead is the modern version of bread and circuses—but something worse. Even as destructive egalitarianism promotes the growth of government as the wiper of every runny nose in society, the logic of radical individualism dismantles every structure aside from the state. We are left as isolated atoms, bereft of the support once provided by churches, families, and other institutions of civil society, completely dependent on ourselves or the agencies of the state. And what is the ideology that motivates that state in its ever more heavy-handed interventions in our lives? Here we come to the last ideology of evil, the one that dominates life in the modern West.

For Further Reading:

T. S. Eliot, *Notes Toward a Definition of Culture* (London: Faber & Faber, 1973).

Edward Feser, *Locke* (Oxford: OneWorld Publications, 2007).

Samuel Gregg, *Tea Party Catholic* (New York: Crossroad, 2013).

Pope John Paul II, *Memory and Identity* (New York: Rizzoli, 2005).

Pope Leo XIII, *Rerum Novarum,* www.vatican.va/holy_father/leo_xiii/ encyclicals/documents/hf_l-xiii_enc_15051891_rerum-novarum_ en.html.

Wilhelm Röpke, *The Moral Foundations of Civil Society* (Brunswick, NJ: Transaction Publishers, 1995).

Alexis de Tocqueville, *The Old Regime and the Revolution* (Chicago: University of Chicago Press, 1998).

Chapter Six

Utilitarian Hedonism

Nietzsche was right: If God is dead, then with him dies any moral block to the will to power. Furthermore, if there is no God to record our innocent sufferings and reward them, then we have no cause to endure them—at least when we can find the means to shunt them onto others. If the world is really Darwin's and Hobbes's rather than God's, and human nature is red in tooth and claw, then all the happy slogans of brotherhood and justice with which we clothe a free society are so many lies we tell ourselves to get through the day. We have already mentioned the long list of victims racked up in the twentieth century by men who thought this logic all the way through to the end, and acted accordingly: the victims of racist nationalism and utopian collectivism paid the price in the millions.

But we need not summon the worst criminals of history to illustrate subhumanism. Such melodramatic comparisons too easily let us off the hook ("I thank you, Lord, that I am not as these commissars who starve kulaks . . ."). Instead, let us look at ourselves, and our friends and neighbors. Let's examine a fact we already mentioned, that more than 90 percent of infants diagnosed with Down syndrome are killed before their birth. The parents who make these decisions are not moral monsters like the men who volunteered for Nazi or Khmer Rouge killing squads. And yet these American parents are using violence to eliminate innocent people. Their motivation is not overtly eugenic or even explicitly selfish; instead, they are acting philosophically, obeying the tenets of a worldview they have adopted, whether or not they have thought it all the way through. The philosophy they are following, which college students soak in through their classes and dorm room bull sessions, which guidance counselors and psychiatrists, ethics professors and public health officials act on without even naming it, is utilitarian hedonism. It has become for most Westerners the moral common currency, legal tender for all transactions, the de facto replacement for what we once called "natural law."

The traditional, Jewish-Christian-classical view of human life sees it as a mixture of suffering and joys underpinned by fundamental principles that weave our anguish into a tapestry that means something—that might even be beautiful. The modern subhumanist creed asserts, by contrast, that life is a series of incidents that are either pleasant or unpleasant, in which we are free (because nothing matters) to try to pile up as many happy moments as possible, while minimizing the unhappy ones. If we choose to be altruistic (if that makes us feel happy), we can factor in the impact of our actions on the "happy-moment" totals of other people, and try our best to do the math, so that we don't steal too many happy moments from others. Because doing that would make us unhappy in the long run. Or so people tell us.

Such a flabby calculus makes a poor substitute for a spine. One's best guess at which course of action might provide the greatest number of chipper, upbeat moments for the greatest number of people will yield very different results from a solid, intransigent moral code. In a pinch, we can always convince ourselves that whatever action we wish to take will actually add to the store of happy moments—at least in the long run. Surely the Chinese Communist Party leaders who imposed forced abortions on millions of Chinese women had convinced themselves that they were acting for the greater happiness of the many. . . . Why else would they have bothered? Likewise the scientists who conducted the Tuskegee Syphilis Study: A few dozen illiterate black men would be left untreated to die in anguish, in order to gain key medical knowledge that might help thousands of others to live. We cannot usefully quarrel with the math, since we cannot see the future. Grant these people their premises, and they might well be justified doing . . . nearly anything to anyone.

Applied to flesh and blood, this seemingly modern, enlightened code of ethics treats human beings like pets—whom we pamper when they are healthy, then euthanize. And it teaches us to see ourselves this way. Is such a self-conception enough to carry us through the tough times in our lives? To make us think it's worth the trouble to have any children? Subhumanist philosophers have already emerged to make the case that it's in fact immoral to have any children, since they are almost certain to experience more unhappy moments than happy ones. Just a few titles in this increasingly popular genre include *Why Have Children?*, *Childfree and Loving It!*, and *Complete without Kids*. Beneath the veneer of cheerful self-seeking, such manifestos affirm something deeply disquieting: That life is not worth living, so much so in fact that we ought not to inflict it on others, but simply wait for it to finally be over. Compared to this philosophy, the most apocalyptic religious cult seems positively hopeful.

In a world where faith-based visions of the Good have been declared unfit for public discussion, and the common understanding of reason that once undergirded a notion of natural law has shattered into a hundred philosophical shards, there are just a few things about which most people can be expected to agree. Post-religious and post-philosophical thinkers can use these shared opinions as the basis for making arguments about what is right and wrong:

1. If you're already alive, you'd rather stay that way, provided that

2. You are physically and mentally healthy, according to your own definition of health, and provided that

3. You are happy—which means that you have more cheerful moments than depressing ones, and your instinctual drives are being adequately satisfied.

To assert that there is any higher good outside of 1, 2, and 3 is commonly held to be an act of dogmatism, which insults the autonomy of others who might not agree—and might even suggest that you wish to enforce your notion of "goodness" on those others. And that is evil. Old fashioned, "live and let live" liberals used to draw the line here at attempts to use the state to enforce one's idea of the Good, but modern liberals go a good deal further. They regard as evil and illegitimate even private pressure, exerted by parents or preachers or other social groups that constitute "civil society." Indeed, it's the open agenda of modern progressives to use the state to dismantle any groups that attempt to use what was once called "constitutionally protected free speech" and "free association" to promote any vision of the Good beyond points 1, 2, and 3. How else can we explain the willingness of legislators to use the sanction of law to force religious hospitals to offer abortion pills, to force religious schools to employ transsexual teachers, to prohibit therapists from helping clients who are troubled by their "sexual orientation"? Here we are far beyond what the American Founders meant by "freedom," and well into the peculiar meaning given that word by Rousseau, who saw the state as a legitimate tool for forcibly dismantling every structure in society—including prepolitical, voluntary groups such as churches and the family. That is, if such groups inhibit the willful self-expression of individuals, or block their quest to pile high happy moments. The core of utilitarian hedonism was best expressed by Pope Francis's first encyclical, *Lumen Fidei*:

> In contemporary culture, we often tend to consider the only real truth to be that of technology: truth is what we succeed in building and measuring by our scientific know-how, truth is what works and what makes life easier and more comfortable. Nowadays this appears as

the only truth that is certain, the only truth that can be shared, the only truth that can serve as a basis for discussion or for common undertakings. Yet at the other end of the scale we are willing to allow for subjective truths of the individual, which consist in fidelity to his or her deepest convictions, yet these are truths valid only for that individual and not capable of being proposed to others in an effort to serve the common good. But Truth itself, the truth which would comprehensively explain our life as individuals and in society, is regarded with suspicion. (25)

Those who argue for such a Truth are not just held in suspicion, but subject to discriminatory measures by the state, whose dominant elites have rejected the classical notion of liberty for the Jacobin, which implies that fines and seizures, police raids and prisons, are worthy means when needed (in Rousseau's words) to "force men to be free."

Can we really be happy if we go through life with this degraded view of others—and of ourselves? Can we be good? When we are faced with the grave temptation to cooperate with evil, to "go along to get along" rather than speak out and take a risk, how will subhumanism help us? Will it gives us the moral fiber to join the resistance, or instead a silken excuse for looking the other way and following orders? The only effective answer to the banality of evil is a thriving, vigorous, spirited sense of what is good. Mankind is good, and it is good that he flourishes in freedom and dignity, even if sometimes he suffers. The attempt to suppress all suffering for ourselves or others, at the cost of our freedom or dignity, will not even lead to our happiness. All it will do is embolden those with the strongest will to power.

And when we seek power, whether to transform human society or simply to make our own lives neater and more convenient, there will be obstacles. Many of those obstacles will not be mountains or forests, but people—self-willed, stubborn human agents who won't or can't serve our utopian (or merely selfish) agenda. So they must be flattened. And we will find ways to do that—as our forebears did throughout the twentieth century. Without red lines etched deep inside our hearts, we will trample each other to death.

For Further Reading:

William Brennan, *Confronting the Language Empowering the Culture of Death* (Washington, DC: Catholic University of America Press, 2008).

J. Budziszewski, *What We Can't Not Know* (San Francisco: Ignatius Press, 2011).

Pope Francis, *Lumen Fidei*, www.vatican.va/lumen-fidei/en/html/.

Abby Johnson, *Unplanned* (Carol Stream, IL: Tyndale Momentum, 2011).

C. S. Lewis, *The Problem of Pain* (New York: HarperOne, 2009).

Dwight Longenecker, "Utilitarianism," in *Disorientation: How to Go to College without Losing Your Mind*, ed. John Zmirak (West Chester, PA: Ascension Press, 2010).

Daniel Mahoney, *The Conservative Foundations of the Liberal Order* (Wilmington, DE: Intercollegiate Studies Institute Press, 2011).

Karol Wojtyła, *Love and Responsibility* (San Francisco: Ignatius Press, 1993).

PART TWO

Whole-Life Principles

In the preceding five chapters, we have surveyed the gravest ideological threats to human life that overwhelmed the world in the past hundred years, and traced their rise from the poisoned waters of subhumanism. We watched these predators wriggle out of the swamp, sprout legs and learn to walk, grow teeth and start to feed. We have chronicled the massive loss of innocent life that these ideologies caused when they came to power. Now it is time for answers. Those won't come in the form of detailed, point-by-point rebuttals of Nazi racism or postmodern hedonism. That is not what we need. In their own times, as they rose to popularity, each of these ideologies was comprehensively refuted. The true humanists won the argument every time. But no one listened. People are not mainly driven by logic or evidence, but rather by their passions and affections, their fantasies and the hopes that churn their guts. We are not computers, but embodied creatures with immortal souls, "thinking reeds" that sway in the wind. We are pilgrims wandering through a world we did not make, though we like to pretend that we did. What we need in these times of profound moral confusion, when left and right, believer and skeptic, do not even seem to be using the same set of maps, is a string of sturdy lighthouses—solid, unmoving points by which we can get our bearings and trace our course in the future.

We need a set of nonnegotiable principles that future generations can stick to—and use to judge each new idea, each intellectual fad, each technological breakthrough and emerging political crisis. Just as the Constitution is meant to guide, govern, and limit each U.S. law, this code of human conduct should live in the back of our minds, and, in moments when difficult questions goad us to seek subhumanist answers, pull us back from the brink.

Earlier, we referred to the lessons of history. A few solid philosophers still talk about "natural law." The moral heart of that law can be boiled down into five "Whole-Life" principles, a name that is doubly apt because these principles apply in every situation of life and every nation, and also because they defend human life at every stage of existence and in every context. They are not imposed from above by a church or a prophet—though people of faith have endorsed the actions they demand. Nor are they the program of some ideological movement, scribbled on a café napkin by activists hungry for power. Instead, these principles are much like what C. S. Lewis called "the Tao" in *The Abolition of Man*—transnational, multicultural truths of the sort that the U.N. ought to be using as its criterion for international policy. They are the distilled insights about the good life and how to protect it that are drawn from a serious study of history, economics, philosophy, and politics.

To show how practical they are, we will illustrate them with stories of men and women who devoted themselves to defending and living them out.

Chapter Seven

Personalism: The Unique and Absolute Value of Every Human Person

If we want our children to inherit a better century, we must rewrite our collective will to include one sacred heirloom that has almost been lost in our time: a sacramental respect for the human person. We must reaffirm the founding truth of humanism—that every human being is important, unique, and dignified. He or she deserves the same reverence we demand for ourselves. We love ourselves with a fierce and primal passion, and such love is the model for how we should try to love our neighbor. This principle is best called Personalism, because it makes the human person the first and primary object of our concern, which should fall short of worship, yet ought to be imbued with a sense of religious awe.

Those of us who read the Bible will know that we are called to love God even more. But we meet our neighbor first, and if we do not love him, our love for God is a sham. The proper, passionate love of our fellow man is the starting point for every other good thing on earth, and any project or program that forgets this will turn to ashes in our mouths. Christians will remember that man is called an "image of God," a thing "a little lower than the angels," who is meant for union with God. Believing in such a theology can make it much easier to remember human dignity, but it is neither necessary nor sufficient. Think of Christians who burned heretics or traded in slaves, and then of the heroic atheist Albert Camus, who served in the French Resistance and later helped to expose the crimes of the Soviet Union.

Making of man an object of solemn reverence is a good deal more difficult than it sounds—in part because of the confused and contradictory notions we have acquired of mankind, courtesy of subhumanism and popular pseudoscience. But there are more basic human reasons why treating each other as truly human entails such heavy lifting.

A sober meditation on the century that unfolded after 1914 would confirm this truth: That human existence is, at root, a paradox. Any answer that fails to admit this is dangerously misleading.

Our lives are a bundle of howling contradictions, of seemingly irreconcilable claims that pull us in different directions like wild horses yoked together, threatening to rip the fragile, complex truth into jagged, hazardous pieces. We are animals and mathematicians, carnivores and pet lovers, tribalists who are haunted by the brotherhood of man. We are Adam newly born from the hand of God, and the sinners who cringe at the Last Judgment. Cain and Abel, Barabbas and Jesus, are equally our brothers.

The great temptation of ideologues is to divide the sheep from the goats—to resolve man's paradoxical nature into brutally stark polarities. We are told that "our people" (our tribe, class, or party) represent what is best in man, and we must unite to purge the "other," a unity that elicits the very basest tendencies we tell ourselves we don't share.

Perhaps the most bitter truth about the human paradox comes from the mouth of a man who did more than almost any other to divide and persecute, Stalin. He was the architect of the Ukrainian famine and the purge, Hitler's willing ally in 1939, and the inventor of the Gulag. He once said, "A single death is a tragedy. A million deaths is a statistic."

Stalin may have been a butcher, but his words ring true. A master of backroom politics and political blackmail, this former seminarian had an intimate knowledge of our soul's darkest unswept corners. If Mother Teresa was right that any one of us (herself included) is capable of committing any crime, then each of us has something to learn from Stalin.

He knew (and in his thuggish way, admitted) something most of us won't put into conscious thought: *Life is at once both sacred and cheap.*

When we let ourselves think it, we know this to be true, both instinctively and from experience. In the first place, we consider our own lives sacred, our own rights inalienable. When we are threatened by violence or are victimized, we swell up with righteous anger and rouse each other to action. Our perception of self-sacredness extends easily to those we love. Some of us have held a tiny child of our own, looked at each of his perfect fingers and gleaming eyelashes, felt the faint flutter of his heartbeat, tended to his needs when he cried. In those moments we are suddenly certain that this innocent life is of infinite importance, and the very thought that someone might snuff it out fills us with rage. Our conviction may even make us willing to sacrifice our own life in order to save his. This is how we typically love a sibling, a parent, a spouse.

Like a drop of ink in a glass of water, the intensity of our empathy tends to diminish as it spreads. For friends and neighbors, for those who look like us, or pray like us . . . and finally for our fellow citizens, we feel some shadow of that same passionate attachment we feel for ourselves and those we love.

With each degree of separation from our ego, conviction fades, until at last we find total strangers at the furthest extent of our empathy—those on the other side of the world with whom we have little in common beyond the human condition. Some may even be our enemies. At this distance our ability to understand the sacredness of human life finds little support in our gut. Suddenly, what we once understood so well requires the active support of our minds, an abstract philosophical or religious opinion. We will ourselves to care, and sometimes we succeed—which is why billions of dollars in private charity flow to foreign countries every year.

Sometimes, however, we fail, and our failure explains the ease with which we overlook or even cooperate in the abuse of humans far from home. "Our people" become drone pilots killing civilians, businessmen poisoning rivers, or social engineers sterilizing poor women "for their own good." Hannah Arendt pointed out forty years ago in *The Origins of Totalitarianism* that well-formed British and French soldiers, who would never have stolen a stick of gum in their mother country, were capable of appalling savagery in "the colonies." In our own history, American white men could not long stand the presence of white indentured servants—so they replaced them with black Africans, who looked different enough to justify two hundred years of servitude and a hundred more of legal discrimination.

If we can manage to stand far enough away, the life we know as sacred appears more and more expendable. We drive past a graveyard full of strangers and react with a melancholy shrug.

Of course there is nothing wrong with loving your family members more than you do a stranger—in fact, if you love a stranger equally, it's probably because you love your own family too little. (Think of Charles Dickens's character Mrs. Jellyby, who denied her own children milk so that she could send their milk money to the African missions.) But if we want strangers—who may feel little for us—to respect our lives as sacred, we must extend to them the same courtesy. This is the bare minimum every human being deserves simply by virtue of being human.

It may sound utilitarian, but respecting human life is not some charade we engage in solely to protect ourselves. Rather, it is an act of the will that cleaves to a fundamental truth—the one truth that can guard us against totalitarianism and imperialism, utilitarianism and eugenics: the infinite moral value of every human being. The fact that the right choice may also seem useful is only evidence of the fact that truth is accessible by reason.

Had the men leading great nations in the bloody twentieth century been convinced of this single truth, there might still have been wars, poverty, and repression, just as there were in the Middle Ages. What would not have happened is the mass destruction of "undesirable" civilians by their own governments, and the callous use of strategic bombing against defenseless populations in enemy countries. Only the most profound failure of empathy could achieve the colossal death toll of the twentieth century.

The more distant, alien, or unattractive we find people, the harder we must work not to act on what we feel but on what we know: That each of these people was once a child whose mother was intimately certain that his life was infinitely precious. That we must will to respect others is a truth that applies equally to soldiers in foreign countries and to the civilians who surround them, to the loved ones we cherish across the dinner table and to the inmates in our prisons, to helpless children in the womb, and to vulnerable Alzheimer's patients.

When we start making exceptions to suit our convenience, we will not stop, since the list of human beings who may prove an obstacle to what we want is as potentially limitless as our desires. History proves the height of this slippery slope. The stern truth that innocent life is sacred is the antidote to tribalist vengeance, ideological hatred, and technological hubris. It was known to the Israelites, whose Commandments said, "Thou shalt not murder," and to the Greeks, whose Hippocratic Oath made doctors promise "to give no deadly medicine."

The gravest, most deadly exception to this fundamental truth was enshrined in U.S. law on a specific day. January 22 is a date many Americans will never forget, along the lines of September 11 or December 7—anniversaries of profound wounds to our country as a whole, even if we didn't lose a relative in those surprise attacks or the wars that ensued. For millions of Americans, however, January 22 portends a loss that is much more rawly personal. One woman in three who came of age after *Roe v. Wade* has exercised the "right" the judges discovered in 1973 to terminate a pregnancy, and millions of men took part in those decisions. (Too often forgotten are men who, like one of the present authors, were bereaved of their preborn children against their wishes.) All those Americans lost a family member because of the events of January 22, and so this day will never slip by unnoticed, as most of us wish it would. We would rather think about almost anything else, be it baseball, stock prices, or shoes.

So let's talk about shoes. One of the authors to whom we owe the most intellectually is the political philosopher Hadley Arkes of Amherst

College. Arkes is the world's leading advocate of the deeply unfashionable principles of natural law. You never hear about natural law anymore, but it played a major role in certain historic events: the American Declaration of Independence, the Abolitionist movement, the U.N.'s postwar assertion of human rights that transcend the laws of nations, and the U.S. civil rights movement. It is almost stunning to think that an idea with such a pedigree could simply be dropped by the world's intellectuals, like a toy that a child grew bored with, but that is what has happened. People will still assert human rights, or insist that our government act with justice, plucking fruit from the branches of a tree they pretend isn't there. In his seminal book, *Natural Rights and the Right to Choose*, Arkes starts by talking not about abstract right and wrong, but about a particular pile of shoes. That has a better philosophical precedent than you might think: One of Heidegger's most influential essays concerns the making of shoes.

Hadley Arkes also talks about German attitudes toward shoes. But Arkes isn't as interested in the philosophical implications of crafting pairs of shoes as in the scrupulous way that certain Germans protected them, kept them safe from heedless destruction in time of war, gathered them carefully, and avoided wherever they could the needless waste of a single shoe—almost as if each pair had a unique and irreplaceable destiny, a dignity no man could rightly ignore. The shoes that interest Arkes were found piled neatly outside the gas chamber at an extermination camp. Those shoes, and other personal items like gold teeth, were removed from the piles of human bodies those plants efficiently processed into smoke. They remain with us as a testimony to modern economy and thrift. We can think of no other single thing—not a skyscraper or a spaceship—that sums up the essence of what it means to be modern as well as that pile of Jewish shoes.

The age we mark as modernity began with grand, exhilarating gestures: discourses on method that would set us free from the dead hand of tradition (Descartes), declarations of the rights of man (the French Revolutionary Assembly), manifestos rejecting the tyranny of mere economic laws over the lives and labor of men (Karl Marx). The grand progression of heroic humanism was full of such golden moments, which moved through the dark night of history like torches leading us ever forward, to a glittering future that would make life at long last worthy of man. At the end of all the struggles, after the next and final conflict, we were promised without any irony a brave new world, an earthly paradise. Descartes had no doubt that science would end disease and aging, so men could live forever. Robespierre offered public safety and a reign of absolute virtue. Marx fought to eliminate war, inequality, and even boring jobs: in the stateless, classless communist endpoint of history, no one would even have to specialize in anything. We could move from one career to another from day to day, and have ample time in the evening to philosophize or write poetry. As Thomas Paine said, "We have it in our power to begin the world over again."

And we did. That's what we spent the nineteenth and twentieth centuries energetically doing. We broke up historic empires into nation-states, where men forgot their loyalty to a tiny village or global Church, and learned to think as members of ethnic tribes or aggrieved social classes. After these collectives had done their work, and proved themselves too dangerous we set about smashing them, too. We broke down the ramshackle, inefficient structure of the old extended family to its minimal, nuclear core. When that didn't seem economically vital, we split it into atoms: When we decided that families have no fiscal impact or social value, we redefined them at last as consensual, temporary alliances of adults, to whom the State contracts the duty of caring for children in the hours when schools and daycare facilities aren't open. We have very thoroughly accomplished the job modernity's founders set us: liquidating every barrier to the assertion of the Self. We are free to make of ourselves exactly what we will. And here we sit with the treasure we've won: this pile of shoes. We have learned to fetishize productivity and freedom, while debasing and disregarding the people who produce things and exercise freedom. We have sold the precious artwork to pay for its glittering frame.

The road we took to get here should be clear: In the high-minded, ruthless war of liberation we fought against the past, against authority, and against every duty or imperative that each of us as individuals had not freely signed on to as consenting adults. We had to destroy the vision of human life our superstitious ancestors clung to, in which a human being was something radical and unique, a hybrid of spirit and flesh whose destiny may have begun inside the uterus, but which stretched on forward into eternity. You would meddle with such a mystery at your peril, remembering that the penalties could haunt your own eternity. So the Russian peasants used to mutter at the soldiers and the secret policemen, who laughed as they carted them off to collective farms or gulags. But these "new men" were unafraid of judgment. In that sense, and that sense only, they were free.

The only support, it turned out, for having a high opinion of other people's lives lay not in the shiny new laboratories or libraries we were building, but in the drafty, candlelit houses of worship we had to bulldoze to make room. The sacred books that old men quoted to thwart the free play of our desires, which we piled in bonfires or smirked at as curiosities, were more important than we realized. They held crucial information, the codes needed to make men treat each other a certain way—a way we had come to take for granted. That way of treating people—protecting the weak, venerating the old, sacrificing for the young—emerged in human history as the side effect of specific assertions about the world. The most important was this one, whose implications are almost infinite: that man is made in the image and likeness of God.

We didn't want to believe this. We resented the rules it imposed on our behavior, the limits it placed on research and productivity. But we craved the rights and dignity that this principle granted us. So we split our minds into two, walling one off from the other.

To suit the way we feel about ourselves, we act as if life is sacred, the individual is precious, and each of us has a dignity no one can deny. What we see in nature is that life is cheap, that all our DNA cares about is replicating itself, and that we are no more than one species among many millions, on a trivial planet in a clockwork universe (one of many) that's gradually running down. We are atheists who want to think of ourselves as angels, but know deep down that we are beasts. We are free of the very things that gave us the right to freedom. We "know" that we are special, and realize that we aren't. But pretense is not enough in times of crisis. When the economy collapses, or war erupts, the only force strong enough to stop us from searching out scapegoats, or matching our enemies atrocity for atrocity, is a solid, immutable moral code—one that we believe in so firmly that it can resist the shrill voice of expedience, or the roars of collective rage.

A once-controversial, now-beloved American president spoke out bluntly about the inexorable creep of darkness only two years after taking office. Too few leaders of his political party, which still venerates his image, remember what Ronald Reagan wrote in 1983:

> Abortion concerns not just the preborn child, it concerns every one of us. The English poet, John Donne, wrote: ". . . any man's death diminishes me, because I am involved in mankind; and therefore never send to know for whom the bell tolls; it tolls for thee."

We cannot diminish the value of one category of human life—the preborn—without diminishing the value of all human life. We saw tragic proof of this truism last year when the Indiana courts allowed the starvation death of Baby Doe in Bloomington because the child had Down Syndrome. . . .

The real question today is not when human life begins, but, *What is the value of human life?* The abortionist who reassembles the arms and legs of a tiny baby to make sure all its parts have been torn from its mother's body can hardly doubt whether it is a human being. The real question for him and for all of us is whether that tiny human life has a God-given right to be protected by the law—the same right we have.[1]

How was it that such a fundamental right could be obscured? This forgetting was willful and conscious, an example of empathy failing in the face of selfish desires wrapped up in utopian slogans. With the rise of contraception and the apparent defeat of "venereal diseases," modern man saw the glimpse of a promised land of sexual freedom that had eluded wistful libertines throughout history. Sex could be freed from its biological moorings and used as a pleasure balloon. Unhinged from commitments that outlast fleeting desire, unburdened by reproduction, without the ballast of guilt and shame, what advocates hopefully labeled "free love" could serve the cause of Progress, dissolving the unwanted social bonds and inherited social structures that the New Left saw as repressive: the nuclear family, the church, and "bourgeois" codes of behavior. Indeed, in the 1960s there were relatively few student activists who were well versed in Marx and Engels, or more than passingly interested in improving the lot of the "workers." Instead, the New Left cannily channeled youthful rebels to knock down the barriers to pleasure. The hard-won peace and prosperity that the generation that survived World War II had scraped together from amidst the graves of more than sixty million dead seemed to prosperous young Westerners a mere entitlement of birth. Few apart from reactionaries and churchmen thought to warn how fragile social order would prove when the wrecking ball of adolescent desire struck its bricks and mortar.

There was just one snake in the garden—the inconvenient fact that human beings are mammals, and reproduce the species through sexual intercourse. The human reproductive system is resilient, and over time will defeat most methods of contraception. The result was that the rise of birth control was accompanied by an explosion of unwanted pregnancies—the increase of promiscuity always outracing the improvements in contraception. By the

---

1 Ronald Reagan, "Abortion and the Conscience of a Nation," *The Human Life Review*, Spring 1983.

middle of the 1960s, the barrier to sexual liberation was no longer the tut-tutting of priests and prudes, or the fear of social disgrace, but a constant crop of squalling, unwanted infants. The progressive movement to free man from every obstacle to his desires was suddenly faced with a purely human obstacle—the reverence that pregnant women felt toward their very own preborn children. A feminist movement that had begun with Susan B. Anthony calling abortion a monstrous crime that men imposed on women adapted instead the ethic that Simone de Beauvoir had cribbed from her faithless lover, Jean-Paul Sartre: a search for self-liberation from every societal bond or external influence, which entailed women reengineering their sexuality to match that of "playboy" males. Abortion went from an illegal convenience mainly favored by single, promiscuous males to a fundamental human right demanded by female activists and favored with quiet philanthropy by population controllers, such as the Rockefeller Foundation—whose alarmist reports, with strong overtones of eugenics, would influence Supreme Court Justice Harry Blackmun, the author of *Roe v. Wade.*

Just as owners of slaves during the Enlightenment found "scientific" rationales for the immoral practice on which their own "liberty" rested, so sexual libertarians looked for support in the tenets of modern subhumanism. Future pope Joseph Ratzinger exposed the dynamics in his famous essay "The Problem of Threats to Human Life":

> If we look briefly at the modern age, we face a dialectic which continues even today. On the one hand, the modern age boasts of having discovered the idea of human rights inherent in every human being and antecedent to any positive law, and of having proclaimed these rights in solemn declarations. On the other hand, these rights, thus acknowledged in theory, have never been so profoundly and radically denied on the practical level. . . .

> The fundamental dogma of the Enlightenment is that man must overcome the prejudices inherited from tradition; he must have the boldness to free himself from every authority in order to think on his own using nothing but his own reason. . . .

> The idea of the good in itself is put outside of man's grasp. The only reference point for each person is what he can conceive on his own as good. Consequently, freedom is no longer seen positively as a striving for the good which reason uncovers with help from the community

and tradition, but is rather defined as an emancipation from all conditions which prevent each one from following his own reason. It is termed "freedom of indifference.". . .

An individualistic type of anthropology, as we have seen, leads one to consider objective truth as inaccessible, freedom as arbitrary, conscience as a tribunal closed in on itself. Such an anthropology leads woman not only to hatred toward men, but also to hatred toward herself and toward her own femininity, and above all, toward her own motherhood.

More generally, a similar anthropology leads human beings to hatred toward themselves. Man despises himself; he is no longer in accord with God who found his human creation to be "something very good" (Gen 1:31). On the contrary, man today sees himself as the destroyer of the world, an unhappy product of evolution. In reality, man who no longer has access to the infinite, to God, is a contradictory being, a failed product. Thus, we see the logic of sin: by wanting to be like God, man seeks absolute independence. To be self-sufficient, he must become independent, he must be emancipated even from love which is always a free grace, not something that can be produced or made. However, by making himself independent of love, man is separated from the true richness of his being and becomes empty. Opposition to his own being is inevitable. "It is not good to be a human being"—the logic of death belongs to the logic of sin. The road to abortion, to euthanasia and the exploitation of the weakest lies open.[2]

The makeshift quality of subhumanist morality would become clear only one year after Ratzinger wrote those words, in the logic of the Supreme Court decision *Planned Parenthood v. Casey,* whose key passage we noted in Chapter Five: "At the heart of liberty is the right to define one's own concept of existence, of meaning, of the universe, and of the mystery of human life."[3]

Think about that assertion for a moment. Does the "heart of liberty" include my "right" to define "my own concept" of liberty, too? And what if my concept doesn't match yours? Whose will prevail? And if each of us defines his own concept of meaning, how do we know what the court's decision

---

2 *L'Osservatore Romano,* April 8, 1991, at www.catholicculture.org/culture/library/view.cf m?id=187&repos=1&subrepos=&searchid=292732.

3 *Planned Parenthood of Southeastern Pa. v. Casey,* 505 U.S. 833 (1992)..

means when we read it? If I have a different concept of "the universe" than you do—as is my right—does that mean I can deny the existence of gravity and shove you out the window? According to the Supreme Court it does, as long as you haven't been born yet.

What the Court presents as the noble logic of American liberty is in fact a string of incoherent babble dressed up in the language of rights, which if taken seriously would make it impossible not just to govern but to communicate or even to think. It is delusion grounded in willfulness, the madness that follows a tantrum. It is what happens when your only axiom, finally, is, "I will not serve."

Elizabeth Anscombe traced the consequences of denying or wishing away the sanctity of preborn life, of persons who are completely helpless, residing in what we think of naturally as the safest place on earth—a mother's womb. As she wrote:

> This lack of reverence, of respect for that dignity of human nature so wonderfully created by God, is lack of regard for the one impregnable equality of all human beings. Lacking it, you cannot revere the dignity of your own human-ness, that is, the dignity of that same human nature in yourself. You may value yourself highly as a tennis player or a natural scientist, but without a change of heart you cannot value yourself as being a human, a *Mensch*. For you have shown the value you set on a human life as such. You are willing to extinguish it as it suits you, or as it suits the people who want you to do so.[4]

But philosophical essays can only go so far in showing the bitter price exacted by man's decision to withdraw his own offspring from the circle of empathy. What is needed is works of art, and we can recommend one: the powerful film *Sarah's Key* (2011). In it, Kristin Scott Thomas plays a middle-aged French journalist, married with just one child—a twelve-year-old daughter. She is working on a story about the deportation of Jews from Paris, which many Frenchmen still like to pretend was forced on France by the Nazis. But records show that it wasn't, that French officials willingly offered those Jews to Hitler, French policemen dutifully rounded them up, and millions of Frenchmen watched without protest while it was done. This is the story Thomas is telling, but along the way she discovers something strange. The

---

4 G. E. M. Anscombe, "The Dignity of the Human Being," in *Human Life, Action, and Ethics*, ed., Mary Geach and Luke Gormally (Charlottesville, VA: Imprint Academic Philosophy Documentation Center, 2005), 72.

quaint old apartment her husband has just inherited from his family fell into their hands during the war—at exactly the time that Jews in their part of Paris were rounded up for the camps. She starts to dig into the family's dirty laundry.

While she's doing the hard journalistic work, Thomas starts to feel physically drained, exhausted, and nauseous. At first she attributes this to the dark material she's exploring, but the doctor informs her otherwise: She is pregnant. Her shock is palpable (and very well played by Thomas in a stellar performance). She and her husband had tried for years to have a second child, even resorting without success to in vitro fertilization. She arranges a cozy, romantic dinner to break the news—and is staggered at his response. He no longer wants a second child. Things have changed in the past few years, he explains, and we built a life that makes both of us happy. You love your work, I love to travel, and our daughter will soon be away at school. We'll be free again, like newlyweds. Do you really want to spoil all that, for . . . this?

Thomas is angry, of course. She feels rejected, ashamed, disgusted. But she cannot deny the force of his arguments. This is an unasked-for intrusion on their lives, a biological accident like leukemia or cancer, a rebellion of mere matter that threatens what's really sacred: their freedom to pursue the lives they wanted. As arbitrary as the dictates of a king or the tenets of a religion, this biological problem threatens to break up her happy marriage—indeed, her husband insists he will leave her if she doesn't terminate the pregnancy. He's within his rights; did he ask her to get pregnant? Did they discuss it beforehand, and both agree to this course of action? Then how could he rightly be bound by her decision? No one has the right to force someone else to become a parent, does she?

Thomas redoubles her work and unearths the story of the Jewish family displaced from her husband's family apartment. She tracks down and follows the fate of each of its members, and confronts her father-in-law about his family's history. She learns to love the little Jewish girl Sarah, pulled out of her family home at nine years old by the neighborhood policeman and shipped off to a concentration camp. She neglects everything else—including her decision about her pregnancy—in search of some trace of Sarah. She learns to see the Holocaust not as some black and enormous monolith, but up close and near-at-hand. She picks up, if you will, a single pair of shoes. She learns what it means. And she chooses life.

That power of choice, that freedom that *Roe v. Wade* held as more sacred than life itself, is nothing to speak of lightly. Liberty is the hard-won product of thousands of years of struggle. It's the logical implication of classical reason and Jewish-Christian revelation. It's the crowning glory of human dignity. It is every single one of these things—or else it is nothing at all, a mere illusion, a flickering of electrical activity in the brain stem of a mammal. We are each of us the envy of angels. Or else we are accidents, as unfree and scraped clean of meaning as a pile of dead people's shoes.

What image of human nature would lead people to assert that their religious freedom and pursuit of happiness are sacred and inalienable rights? Rather an exalted image—one quite incompatible with the idea that we are mere cosmic byproducts, or extremely clever monkeys. Such a creature, whose rights are solemn and ought to be inviolable, surely ought not to be killed in the womb for the convenience of his or her parents. Deny the sanctity of life (in order, say, to allow women the "right" to abortion), and you remove any consistent argument against the State (or the Party, the Race, or some scientific elite) overriding every other human right. A state that allows abortion has no good argument against requiring it (when it suits the public interest)—or forcing particular women to bear children and preventing others from doing so. In the long run, even in the medium run, there is no middle ground between the old Judeo-Christian world and the Brave New World. Stumble out of the first, and you are already headed into the second.

* * * * *

A uniquely eloquent advocate for the sanctity of the human person in our lifetime was the pediatrician and geneticist Dr. Jérôme Lejeune (1926–1994). We cannot do full justice here to his story, which is best told in the tender memoir *Life Is a Blessing*, by his daughter Clara Lejeune-Gaymard.[5] In it, she recounts her father's groundbreaking medical discoveries, which were driven by his profound respect for the specialness and sanctity of every human life—however young, sick, or vulnerable. Lejeune's most important breakthrough was to uncover the genetic basis for Down syndrome, the presence of an extra chromosome in the DNA of children born with that condition. This discovery by itself helped transform the lives of patients and their families, who had for decades lived under a false moral stigma, since it was widely believed that Down syndrome in a child was the side effect of syphilis in the mother, which was associated in the popular mind with

---

5 Philadelphia: National Catholic Bioethics Center, 2010.

prostitution. By offering proof of a biological cause, Lejeune helped the parents of affected children move out of the shadows. He went on to uncover the genetic basis for another devastating birth defect, Cri-du-Chat syndrome, and made advances in understanding the causes of Fragile X syndrome. He also anticipated by decades the rest of medical science in his insistence on the importance of folic acid in reducing the risk of many birth defects.

Lejeune's discoveries won him early academic acclaim. In 1962, he was honored by President John F. Kennedy with the first Kennedy Prize. He was appointed the first Professor of Fundamental Genetics at the Faculty of Medicine of Paris in 1964, and in 1969 he received the most prestigious honor in his field from the American Society of Human Genetics, the William Allan Award.

Unlike many scientists of his era, Lejeune saw his work as deeply rooted in his relationship with patients and their families. He referred to his Down syndrome clients as "my little ones," and worked with their families to help them find educational and work opportunities, consistently taking time away from his research (and turning down opportunities to vastly increase his income) to see patients at his low-cost private clinic. Lejeune's research for the next thirty years was devoted to understanding the causes of genetic disorders and finding the means to treat these conditions in utero, as well as mitigating the effects of the disorder in children and adults. His goal was to gain the best and richest life possible for each patient.

Lejeune took with religious seriousness the medical vocation and the ethic that has undergirded it since Hippocrates: to do no harm, to serve the cause of life, and to put the interests of the individual patient first.[6] He watched with an almost uncomprehending horror in the 1960s and 1970s as the majority of his colleagues rejected key elements of this heritage and embraced a utilitarian, hedonist creed that accepted abortion and allowed Lejeune's "little ones" to be seen not as patients deserving treatment, but as problems that should be prevented.

In a bitter irony, the research Lejeune pioneered also led to the development of prenatal screening tests, now used by doctors to detect Down syndrome in preborn babies—most of whom are aborted. Lejeune denounced this abuse of science as "chromosomal racism." The first laws

---

6 Indeed, in the traditional Hippocratic Oath, new physicians specifically promised not to take part in abortions; in 1964, Dr. Louis Lasagna of Tufts University School of Medicine composed a watered-down version that specifically allowed for abortion—a rewrite that is used at most secular medical schools today.

in France permitting abortion, passed in 1975, were promoted as a means to help parents abort "defective" fetuses, and Lejeune was one of the few prominent scientists in France to lobby against them. In 1981, he testified before a U.S. Senate Judiciary Subcommittee on the "question" of when human life begins. After recounting the overwhelming biological evidence that the answer is "at conception," Lejeune revealed a little of the personal tenderness and wonder the preborn life evinced in him:

Thanks to a refined sonar-like imagery, Dr. Ian Donald, from England, a year ago succeeded in producing a movie featuring the youngest star in the world, an 11-week-old baby dancing *in utero* (in the uterus). The baby plays, so to speak, on a trampoline! He bends his knees, pushes on the wall, soars up and falls down again. Because his body has the same buoyancy as the amniotic fluid, he does not feel gravity and performs his dance in a very slow, graceful, and elegant way, impossible in any other place on the Earth. Only astronauts in their gravity-free state can achieve such gentleness of motion. (By the way, for the first walk in space, technologists had to decide where to attach the tubes carrying the fluids. They finally chose the belt buckle of the suit, reinventing the umbilical cord.)

When I had the honor of testifying previously before the Senate, I took the liberty of referring to the universal fairy-tale of the man smaller than the thumb. At two months of age, the human being is less than one thumb's length from the head to the rump. He would fit at ease in a nutshell, but everything is there: hands, feet, head, organs, brain, all are in place. His heart has been beating for a month already. Looking closely, you would see the palm creases and a fortune teller would read the good adventure of that tiny person. With a good magnifier the fingerprints could be detected. Every document is available for a national identity card.

With the extreme sophistication of our technology, we have invaded his privacy. Special hydrophones reveal the most primitive music: a deep, profound, reassuring hammering at some 60–70 per minute (the maternal heart) and a rapid, high-pitched cadence at some 150–170 (the heart of the fetus). These, mixed, mimic those of the counterbass and of the maracas, which are the basic rhythms of any pop music.

We now know what he feels, we have listened to what he hears, smelled what he tastes and we have really seen him dancing full of grace and youth. Science has turned the fairytale of Tom Thumb into a true story, the one each of us has lived in the womb of his mother.[7]

Lejeune would return to the United States to testify in the "frozen embryo" case, *Davis v. Davis*, that every embryo should be treated as a patient, not a commodity. He correctly foresaw the outcome of designating tiny human beings as property, not people. "Unclaimed property" is the current legal status of the hundreds of thousands of frozen embryos now languishing in a technological limbo across the world, embryos that scientists are hungrily seeking out for use in stem cell research. These infinitesimal human beings will either sit in freezers indefinitely or be cannibalized for parts.

As his daughter documents, Lejeune's activism led directly to his loss of research money, the end of his academic advancement, and a professional isolation that would prevail until the end of his life. As she wrote of her father's fate:

But here is a man who, because his convictions as a physician prohibited him from following the trends of his time, was banned by society, dropped by his friends, humiliated, crucified by the press, prevented from working for lack of funding. Here was a man who became, for certain people, a man to be beaten down; for others, a man not worth jeopardizing your reputation with; and for still others, an incompetent extremist.[8]

Lejeune-Gaymard recounts that even she found herself shunned at her university because of her father's activism, as if the guilt from "crimes" against public opinion had been transmitted genetically to her.

What recognition Lejeune still received began to come from those who shared his concern for the sanctity of life. In 1981 he met with Pope John Paul II—as it turned out, just a few hours before the attempt on the pontiff's life—and he joined the Pontifical Academy for Science. In 1994, John Paul would name him head of the newly established Pontifical Academy for Life. Lejeune would not be able to accomplish much in that position, as he was already dying of cancer. After a long and agonizing illness, he died on Easter Sunday, 1994. One of his last requests, his daughter reports, was that spaces

---

7 www.principlesandchoices.com/students/quick-code-library/pcs344/.
8 Lejeune-Gaymard, 94–95.

be saved at his funeral for his "little ones," the patients whom he loved so truly, to the end.

For Further Reading:

G. E. M. Anscombe, *Human Life, Action, and Ethics* (Charlottesville, VA: Imprint Academic Philosophy Documentation Center, 2005).

Hannah Arendt, *The Origins of Totalitarianism* (New York: Harcourt, Brace, Jovanovich, 1973).

Hadley Arkes, *Natural Rights and the Right to Choose* (Cambridge: Cambridge University Press, 2004).

Tatiana De Rosnay, Serge Joncour, and Gilles Paquet-Brenner, *Sarah's Key* (video), directed by Gilles Paquet-Brenner (Paris, Hugo Productions, 2010).

Peter Lawler, *Modern and American Dignity* (Wilmington, DE: ISI Books, 2010).

Clara Lejeune-Gaymard, *Life Is a Blessing* (Philadelphia: National Catholic Bioethics Center, 2010).

Robert P. George, *Conscience and Its Enemies* (Wilmington, DE: ISI Books, 2013).

Jason Jones, Eduardo Verastegui, and Pattie Mallette, *Crescendo* (video), directed by Alonso Alvarez (Los Angeles, Movie to Movement, 2012).

C. S. Lewis, *The Abolition of Man* (New York: HarperOne, 2009).

Ronald Reagan, *Abortion and the Conscience of a Nation* (Sacramento, CA: New Regency Communications, 2001).

Chapter Eight

The Existence of a Transcendent Moral Order

One of the most insightful things ever said about America is G. K. Chesterton's quip that it is "a nation with the soul of a church." Chesterton said that in 1922, at a time when much of Europe was made up of new, unsteady democracies that had been cobbled together from the shards of multicultural empires destroyed during World War I, and Russia was undergoing the laboratory experiment of dictatorial socialism. The United States had been the chief instigator of the breakup of those empires; Woodrow Wilson's late intervention in the war had thrown an unexpected and decisive victory to the Entente powers of Britain and France, and one of his peace conditions was the fracturing of the Austro-Hungarian Empire into homelands for its largest ethnic groups. Wilson's "Fourteen Points" were a model of American Progressivism, a secularized offshoot of the this-worldly, reformist Protestant movement called the Social Gospel—the religious tradition that had formed the pious, self-righteous Wilson. In essence, the Social Gospel theologians responded to doubts about the reliability of the Bible induced by Darwinian science by relegating Christian doctrine to the background, and focusing instead on Christian ethics—which Progressives argued could best be implemented through the mechanisms of the modern socialist state.

The power that the Social Gospel movement and its Progressive offshoot acquired in America bore witness to the deep wells of Protestant faith that remained in the country, and the strong impetus Americans feel to justify their political activity by some higher moral criterion than expediency or national interest. The fatal flaw in these movements is that the Social Gospel's ethical program was based not on solid, rationally defensible assertions about who man is and how he should live, but rather on vague, inherited Christian sentiments and social mores. Sentiments and mores are not enough in times of crisis, and a movement that relies on them is easily hijacked by activists who do possess a firm guiding philosophy—which might well be completely contrary to the worldview of the people who launched the movement. (Thus well-meaning liberal Christians who cooperate with

Communists find, over time, that their ideological allies eventually morph into their masters.) Without a firm anchor in metaphysical truth, tenderness can lead (as Flannery O'Connor famously said) to the gas chamber. What is needed instead of fragile prejudice and warm, fuzzy aspirations is a firm and defensible code of moral law, which transcends time and place and applies to every human being equally. Only such a code, carved in stone with the chisel of rigorous reasoning, will serve to restrain selfish interests and ideological passions, and preserve the dignity of every human person.

Applied to peacemaking, Wilson's missionary Progressivism drove him to try to edit out the bumps and scratches of history and eliminate self-interest and power politics from the relations between sovereign nations. Inevitably, his idealistic Fourteen Points were applied very unevenly, and ethnic self-determination was denied to millions of Germans, Austrians, Hungarians, and other "guilty" nationalities. What was worse, newly configured nations such as Czechoslovakia, Yugoslavia, and Poland were rife with their own dissenting minorities whose rights were barely protected by ineffectual treaties. These nations were unstable and militarily weak, and it took a truly utopian mind to imagine that even in alliance with a bloodied, exhausted France, they could contain a resurgent Germany or a rising Soviet Union. The toothless League of Nations, and utopian international pacts to "outlaw war," were the paper walls that were meant to hold out the storm of national rivalry and ethnic rage that the "war to end all war" had aggravated. The loftiness of Wilson's rhetoric comported badly with the cynical realpolitik that dictated the Treaty of Versailles, piling the guilt for the war on Germany and crippling that fledgling democracy with reparations it could not pay—which were meant to fund the British and French attempts to settle their enormous war debts to the United States.

But across the Atlantic, in the nation that had ended the war and set the tone (if not the terms) of peace, things looked a good deal more hopeful. America's losses in the war had been few (not quite 117,000 Americans had died in combat, compared to almost 1.4 million French), and its economy was booming. The population was growing, and instead of trying to control ethnic minorities who wanted to flee or secede, the United States was struggling with the sheer number of foreigners who clamored to enter the country.

In domestic policy as in diplomacy, Progressives were optimistic that they could solve age-old human problems through the application of research, social science, and the power of the state. This confidence was only somewhat more intense among the Bolsheviks in Russia, whose victory was greeted with enthusiasm by the likes of John Dewey and many of his followers—though many would be later disillusioned. (For an account of how slowly and reluctantly such fellow travelers would admit that the Soviet experiment was a monstrous failure, see Paul Kengor's *Dupes*.) While labor unions pressed for needed legal regulation of working conditions and picketed for higher wages, some elite reformers sought to attack poverty and social dysfunction at what they thought was its taproot: the birth of children to "unfit" parents (see Chapter 3).

In *Blessed Are the Barren: The Social Policy of Planned Parenthood*, Robert Marshall and Charles Donovan document in painstaking historical detail how the eugenics movement marched through the parlors and church halls of America's liberal Protestant elites, its advocates using native-born Americans' fear of displacement by teeming, fertile Jewish and Catholic immigrants to win influential converts to their cause. The main obstacle eugenicists faced among these churchgoers was the centuries-old condemnation of the means required to make eugenics work—contraception. This practice was condemned by every orthodox Protestant church, as it had been by Luther and Calvin, who passed along the opinion of the Fathers of the Church to their own spiritual descendants. However, the Protestant case against contraception was based entirely on theological tradition and the reading of biblical passages whose meaning could be contested; the Aristotelian body of natural law arguments that convinced Roman Catholics to reject this practice had languished in Protestant Europe. The fear of ethnic displacement, the happy collapse of infant mortality, the teeming slums of America's cities, and the hard-luck stories of large, impoverished families recounted by Margaret Sanger and her supporters proved quickly sufficient to overcome the inherited prejudice against contraception, and by 1930 the bishops of the Anglican Church broke the logjam, becoming the first Christian denomination to offer approval to the practice. (By 1968, the Catholic Church would be almost alone in maintaining the ancient teaching.) In the 1920s, America's Catholic bishops were among the only prominent voices opposing mandatory sterilization conducted in the name of eugenics. They argued against it in the name of the transcendent moral order (or natural law), claiming not only that its means were intrinsically evil, but that its ends were unjust. Human beings are not raw material to be molded by the state for its own purposes, and procreation and parenthood are sacred mysteries proper to married couples, which their neighbors have no business attempting to control.

Many of the same people who favored eugenics laws also thought that state action could solve the timeless human problems of substance abuse and addiction. America's draconian drug laws date from the Progressive Era, whose most famous policy failure was Prohibition. When it came to restricting alcohol, Progressives could count on another wellspring of support: the newly vibrant movement of Protestant fundamentalism. Wine-making Italians and beer-drinking Slavs were also seen as a threat to America's "Nordic" integrity, and strict immigration quotas were imposed in 1926 along frankly ethnic lines intended to preserve the ethnic balance in the United States, as well as to keep out the large numbers of long-mistreated, sometimes radicalized Jewish migrants who had fled Eastern Europe.

Chesterton was no ideologue, and he also saw the virtue in America's churchy soul. As you'd learn from reading *What I Saw in America* (1922), the democratic Chesterton was deeply impressed by Americans' commitment to fair play. Apart from the ugly reality of racial segregation, America was the place in the world that most disdained inherited prestige or unearned political privilege. Our culture and economy were built on the presupposition that any person, through hard work and talent, could rise to be the equal of anyone else. It didn't matter who your grandfather was, or whether you spoke with a "posh" accent. America cared what was inside a man, and what he was willing to do. As a self-made man himself, Chesterton respected that culture of openness, that love of justice. He also knew where it came from.

Over and over again throughout our history, Americans have been moved to test themselves against abstract ideals, sometimes at the expense of our short-term self-interest. The American Revolution was driven not so much by outrage at trivial taxes on stamps or sacks of tea, as by the sense that King George and his Parliament had no moral right to tax the colonies without allowing them representation. This violated the traditional rights of Englishmen, but as Thomas Jefferson carefully explained in the Declaration of Independence, it also flouted the laws of "nature's God." He built his rationale for the bloody, risky venture of American independence on the groundwork of "unalienable rights" endowed by our "Creator." It was to defend these rights that the signers of the Declaration pledged "our Lives, our Fortune, and our sacred Honor."

In other words, the very foundation of the United States rested on a proposition about reality: the existence of an objective, transcendent moral order. By making the rights of the person the cornerstone of the national edifice, Jefferson won sympathy from like-minded people across the world, who might otherwise not have cared about a tax dispute. He also planted a time bomb, an intellectual premise that would be used again and again to challenge unjust institutions—including slavery, the system that made

Jefferson's life of leisure possible. While it would have been impossible to unite the colonies and simultaneously abolish slavery, by making "unalienable rights" the core American principle, Jefferson wrote slavery's epitaph in advance.

As we have already explained (see Chapter Five), the content of "nature's laws" has been an endless source of argument in American politics. The phrase itself was intentionally ambiguous, in the same sense that Jefferson's chief intellectual influence, John Locke, had been equivocal in his writings on natural law. The Lockean-Jeffersonian account of natural law is one that philosophers would call "thin," containing little or no normative substance about what man is or how he ought to live if he hopes to thrive. Instead, the Enlightenment code merely prescribes a set of rules by which men should interact, based on rights that are not grounded in any metaphysics of human nature; these rights are simply asserted as "self-evident" and "unalienable." Such vagueness makes for effective political rhetoric, but tells us little about how to frame or interpret our laws, much less about how they relate to human flourishing—that is, to the authentic pursuit of happiness.

To understand why such a bold expression of the rights of the individual could serve as effective political rhetoric in eighteenth-century America and Europe—as opposed to the Ottoman Empire or the Empire of Japan—we must look to the broader cultural and religious context: an overwhelmingly Christian West, with its elevated idea of the person, and its history of the separation of spiritual and temporal powers.

Whatever his moral authority at the height of historical Christendom, the pope never ruled over Europe as a theocrat (as the caliphs had in Islamic lands) or claimed the status of incarnate god (as the emperor of Japan would until 1945). While popes fitfully attempted to assert their superior authority over secular Christian monarchs—for instance, by deposing certain rulers and absolving their subjects of their duty to obey them—such efforts often failed. What is more, the pope was bound in his interactions with rulers by the universal European assent to a body of common law that was grounded in a lively tradition of natural law. That natural law was not the fruit of divine revelation, although some of it was echoed in the Bible; rather, it was the organic product of thousands of years of reflection by philosophers and statesmen (especially Aristotle and Cicero), whose arguments were drilled into the heads of prospective clergymen and bureaucrats through Scholastic disputation at centers of learning such as the universities of Paris, Oxford, and Bologna. No pope claimed the power to revoke or override the natural law, and even his divinely guaranteed authority was bounded in its exercise by the common opinion of scholars and theologians concerning that natural law. On matters of revelation, too, the pope was constrained by tradition and could be corrected: Pope John XXII (1244–1334) famously developed a personal heresy that asserted that human souls "sleep" at the moment of death and are only awakened again at the day of judgment. Members of the College of Cardinals, alarmed by his public discourses asserting this opinion, intervened and compelled him to silence.

In the wake of the Reformation, the West no longer had a commonly accepted highest authority who could settle disputed questions of natural law or revelation, but the sources that academics cited remained largely the same: classical philosophers and the Fathers of the Church. Along with the authority of the Church, the persuasiveness of medieval precedents and the Aristotelian tradition came under question in the Enlightenment, as political philosophers such as Hobbes and Locke followed Descartes's example in claiming to assert only what unaided reason could convincingly prove. But the men who signed the American Declaration of Independence, and those who later wrote its Constitution, were by no means a mass of skeptical Enlightenment *philosophes* who dismissed the verdict of history and tradition, along with the Aristotelian tradition of natural law reasoning. The Deists among the Founders were a small and cautious minority among an overwhelmingly orthodox Protestant body. If we seek to interpret America's founding documents according to their original intention, we must see that its concepts of "liberty" and "equality" were meant to be read in a Christian context that took for granted the traditional tenets of natural law. The meaning we give to "liberty" and "the pursuit of happiness" must be colored by that tradition. "Liberty" in this sense is the freedom to exercise one's natural powers as they were intended by the Creator, and as reason tells us human beings ought to use them. (Suicide and drug addiction and prostitution are not activities that our liberty grants us the God-given right to practice.) Likewise, the "happiness" we must be free to pursue is the happiness proper to a human being—which is incompatible with life as a chattel slave, or as a member of an ethnic group subject to segregation.

The founders of America's free government firmly believed in both the dignity of the person (see Chapter Seven) and the existence of a timeless, rationally knowable natural law that reflected the intentions of the Creator— which most of them thought could be known even more reliably through the study of sacred Scripture. Indeed, the Constitution's famous refusal to establish a single church in the United States was the fruit of a well-founded Protestant concern for liberty of worship—and not of a Deist disdain for Christianity.

The legitimacy that most Americans throughout our history granted to religious sources as means to interpret our constitutionally guaranteed rights can be seen in the extended national argument over slavery. In the course of this decades-long debate, pamphleteers, scholars, and legislators made repeated appeals to the Bible, both in defense of slavery, and in building up the powerful abolitionist movement, which found its most reliable spokesmen among the ministers of New England. So critical were churchmen to the political debate over the moral status of slaves that religious denominations, such as the Baptists, split into southern and northern denominations over this question. Classical formulations of natural law, such as Aristotle's, had made room for slavery—the cornerstone of the social order in classical Greece, which only the radical Sophists would dare to question. But the Christian notion of the person as the image of God, redeemed and elevated to sonship with God through the incarnation of the Son of God in the form of a human person, had rendered slavery an anomaly, a pagan holdover that could be rendered repugnant to Christians through prophetic speech and action. The first great abolitionist movement, which arose in England under the leadership of William Wilberforce, was wholly the product of the Methodist movement in English churches.

As the abolitionist movement grew in strength, its leaders would use the Declaration as its chief rhetorical weapon, pointing out the stark hypocrisy of slave masters who cherished their "liberty." Although they never won a national consensus for outlawing slavery, the abolitionists did successfully render that institution disgraceful to most non-Southerners—such that Americans of other regions opposed its expansion into new, Western states, and were outraged when the Fugitive Slave Act compelled Northern, free states to act as slave catchers. The election of Abraham Lincoln was the expression of this outrage. Although he fought first to save the Union, Lincoln saw in the midst of war an opportunity: by tying the fight for union to the cause of emancipation, he made of the Civil War a crusade for America's founding principles—which relied for their legitimacy on the existence of a transcendent moral order (the laws of "Nature's God").

The postwar Jim Crow laws that were enacted throughout the country (not just the South) prevented the full recognition of the rights of nonwhite persons. It would take another century for the Civil Rights movement to force Americans to take a more rigorous look at the principles upon which our country rests. Many of their opponents tried to paint the Civil Rights protestors as anarchist or communist agitators—citing the cynical use by the American Communist Party of real racial grievances to recruit new party members. But because our very existence as a nation was only justified by this set of transcendent moral laws, Dr. Martin Luther King Jr. was able to make the case that equal rights for all was a patriotic principle. Despite the bitter resistance that claimed King's life, America was able to enact full, legal equality for all without tearing itself apart.

Martin Luther King Jr. did not rely on Marxist class analysis or ethnic self-seeking when he called for civil rights from Birmingham Jail, but cited the great Western and Christian tradition:

> A just law is a man-made code that squares with the moral law or the law of God. An unjust law is a code that is out of harmony with the moral law. To put it in the terms of St. Thomas Aquinas: An unjust law is a human law that is not rooted in eternal law and natural law.[1]

Because he cited the core principles of our country and our culture, King's arguments prevailed.

America is not the first or only country to recognize a transcendent moral order. In fact, the realization that positive laws must accord with (or bow to) the laws of heaven goes all the way back to the roots of Western culture—to classical Greece. Sophocles put this awareness of a transcendent law in the mouth of Antigone, who sacrifices her life to disobey King Creon's unjust edict. In the play, her brother, Polynices, committed treason by attacking the city of Thebes, and died in battle. Creon decides to impose on Polynices the ultimate punishment—to deny his soul rest in the underworld by refusing him proper burial. His body is left to the dogs and crows, and the death penalty is promised for anyone who dares to bury him. Antigone confronts the king, whose power is theoretically absolute, and insists that his laws are subject to a transcendent authority, the laws of the gods. Interestingly, Antigone cites not so much the "higher" law of the Olympian gods as the "lower" or primordial law of the gods of the underworld. This literary device points up the fact that a transcendent moral order is not only the proper criterion by which earthly laws can be judged; it is also the ground from which they grew. She tells Creon that she defied his decree because it

> . . . was not a law decreed by Zeus, nor by Zeus' daughter, Justice, who rules with the gods of the Underworld. Nor do I believe that your

---

1 Martin Luther King Jr., "Letter from Birmingham Jail," April 16, 1963, http://mlk-kpp01. stanford.edu/kingweb/popular_requests/frequentdocs/birmingham.pdf.

decrees have the power to override those unwritten and immutable laws decreed by the gods.

> These are laws which were decreed neither yesterday nor today but from a time when no man saw their birth; they are eternal! How could I be afraid to disobey laws decreed by any man when I know that I'd have to answer to the gods below if I had disobeyed the laws written by the gods, after I died?[2]

Creon's claim to flout the eternal law and dishonor the dead rests on his embrace of what we might anachronistically call legal positivism, a philosophy of jurisprudence that regards only official, codified laws as having any authority, regardless of their adherence to moral principles. Previously in the play, the Chorus has endorsed this theory, telling Creon, "You have the right, son of Menoeceus, to do as you please and to decree what laws you want, both, for the dead, as well as for the living." In an authoritarian context, this argument rings hollow to us today, but keep in mind that we, too, have a principle of legitimacy: democratic assent. In a modern setting, a government that sought to override the precepts of the moral law would cite not the will of the monarch but of the majority, claiming that "the American public demands" and that "only extremists and fundamentalists oppose" a proposed course of action. Creon also argues from expediency, from the necessity for the safety of the city, to set an appalling example of a traitor's ultimate fate. In other words, Creon defends his actions in terms that would recur throughout history whenever legal regimes attempt to override the fundamental precepts of the timeless moral order.

Antigone does not enter the dispute on Creon's terms. She asserts that he simply lacks the jurisdiction to make decisions that affect a man's eternal destiny. Such choices are beyond politics, beyond even the power of kings. The dead have an absolute right to burial, which no human ruler can revoke.

Returning to our history, the debate over slavery in America hinged, in the end, on whether the positive law of the Constitution (which explicitly allowed for the institution of slavery) would be allowed to stand, or whether that law was intrinsically unjust according to the higher standard of the natural law—in which case that law was null and void and should be repealed, and in the meantime could be disobeyed. This conflict was decided in favor

---

2 Sophocles, *Antigone*, trans., George Theodoridis, 449ff., www.poetryintranslation .com/PITBR/Greek/Antigone.htm.

of positive law by the Supreme Court in the 1857 Dred Scott decision; it took an appallingly bloody civil war to overturn that verdict.

Similar debates occurred among Americans during the Civil Rights movement, when blacks who tried to use segregated facilities were denounced as "lawbreakers," and they have arisen again thanks to the Supreme Court's 1973 judicial fiat, *Roe v. Wade*—a ruling that stated that the "privacy" rights granted by the positive law of the Constitution trumped the intrinsic right to life of a preborn child, which the law does not recognize as a person.

Perhaps the most dramatic confrontation of positive law and natural law arose in the wake of World War II, when the victorious Allies sought to mete out justice to the leaders of the defeated, disgraced Third Reich. Throughout the course of the war, the Western Allies had repeatedly denounced Axis atrocities against civilians, and promised that after their defeat the responsible parties in the governments of Germany, Italy, and Japan would face a court of justice. At first, President Roosevelt had announced the intention of trying Nazi generals and bureaucrats according to the legal systems of the occupied countries in which their crimes had been committed, but this quickly showed itself to be impractical; the same SS commander might have executed hostages, deported Jews, and starved civilians in Belgium, Poland, and Greece. Trying him successively in each of these countries was not a realistic option. The Soviets preferred to try the German war criminals they captured in their own courts, on the model of the "show trials" that had marked Stalin's Terror. The Allies knew that such political trials would be transparently biased and hold no moral legitimacy in the eyes of the world, and that the spectacle of Stalin's criminals putting Hitler's criminals on trial might even evoke some sympathy for the devils. Concerned to avoid such a spectacle, some British leaders favored summary justice—execution upon apprehension of Nazi leaders and commanders. The Americans, however, thought that this form of victor's justice would bring with it the same moral hazards as the approach the Russians proposed.

So Roosevelt (and after him, Truman) insisted on international tribunals that would be conducted with every concern for fairness and the rights of the accused, which would record for the eyes of history the precise details of the crimes the Axis leaders had committed, and shame the members of the respective aggressor nations who had supported their governments' policies. A number of obstacles presented themselves to the prosecution of war criminals, such as the differences between Anglo-American and Continental legal systems and standards of evidence, and the politicized nature of Soviet trial proceedings and jurisprudence. But the most important problem was philosophical: How could the Allies prosecute individual officers and officials for acting on behalf of a government—"following orders"—and doing things that had not been illegal in their own country at the time, such as organizing a genocide or conspiring to fight an aggressive war? For a comparative case, imagine that the U.S. government after 1865 had prosecuted former slaveholders, or that a future U.S. government tried to prosecute doctors for performing abortions after 1973. The prohibition of "ex post facto" prosecution is in fact a core principle of English common law—the system that largely prevailed at Nuremberg, at the insistence of the United States.

There was only one logical solution: To assert that the war criminals had in fact broken laws that preexist and transcend the positive laws of any regime, such as Nazi Germany or fascist Italy, laws that any rational human being should be able to perceive and know are binding. The Allies were forced to acknowledge a principle that had largely dropped out of Western jurisprudence: the existence of a transcendent moral order. However, the intellectual taboo against explicitly asserting such an order was powerful. The modern philosophical skepticism about there being a rational order that pervades the universe, much less one that aptly describes human nature, rights, and duties, had permeated the legal field as thoroughly as any other— not just in Germany, but throughout most of the West. (It was mostly in Catholic universities and in faculties of international law that the tradition of natural law was passed along to students.) The Allies rightly condemned the Axis officials for "crimes against humanity," but lacked an explicit account of what humanity is, and what humans deserve. The newly created United Nations would offer such an account in the 1946 Universal Declaration of Human Rights, a document that showed significant natural law influence, thanks to the insistence of drafters such as France's René Cassin and Lebanon's Charles Malik.[3]

But even the outrage of the victorious Allies after six years of grinding conflict that had claimed more than forty million lives was not sufficient to revive in legal circles the concept of natural law, and relativist objections to even the concept of "supra-positive" law would dog prosecutions of war criminals for years. In the Israeli trial of Holocaust architect Adolf Eichmann, for instance, the defense attorneys would claim,

---

3 Allan Carlson, "Globalizing Family Values," a talk for the Charismatic Leaders' Fellowship, January 12, 2004, profam.org/docs/acc/thc.acc.globalizing.040112.htm.

A solid awareness of values, which alone could make such supra-positive ideas binding and at the same time enforceable in law, does not exist at present—and not only in the national but also in the international sphere. Thus, for instance, Jescheck [a legal scholar of the day] has raised doubts "whether supreme legally protected interests of the community of international law, recognized by the whole of mankind as absolute values, do exist at all." Schwarzenberger has confirmed these doubts in his book *Power Politics*. At the outset, he emphasizes the religious origin of most ethical systems which, by a process of secularization, have developed, later on, a more or less greater degree of "autonomy" from their religious origin. Schwarzenberger then asks the following question:

"Does not this very origin of moral rules establish a presumption against the existence of an universal code of international morality? Do not necessarily Western, Soviet and Far Eastern statesmen mean very different things when they speak of justice, equity, honour or friendship between States?"[4]

Sadly, there is some validity to this ploy on the part of a mass executioner's defense attorneys. The West had spent the better part of the Enlightenment dismantling the metaphysical underpinnings of a transcendent moral order, even as ethically minded secular philosophers such as Immanuel Kant struggled manfully to manufacture a code of universal morality that could stand atop the void created when God was banished and ultimate reality was deemed beyond the powers of man to know with certainty. By the nineteenth century, few jurists or philosophers of law in Europe were inclined to rule much differently from the U.S. Supreme Court's chief justice Roger B. Taney, whose decision in *Dred Scott* had ignored the transcendent truth of the humanity of slaves, to affirm their positive legal status as no more than chattel. The collapse of a common sense of international morality was surely a contributing factor to the brutality with which both World War I and II were waged—and indeed, to the surges of fanatical nationalism that made such wars themselves inevitable.

The melancholy story of how the West forgot its reasons for deeming wrong aggressive war, genocide, and the murder of civilians has been chronicled in exacting scholarly detail. But the best account of it does not date

---

4 The Trial of Adolf Eichmann, "Defence Submission 2," www.nizkor.org/hweb/people/e/eichmann-adolf/transcripts/Sessions/Defence-Submission-02-02.html.

from after World War II and the Nuremberg Trials. In fact, it was published in 1936 by an ordinary German lawyer named Heinrich Rommen, who had watched with horror for three years as erudite jurists, philosophers of law, and prominent attorneys disgraced themselves with their willingness to accommodate the Nazi seizure of power and the perversion of the centuries-old system of German justice to suit the arbitrary dictates of a totalitarian ideology. Rommen served as a prophet at the risk of his career and even his freedom, in the full knowledge that opponents of Nazi ideology were already languishing in concentration camps such as Dachau. His signature work, *The Natural Law: A Study in Legal and Social History and Philosophy*,[5] managed to escape prior censorship, but it ended Rommen's legal career, forcing him to flee Nazi Germany in 1938. He would later teach legal theory at prominent American universities, including Georgetown. In that book, Rommen traces the historical duel between advocates of natural and of purely positive law, from ancient Greece up through Weimar Germany—showing in painful detail how the abandonment of natural law in favor of legal positivism tends to serve the interests of tyrannical regimes, and laying out with considerable philosophical sophistication the intellectual reasons why one theory or another came to dominate. In essence, Rommen writes, the difference between positivism and natural law comes down to a theory of origins: What is the first principle in nature and the universe? Is it power or is it reason? He shows how Christian nominalists, orthodox Muslims, and materialists such as Hobbes and his successors agree in embracing power—either the arbitrary will of an inscrutable God whose decisions are absolute, or the blind forces of nature, which include the irrational passions of instinct-driven human mammals. Plato, Aristotle, the Roman Stoics, the Catholic Scholastics, and those Protestants who carried on the natural law tradition by contrast saw divine reason as the guiding force of the universe, holding that God binds himself and his own decisions by the self-consistent rules of the reason that inheres in his very being. Likewise, humans can see, through their own God-given reason—which is impaired but not obliterated by sin—the structure, purpose, and proper shape of human life. What we learn from reflecting on man's own nature, from what he needs to fulfill it and live it integrally, provides the meat of the natural law, which statesmen are bound to embody in the positive laws they promulgate, and which must guide our own daily decisions. Laws that imperfectly embody the natural law ought generally to be obeyed, in the interest of maintaining the great

---

5 English edition, trans., Thomas R. Hanley, OSB (Indianapolis: Liberty Fund, 1998).

good of public order; but laws (such as the Nazi race laws) that flagrantly contravene the basic principles of human dignity ought to be resisted as vigorously as prudence permits. They are the unjust laws that Aquinas (and later, Martin Luther King) would call "no law at all."

Because of his almost reckless courage in denouncing the lawless laws of the Nazi dictatorship while living at its mercy, Rommen is the man we hold up for emulation as the icon of the transcendent moral order. Here is his precise summary of the high point of natural law thinking in the writing of Aquinas, which Rommen cited in the face of Nazi irrationalism, perverted Romanticism, and blind worship of power:

> In the essential nature of the created world, as it came forth in conformity with the will of the Creator, are imbedded also the norms of its being. In the essential nature is likewise founded essential oughtness, the eternal law, which is God's wisdom so far as it directs and governs the world as first cause of all acts of rational creatures and of all movements of irrational beings. The eternal law, then, is the governance of the world through God's will in accordance with His wisdom. This law is thus the order of this world. Creatures fulfill this law in conformity with their nature as it has been fashioned by God: from the lifeless and inorganic realm of creation, through the living but dumb creatures, to the rational and free beings. . . .

Had Germans in 1936 awakened their consciences and rejected the seductive excuses of legal positivism and metaphysical skepticism, few of them could have continued to cooperate in the preparation of aggressive war, mass genocide, or any of the other crimes that Hitler had openly promised to commit in his political manifestos and fervid speeches. There was still time to resist, and there were powerful elements in the German Army who were prepared to launch a coup against Hitler's regime, provided they saw sufficient public support for such a move. The seamless cooperation of Germany's famous bureaucracy, its punctilious judges and lawyers, and the faculty of its universities, was essential to maintaining and solidifying the Nazi regime.

Likewise in our time, crimes against the human person are only made respectable and raised to legality with the aid of highly educated collaborators—from the lawyers who work pro bono for Planned Parenthood, to the bioethicists who make excuses for euthanasia, to the political figures who justify torture and preemptive war. If we have any hope of preventing in the twenty-first century a higher-tech repetition of the crimes and outrages that bloodied the twentieth, we must regain a lively sense that our actions have intrinsic moral value—a positive or negative one that transcends the words of the Constitution, the letter of federal law, the shifting winds of elite and mass opinion, and even the urgent demands of so-called necessity. We must be willing to stand with Antigone, and even be prepared in extreme cases to die alongside her rather than to join, assist, applaud, or merely enable her killers.

For Further Reading:

Hadley Arkes, *First Things* (Princeton, NJ: Princeton University Press, 1986).

G. K. Chesterton, *What I Saw in America,* in *The Collected Works of G. K. Chesterton, Vol. 21: What I Saw in America / The Resurrection of Rome / Side Lights* (San Francisco: Ignatius Press, 1990).

John Finnis, *Natural Law and Natural Rights* (Oxford: Oxford University Press, 2011).

Richard M. Gamble, *The War for Righteousness* (Wilmington, DE: ISI Books, 2003).

Russell Hittinger, *The First Grace: Rediscovering the Natural Law in a Post-Christian World* (Wilmington, DE: ISI Books, 2007).

Robert Marshall and Charles Donovan, *Blessed Are the Barren: The Social Policy of Planned Parenthood* (San Francisco: Ignatius Press, 1991).

Eric Metaxas, *Amazing Grace: William Wilberforce and the Heroic Campaign to End Slavery* (New York: HarperOne, 2007).

Heinrich Rommen, *The Natural Law* (Indianapolis: Liberty Fund, 1998).

Sophocles, *Antigone*, trans., Martin L. D'Ooge (Minneapolis: Dover Thrift Edition, 1993).

Leo Strauss, *Natural Right and History,* (Chicago: University of Chicago Press, 1965).

Chapter Nine

Subsidiarity: The Duty of Governments to Defend Civil Society

The historian Lord Acton is famed for reflecting that "power tends to corrupt." This is less an observation about power itself than it is about human nature and its vulnerability. Whatever our aspirations toward ideals, we are also goaded by instincts, biased by prejudices, and prone to self-serving rationalizations. To use an old-fashioned expression, man is fallen.

Our imperfect and egocentric nature makes it perilous for any of us to gain coercive power over our fellow men, since such power lets us indulge in selfishness, hubris, sadism, and other symptoms of the hunger to be "as gods." Give someone the power to dominate, and these dark drives will rise and begin to corrupt the man, who might have otherwise been virtuous, until (as Acton warned) "absolute" power corrupts him "absolutely."

Clearly, this statement alone is a little too pessimistic, and if applied too crudely might be misleading. A parent deserves the power to coerce her minor children, a general to coerce his soldiers, and a policeman to force a tipsy driver out of his car. Although such powers can be (and frequently are) abused, only a truly delusional utopian would imagine that human society can liquidate every trace of hierarchy or compulsion. It is a sad fact that many of the most destructive ideologies that emerged to mar modern life found their first motives in the urge to eliminate injustice and the abuse of power, only to become themselves more destructive than any of the old abuses. In twentieth-century politics as in nineteenth-century medicine, the cure was often worse than the disease.

Justified complaints about the coercive powers of fathers and husbands helped to generate current forms of feminism that threaten to liquidate family life altogether—and we have seen it, in fact, disappear from major sectors of Western society, with large swathes of the poor born to single mothers, dependent on distant government aid instead of husbands and fathers.

Outrage at abusive work relationships and unjust working conditions gave birth to the various forms of socialism, from the murderous Marxist-Leninism that collapsed in 1989, to the stagnant modes of socialism that prevail now in Western Europe, which make it so hard to fire any employee that it is hazardous even to hire one, and cocoon every citizen with guarantees and subsidies that have now become "human rights."

The racial biases and petty tyrannies that sometimes marked local government in America have encouraged two equal and opposite errors: the radical libertarianism that seeks to dismantle the state altogether, and its evil twin, the fervent centralism that would concentrate all power in the hands of federal bureaucrats charged with enforcing a uniform, utilitarian code of conduct on every community in America.

This last tendency, bureaucratic centralism, is a growing menace in America, as our federal government cheerfully contemplates the prospect of closing every Catholic institution in the country rather than let employers follow their consciences on what kind of health care they will offer. Reformers who see in every kind of existing inequality prima facie proof of injustice are willing to steamroll over religious freedom, property rights, and economic freedom in their relentless drive to ensure that every citizen receive a full menu of "basic human rights" that accrues at the moment of birth (and not, we must note, at conception) without imposing any responsibilities beyond one's duty to pay his taxes. The state will take care of the rest, and it will see to it that there is no escape from its all-encompassing power, which invades every nook and cranny of private life, demonizes and then suppresses dissent, until the agenda of those who control the central power has imposed its ultimate goal: a total political and intellectual uniformity.

Much of the West already is subject to such regimes; Western European countries we still call "free" are devoid of private schools and colleges, bare of private charities, unfriendly to parents' rights in education (some, such as Germany, jail homeschoolers and take away their children), and willing to punish impolitic speech with terms in prison. It is our task as sober defenders of ordered liberty to recognize real injustice where it occurs, and to offer solutions that do not cause more harm than good.

So how do we navigate among all the various destructive extremes that fail to do justice either to our unalienable individual rights or to our nature as social creatures whose very identities are formed by family and community? This issue divides political movements across the contemporary spectrum— and we do not pretend to offer a comprehensive answer. Instead, let us offer some principles of discernment, which any citizen can use in analyzing political questions as he encounters them. It is best to begin with a question:

At what point in an argument is it right for me to pull a gun? Or call the cops, so they can pull out their guns? The answer you give to this question determines pretty much what system of government you favor, what kind of economic and social policies, and even what level of taxes and regulation. In fact, most of the disputes in politics can be boiled down to the issue of which social, moral, and economic goods ought to be defended by police force and backed up by the threat of prison. When should you call in the police and threaten your neighbor with jail time because his actions don't conform to your vision of the good? On any given issue (drug use, abortion, wage levels, pollution, discrimination, "hate speech"—fill in the blank), there are three possible judgments a person could make:

1. This is morally indifferent; the natural law (see Chapter Seven) doesn't teach that one course of action or another is required. You are free to act as prudence tells you.

2. There is a right course of action here, and as a matter of justice and the common good, the state must be willing to enforce that course of action and punish those who act otherwise.

3. There is a right course of action here, and a wrong one. But getting the state involved would be imprudent because it would violate other goods that are too important.

Examples of issues that fit the first category are easy to think of. Should you direct your charity toward soup kitchens or crisis pregnancy shelters? Should Billy go to graduate school or join the army? And so on. Large segments of life fall into this category, which we might label "neutral." Obviously, no one but a totalitarian would wish to politicize decisions such as these.

Problems arise when we try to distinguish what belongs in the second category from what really belongs in the third. The great divide between illiberal, paternalistic governments (e.g., feudal, theocratic, or socialist) and free governments rests on how we routinely settle this question. Do we assume as a matter of course that the state ought to promote the good by using its coercive power to seize our property and march us at gunpoint to prison? Or do we see the use of coercive power as a necessary evil and try to minimize it as much as possible? Our focus in this chapter is on how to resolve such questions intelligently, and apply the answers to practical questions of politics.

While the state might still exist even absent the fall of man—Aquinas, following Aristotle, thought it would have—it is only because of the fall that the state requires the use of violence, both to prevent and correct injustices and to wage war in self-defense. Traditional just war theory (see Chapter Two) insists that the use of violence by the state is properly a last resort, when every other means to resolve a conflict has failed. Of course, governments have routinely violated this principle over the centuries, waging wars they insisted were "just" for trivial or arbitrary reasons, and fighting in ways that failed to respect the rights of unarmed civilians. Nevertheless, the fact that just war principles have been routinely flouted does not invalidate them, as Machiavelli and other practitioners of realpolitik came to assert. We saw in the bloody twentieth century what results when men in power give up even the pretense of respecting justice and equity in the conduct of international politics and the waging of war— and we punished such men at Nuremberg.

It is no coincidence that the regimes that abandoned any principle of restraint in waging war had previously discarded norms restraining the power they wielded over their own citizens in peacetime. Total war walks hand in hand with the "total" or totalitarian state, whose governing principle Benito Mussolini summed up in a 1928 speech: "All within the state, nothing outside the state, nothing against the state."[1] The regimes in Germany and Russia were much more rigorous in applying this principle than the creaky Italian dictatorship, and it is no coincidence that they were also more effective at liquidating internal political opponents and "unwanted" ethnic minorities, and at waging total war.

Since the structure of totalitarian governance seems to mirror total war, it is worth considering that the proper answer to resisting and restraining the abuse of government power in peacetime would resemble just war teaching. Could we come up with an equivalent moral principle to govern the proper use of state coercion outside of war—a "just peace" theory, if you will?

It turns out that we don't need to. Such a doctrine already exists, and has a name. The principle of subsidiarity amounts in fact to the application of the same principles that govern just war theory to the ordinary business of lawmaking and government. Precursors of the idea of subsidiarity were influential over the centuries and arose in a number of countries. The concepts of federalism in America, and decentralism in Switzerland, aimed at the same goals we now subsume under subsidiarity—a term that was popularized by Pope Pius XI in his encyclical *Quadragesimo Anno*.[2] This document was published in 1931, when totalitarian parties already governed Italy and

---

1 Harwood Lawrence Childs, ed., *Propaganda and Dictatorship* (New York: Arno Press, 1972), 48.

2 www.vatican.va/holy_father/pius_xi/encyclicals/documents/hf_p-xi_enc_19310515_quadragesimo-anno_en.html, 79.

Russia, and brawled in the streets of Germany, seeking absolute power. Pius XI laid out the principle of subsidiarity in clear and straightforward terms:

> Just as it is gravely wrong to take from individuals what they can accomplish by their own initiative and industry and give it to the community, so also it is an injustice and at the same time a grave evil and disturbance of right order to assign to a greater and higher association what lesser and subordinate organizations can do. For every social activity ought of its very nature to furnish help to the members of the body social, and never destroy and absorb them.

The pope did not derive this principle from some tenet of Christian theology that nonbelievers could be expected to reject, but from a sober consideration of the natural law tradition in the light of the social problems of his day; moreover, he cited it as a timeless principle, which held true implicitly wherever human beings live in community.

Let us translate this principle into contemporary language and concerns. Subsidiarity demands that social problems be resolved, whenever possible, by free individuals working together as families, charities, churches, or other units of "civil society." Only when it is obviously clear that a vital good, or a norm of justice, cannot be maintained without the use of government force are we even permitted to call in the police. And wherever possible, the person we call should be the sheriff—not the FBI or the United Nations. In other words, subsidiarity dictates that any problem addressed by the state should be resolved at the local level, by the relevant town or county. Only issues that cannot be fixed this way should be referred to the next highest level of power, the state or province. If a problem eludes the power and expertise of New York or Ontario, only then should it be referred to the federal government. Issues that reach beyond even what national governments can resolve must be addressed by the United Nations or through treaties.

Just as rulers throughout the centuries have flouted just war teaching, governments have trampled all over the truths about human rights summed up in subsidiarity. A student of history need only consult the record of early modern "absolute" monarchs to see the inexorable liquidation of local autonomy, and the gathering in of coercive power over the lives of citizens by the centralizing states that dominated most of Europe. Political writers served the interests of monarchs who sought to accumulate power, from England's James I to France's Louis XIII, and to this end they revived and modernized the paternalistic political theories of classical Greece, applying to the vast expanses of national empires ideas that had been conceived for tiny, compact city-states. While of course we can't presume here to sum up the philosophies of government of Plato and Aristotle, we can identify a key element that distinguishes their thought from the Christian liberal tradition that shaped the founding of the United States: a top-down philosophy of government, which centered on the "rights" of lawgivers and rulers to enforce their vision of the good in citizens' lives instead of the rights of citizens against the powers of the state. A rival, personalist politics of liberty also arose from Christian sources, to match the exalted Christian idea of each human being, and was expressed in institutions like English common law and Swiss democracy. It coexisted with the older, pagan authoritarian strain, and in a few countries, such as England and Switzerland, the idea of liberty won out against its rival—largely because of historical accidents such as extreme religious divisions in the countries that demanded the separation of powers or decentralist policies. Similar divisions, and the strong influence of the liberal tradition in England, led America's founders to embrace a highly decentralized form of government, with branches of government that were intentionally set up in opposition to each other to restrain the activist temptation to which political leaders are too often prone.

With this core principle in mind, of a preferential option for nonviolence and noncoercion, we should look with prudent care at every social and political issue, from economic inequality to health care, from drug laws to foreign policy. We must avoid the intellectual traps that lie on every side of the truth. Too many modern Westerners use liberty as a pretext for sliding into relativism, letting their healthy aversion to calling the cops and throwing their neighbors in jail corrupt their sense of what is good and true. Just because the state is not permitted to enforce religious orthodoxy does not mean that religious truth is of no importance. The state may not imprison people for adultery as the U.S. military still does, but that fact does not ratify as good every "sexual choice" of each "consenting adult."

Some indignant religious conservatives fall not into relativism but illiberalism, concluding that whatever is morally good ought to fervently promoted with all the blunt force of the state. For instance, God's existence can be known by reason alone; hence atheism flies in the face of the natural law. So an atheist raising his children in unbelief could be said to be flouting that law. Does that mean the state should intervene and take them away? Of course not, because the good of family life is too vital to be disturbed in this way. Some sexual acts violate the natural law. Would we favor hidden cameras in every citizen's home so that violators can be arrested and imprisoned? No, we would not. Does that refusal to violate privacy and grant enormous power to legislators and bureaucrats imply that we are sexual libertines? No, it does not.

Liberty is a vital good, especially given the fact of human fallenness. The men who draft and enforce a law are every bit as rife with original sin as any citizen. Power may not in every case corrupt, but it is always a near occasion of sin, which ought to be treated warily. This is the lesson the American founders took to heart, and which too many Americans are now lazy enough to forget.

Even as we join the libertarians in defending the individual from tyranny and fighting the growth of Leviathan, we also must see that the isolated individual is not the hero of our story. Cut off from family, church, and culture, he is an atom whirling in the void—an all-too-tempting target for manipulation and control by a power-hungry state. It is only in the context of healthy nonstate civil society, and a participatory local government, that persons can live a fully human life, blunt the jagged edges of Darwinian competition for success, and find the meaning that "mass man" has learned to see in the state, the party, or the race.

We propose instead to embrace decentralism, diversity, and the gorgeous mosaic of unequal outcomes that such a bottom-up approach to government power will generate, as the fifty states, and thousands of towns, act as laboratories of modern, democratic living. Let the people of Vermont towns ban stores like Walmart if they wish, while Texans carry loaded guns and Coloradans smoke whatever pleases them. Only a broadly decentralized power that lets the diverse body of Americans vote with their feet on how they wish to live can accommodate a country as wild and woolly as ours, without homogenizing by force the many strands that make up our society. The mores of cosmopolitan towns should neither dominate nor liquidate those of rural communities, and life in America should thrive as a vibrant patchwork, instead of a drab uniformity imposed on all from above. That model alone will avoid tyrannizing minorities or persecuting dissent. Happily, it is the very model our Constitution envisioned, and it is one that is within our reach if we have the courage to grasp it.

Given the tenacious nature of poverty in America, and the growing social dysfunction of the people who make up the poor—the fracturing of their families, their lack of class mobility, the almost hereditary nature of reliance on public assistance—it should be clear that the approach our country is taking toward addressing poverty is not working. Decades of research have shown the failures of programs such as the Great Society, which have served less to mobilize the poor and move them upward than to tame them and make them manageable. We have no more urban riots, as we did in the 1960s before the Great Society's advent. But the lives and the prospects of America's poor have not improved, and in many ways are growing worse—as Charles Murray documents in his alarming recent study *Coming Apart*, which notes that the level of family breakup and other social problems among America's white majority is currently at the level that so alarmed Daniel Patrick Moynihan when he saw it in the African American minority in 1965. What was tragic when it befell a single community is downright menacing when it spreads to the rest of society.

When what you have been trying has clearly failed over the course of five decades, and in fact appears to be making matters worse, it is only sane to reexamine the very premises of your efforts. We would like to suggest that the reason America's poverty programs fail is that they violate the truths about human nature that subsidiarity recognizes, and inadvertently reinforce and encourage the self-destructive habits that they were meant to help people overcome—such as illegitimate childbearing, the failure to marry, and the absence of paternal role models in the homes of poor families. Our system, in the laudable effort to provide nutrition and health care to the children of the poor, lets their fathers entirely off the hook, and thus removes the strongest incentive young women have historically felt for avoiding sexual conduct until they are married. As George F. Gilder observed back in 1973 in *Sexual Suicide*, the welfare state steps forward as the surrogate father, the default provider for every deadbeat dad—and needless to say, it does not offer all the human and moral benefits of an actual human father. A teenage girl who gets pregnant can apply for a range of benefits that make it possible for her to move out of her parents' home and begin her own household, fully supported by the government. If our national goal was to increase the incidence of teenage pregnancy and suppress the marriage rate among the poor, how exactly would we do things any differently?

It is hard to see how a government-sponsored program, in our age of postmodern, subhumanist morality, could possibly act otherwise. It allots the poor financial "entitlements" and cannot inquire how they are putting them to use. Apart from minor, easily flouted restrictions on the use of things like "food stamps," government programs do not and cannot offer incentives that spur the poor toward less self-destructive behavior. Each subsequent out-of-wedlock child that a young woman has will bring with him a new set of benefits, since we rightly do not wish to punish innocent children for their mother's mistakes. But in setting up such a system, we mask the fact that such decisions are mistakes. We put a Band-Aid on the short-term problem of how a young mother will feed her children and get them health care, and disguise the long-term ills that such children suffer from growing up without fathers, and with mothers whose experience of the world of paying work will be intermittent at best.

The answer to this problem is not some eugenics-infected program to place "welfare mothers" on more effective birth control, nor sudden cuts in public welfare programs that leave the poor unprovided for. Instead, we should prepare the way for a gradual rollback of public welfare benefits, by building a new safety net, one that is funded and administered by private agencies—some of them faith-based, all of them informed by a more elevated view of the human person as a responsible adult who can make rational choices.

In a justly famous article, William J. Stern of *City Journal* documented in detail how such a benevolently paternal, private charity system worked: how it addressed the crippling social pathologies suffered by the Irish who had escaped the Potato Famine and landed in New York City. It is worth quoting him at length:

> New York's Irish truly formed an underclass; every variety of social pathology flourished luxuriantly among them. Family life had disintegrated. . . . In *The New York Irish*, Ronald Bayor and Timothy Meagher report that besides rampant alcoholism, addiction to opium and laudanum was epidemic in these neighborhoods in the 1840s and 1850s. . . . An estimated 50,000 Irish prostitutes, known in flash talk as "nymphs of the pave," worked the city in 1850, and Five Points alone had as many as 17 brothels. Illegitimacy reached stratospheric heights—and tens of thousands of abandoned Irish kids roamed, or prowled, the city's streets. . . . Death was everywhere. In 1854 one out of every 17 people in the sixth ward died. In Sweeney's Shambles the rate was one out of five in a 22-month period. The death rate among Irish families in New York in the 1850s was 21 percent, while among non-Irish it was 3 percent. Life expectancy for New York's Irish averaged under 40 years. Tuberculosis, which Bishop Hughes called the "natural death of the Irish immigrants," was the leading cause of death, along with drink and violence.

The man who took it upon himself to address this appalling problem was not a government official but a private citizen acting on behalf of a free institution of civil society—Bishop John Hughes, the Catholic prelate of New York.

Because he did not represent a modern, morally neutral welfare state but a Church with a crystal-clear code of virtuous living, Hughes was free to build a program of social restoration that drew on the fuller, more accurate vision of human life to be found in classical natural law—a vision that forced recipients, on pain of being cut off, to assume responsibility for themselves and become self-reliant citizens–in other words, to claim the kind of "freedom" that the U.S. founders actually fought to defend. As Stern explains,

> Hughes's solution for his flock's social ills was to re-spiritualize them. He wanted to bring about an inner, moral transformation in them, which he believed would solve their social problems in the end. . . . With unerring psychological insight, Hughes had his priests emphasize religious teachings perfectly attuned to re-socializing the Irish and helping them succeed in their new lives. It was a religion of personal responsibility that they taught, stressing the importance of confession, a sacrament not widely popular today—and unknown to many of the Irish who emigrated during the famine, most of whom had never received any religious education. . . . Hughes proclaimed the need to avoid sin. His clergy stated clearly that certain conduct was right and other conduct was wrong. People must not govern their lives according to momentary feelings or the desire for instant gratification: they had to live up to a code of behavior that had been developed over thousands of years. This teaching produced communities where ethical standards mattered and severe stigma attached to those who misbehaved.
>
> The priests stressed the virtue of purity, loudly and unambiguously, to both young and old. Sex was sinful outside marriage, no exceptions. . . . The Church's fierce exhortations against promiscuity, with its accompanying evils of out-of-wedlock births and venereal disease, took hold. In time, most Irish began to understand that personal responsibility was an important component of sexual conduct.
>
> Since alcohol was such a major problem for his flock, Hughes—though no teetotaler himself—promoted the formation of a Catholic abstinence society. In 1849 he accompanied the famous Irish Capuchin priest, Father Theobald Mathew, the "apostle of temperance," all around the city as he gave the abstinence pledge to 20,000 New Yorkers.[3]

---

3 William J. Stern, "How Dagger John Saved New York's Irish," *City Journal*, Spring 1997, www.city-journal.org/html/7_2_a2.html.

Today's American "underclass" suffers from the exact kind of social chaos that afflicted Hughes's desperate New York Irish. The value-neutral welfare state, which is prohibited by a wide array of policies and court decisions from promoting any other notion of human flourishing apart from utilitarian hedonism, can blunt the impact of economic scarcity. But insofar as it will not and cannot foster the necessary character virtues that history has shown make the climb out of poverty possible, the welfare system in effect enables and subsidizes dysfunction. Given how dominant utilitarianism is in so many sectors of American life, it would seem arbitrary (and hence politically unthinkable) to demand of those on public assistance that they hew to a higher standard as the price of receiving aid. The welfare system is doomed by its very nature to reinforce the social chaos that it was meant to ameliorate. When liberals are in power, it can do so generously and recklessly; when fiscal conservatives dominate, it can do so stingily and punitively. But the welfare system, because it has no coherent, true philosophy of human flourishing, can never serve the actual welfare of its recipients. It was not built to do so, but rather to make the poor less dangerous to the rest of society.

The same profound, unfixable problems need not afflict private charities, as the example of Archbishop Hughes's efforts in New York City indicates. Just as parochial schools are able to maintain better order and achieve superior academic outcomes than public schools in blighted urban areas, so private charities can practice a wholesome paternalism and firmly guide recipients toward morally healthier behavior. The aid that private charities dispense is not a legal "entitlement" but a free gift that can be withheld or increased, at the discretion of administrators who speak to recipients face-to-face, and who are guided by a richer, more comprehensive, and fully human view of how people flourish and what holds them back from success. While many might bristle at the notion of church-based charities conditioning aid on the moral behavior of those whom they try to help, this in fact is a far more human model of compassion, one that treats poor people as responsible adults whose actions have consequences, and who are free to make consequent choices and are responsible for dealing with those consequences. That is how life works in the world of work, and we do the poor no favors by treating them as wayward pets, or "blind mouths" that must be warehoused, controlled, and fed.

In a bitter historical irony, just at the moment when we most need the free agents of civil society such as the churches to adhere to a more elevated vision of the human person, the agencies of government are restricting their freedom to do so. "Common Core" requirements are impinging on the liberty of parochial schools to set their own curricula. Discrimination lawsuits are punishing business owners who decline to cooperate with a new, state-imposed vision of marriage. Increasing tax burdens made necessary by massive government deficits dry up the resources for private charity. But worst of all, direct mandates that are not even conditioned on accepting government funding are being directed at private businesses and church-run agencies in the form of the Health and Human Services requirement that virtually all employers provide insurance coverage that pays for both contraceptives and drugs that induce abortions. This mandate came as a surprise to the U.S. Catholic bishops, who had previously supported the passage of President Barack Obama's Affordable Care Act—though not to small-government advocates, who warned that when one-sixth of a nation's economy comes under the direct control of the federal government, subsidiarity must suffer. A courageous group of religious institutions have initiated lawsuits to defend their freedom of action against this mandate, as have some private businesses. As our heroes of subsidiarity, we would like to highlight one of these small businesses—a family-owned firm that has risked its very existence in defense of its owners' freedom of conscience.

Mary Anne and Christopher Yep are the proprietors of Chicago-based Triune Health Group, which they founded in 1990, and which employs almost a hundred full-time workers. As *Crain's Chicago Business* reported, "The couple raised eight children and simultaneously built their business, starting from the basement of their home."[4]

In 2012, the Yeps were informed along with thousands of other business owners that they would have to provide medical insurance that covered contraception, sterilization, and the abortifacient "morning-after pill." With their own limited resources, they decided to defend themselves by initiating a lawsuit against the federal government. The Yeps were able to attract support from other institutions of civil society, the Thomas More Society, Kevin Edward White and Associates, and the Jubilee Campaign's Law of Life Project, which offered legal expertise "My stance on this issue is that we're fighting for religious liberty for men and women," Mary Anne told the *National Catholic Register.*[5] "And that's what was guaranteed to me as a woman in the Constitution," she said. As a sidenote, it is worth pointing out

---

4 "Best Workplace for Women: Triune Health Group," by Meg McSherry Breslin, *Crain's Chicago Business,* May 7, 2012, www.chicagobusiness.com/article/20120505/ISSUE02/305059993.

5 "Catholic-Owned Health Group, Voted 'Best Place to Work for Women,' Sues Over HHS Mandate," EWTN News/Catholic News Agency, August 24, 2012.

that Triune Health Care was voted in 2012 one of Chicago's "best workplaces for women." In their legal complaint, the Yeps request relief

> from grave and ongoing infringement of their fundamental constitutional rights under the First Amendment of the United States Constitution and the corresponding provisions of the Illinois Constitution of 1970, as well as their statutory rights arising under other provisions of federal and Illinois law, to engage in the free and robust exercise of their religious beliefs, in strict and faithful adherence to the deepest dictates of their private conscience as well as their publicly professed religious beliefs and the religious dimension of their corporate mission. . . .
>
> In particular, plaintiffs deem it abhorrent and evil that they find themselves now doubly mandated—by federal and Illinois law alike—to provide other human beings, their cherished employees, with drugs and services relating to abortifacients, sterilization, and artificial reproductive and contraceptive technologies, which are inimical to their health and well-being, as well as being fundamentally at odds with plaintiffs' religious faith and corporate mission. . . .
>
> They believe that the inherent dignity, and indeed the inviolable sanctity, of each and every human being rests ultimately on the immutable truth that each person has been *created* in the image and likeness of God, before whom they stand as equals, endowed with inalienable rights. Consequently, they believe that the life of each and every human being must be protected, cherished, and even fostered from the moment of his or her conception until natural death, no matter whether that human being may be flawed or flawless, rich or poor, humble or exalted.[6]

Christopher Yep told *Legatus* magazine, "Most people don't understand what is going on. But it's an argument that can be won in five minutes. Once people understand the HHS mandate, they can't believe it and they can't believe this is happening. We need to engage others. If the government is successful, they

---

6 Complaint against United States Department of Health and Human Services et al., www.scribd.com/doc/103687004/Complaint-against-United-States-Dept-of-HHS-Treasury-and-Labor-and-the-Illinois-Dept-of-Insurance.

will force Catholics and Christian business people off the playing field and weaken our culture. It's a battle we have to win."[7]

Indeed, it is crucial that citizens such as the Yeps preserve their freedom to follow their consciences. We cannot speak of living in a free society when an appointed official of the executive branch of government can, with the stroke of a pen, promulgate a regulation that compels religious believers to pay for medical procedures that they consider evil, on penalty of fines designed to bankrupt their businesses. The role of the federal government is not to impose a uniform standard of day-to-day conduct encompassing every aspect of human life upon our vast and diverse country, punishing dissenters with threats of fines or imprisonment. The experience of national Prohibition laws should be enough to show us the costly consequences of making such an attempt: a massive loss of liberty, followed by widespread lawbreaking, and contempt for the rule of law. The courage of ordinary small-business owners such as the Yeps is all that stands between us and such an ugly outcome. But that is fitting: subsidiarity asserts that power flows from the bottom up, and it has always been best protected by grassroots activists and doggedly independent citizens.

Defenders of the HHS mandate have claimed that because women alone can become pregnant, refusal to cover "reproductive services" (including those that prevent or abort pregnancies) amounts to unconstitutional discrimination between the sexes, and that opposition to the mandate is part of a Republican "war on women." More ominously, some advocates have countered the religious liberty argument offered by churches and believers with a novel interpretation of the Constitution's First Amendment. These revisionists have claimed that what the Constitution really protects is merely "freedom of worship," and not the full exercise of freedom of conscience in the course of daily decision-making. Bolstered by Supreme Court decisions refusing the right of certain Indian tribes to use peyote as part of spiritual ceremonies, "freedom of worship" advocates (who include Hillary Clinton) argue that the religious motivations of a citizen's behavior are no more protected than any other arbitrary reasons why someone would make a decision. This narrow right to religious rites, but not to the practice of a fully religious lifestyle, resembles nothing if not the condition of dhimmitude, the second-class status granted to non-Muslim monotheists in sharia states, where Christians are also free to worship (often in unmarked buildings

---

7 "The Big Fight," by Sabrina Arena Ferrisi, *Legatus*, March 1, 2012, www.legatusmagazine.org/the-big-fight/.

with neither towers nor bells), but must accept their subordination in every area of life to the dominant creed. When one sector of society imposes such conditions on other sectors of people who disagree, "freedom" loses much of its meaning. If aggressive secularists can use state regulations to force every business owner in America to disregard his conscience, then the very independence of civil society will become a meaningless fiction, as businesses, schools, and finally even churches lurch ever closer to acting as agencies of the federal government.

What is lost when such a federal power grab succeeds? Many things, including social diversity, freedom of conscience, freedom of association, and other goods essential to a thriving democracy. The importance of subsidiarity becomes clear when we look at a few historical instances in which that principle served as a crucial backstop in the defense of fundamental human rights. The best example in America can be seen in the resistance that local and state governments outside the South put up against the infamous Fugitive Slave Act (1850). In many locales, especially in New England, sheriffs and other law enforcement personnel simply refused to use their legal authority to capture, imprison, and transport back to slavery human beings who had escaped their condition of bondage. Had the United States been governed as a rigidly centralized state on the model of Tsarist Russia or republican France, local officials would have lacked the independence to take stands of conscience.

Much more dramatic is the case of the Kingdom of Denmark during the German occupation (1940–45), which author Bo Lidegaard recounts in his history *Countrymen*. As Michael Ignatieff writes of Lidegaard's findings,

> When, in October 1943, the Gestapo came to round up the 7,500 Jews of Copenhagen, the Danish police did not help them to smash down the doors. The churches read letters of protest to their congregations. Neighbors helped families to flee to villages on the Baltic coast, where local people gave them shelter in churches, basements, and holiday houses and local fishermen loaded up their boats and landed them safely in neutral Sweden. . . .
>
> Both the Danish king and the Danish government decided that their best hope of maintaining Denmark's sovereignty lay in cooperating but not collaborating with the German occupiers. . . . From very early on in this ambiguous relationship, the Danes, from the king on down, made it clear that harming the Jews would bring cooperation to an

end and force the Germans to occupy the country altogether. The king famously told his prime minister, in private, that if the Germans forced the Danish Jews to wear a yellow star, then he would wear one too. . . . [T]he institutions of Danish society all refused to go along [with the persecution of Jews]. And without their cooperation, a Final Solution in Denmark became impossible.[8]

In the case of Denmark, as in that of antebellum America, the actions of subsidiary institutions—local governments and units of civil society—proved absolutely critical in resisting the evil intentions of governments that tried to enforce unjust laws. In a rigidly centralized state, where all power descends from the top instead of bubbling up from the roots, the safety and liberty of any citizen depend on the goodwill of a single person or a small cabal. In a decentralized system, thousands of people have the wherewithal to resist and obstruct the progress of evil.

Many of the grossest human rights abuses of the twentieth century would have proven impossible to carry out had the power in the respective countries not been relentlessly gathered into the hands of centralized governments decades before. When a vicious ideologue gained power in Germany in 1933, the smooth apparatus of a rigidly centralized state fell into his hands, and Hitler as chancellor was able with the stroke of a pen to impose his toxic views on the whole of German academia, media, and society. Likewise, local leaders in Ukraine had no independence of action to counter the famine that Stalin's policies imposed on that battered region.

In our own country, legal abortion had only been approved by a few states in 1973 when the Supreme Court removed from the states the right to legislate on this matter. This made the abortion debate in the United States more polarizing and bitter than it was in almost any other Western country and saddled the country with what are still the most lax abortion laws in the world. These laws are the same in Mississippi as they are in California, despite the wishes of voters in either state. Much of the rage that social conservatives came to feel toward the federal government can be traced to this and similar legislative decisions that arrogated the power over critical legal and moral issues to a tiny, appointed elite of judges who are unaccountable to voters. American democracy was not designed to operate on such a model, and the result has been the collapse of bipartisan cooperation

---

8 "One Country Saved Its Jews. Were They Just Better People? The Surprising Truth about Denmark in the Holocaust," *New Republic*, December 14, 2013.

in our Congress—as the two parties increasingly seem to represent starkly different peoples, with irreconcilable views. In a rigidly centralized system, local elections—traditionally the laboratories of democracy—begin to seem ever less meaningful, while national votes come to resemble plebiscites that choose between opposing ideologies. Political rivals gradually are polarized into enemies, and the once robust structures of government turn brittle. The more power the state has over its people, the higher the stakes of winning. The more centralized that power is, the uglier the contests will become, because so much—far too much—is at stake. Each side in our elections becomes increasingly desperate to keep such excessive power out of the hands of its enemies, and each side that does win is prone to the corruption that unchecked power brings.

For Further Reading:

Lord Acton, *Essays in the History of Liberty: Selected Writings of Lord Acton,* Vol. 1 (Indianapolis: Liberty Fund, 1985).

Charles Chaput, *Render unto Caesar* (New York: Image, 2009).

M. Stanton Evans, *The Theme Is Freedom* (Washington, DC: Regnery Publishing, 1996).

George F. Gilder, *Sexual Suicide* (Chicago: Quadrangle, 1973).

Alexander Hamilton, John Jay, and James Madison, *The Federalist* (Indianapolis: Liberty Fund, 2001).

Bo Lidegaard, *Countrymen* (New York: Knopf, 2013).

Charles de Montesquieu, *The Spirit of the Laws* (Cambridge: Cambridge University Press, 1989).

Charles Murray, *Coming Apart* (New York: Crown, 2013).

John Courtney Murray, *We Hold These Truths* (New York: Sheed & Ward, 2005).

Pope Pius XI, *Quadragesimo Anno.* www.vatican.va/holy_father/pius_xi/ encyclicals/documents/hf_p-xi_enc_19310515_quadragesimo-anno_ en.html.

Wilhelm Röpke, *The German Question* (Birmingham, AL: Ludwig von Mises Institute, 2008).

Chapter Ten

Solidarity: The Moral Unity of the Human Family

If there is a single, core moral truth that was forgotten in the bloody twentieth century, it was this one. Solidarity refers to the debt of respect that each of us owes every other person, and that forbids us from using him as merely a means to an end. Even in the most pragmatic, urgent endeavor like fighting a fire or waging a war, we must know in our hearts that each human being is an end in himself—a person of real and transcendent dignity of equal worth to ourselves and each of our loved ones. Because our wills are fallen and resources are limited, it is all too tempting to lie to ourselves, to live in denial of the truth that forbids this moral shortcut or that pragmatic compromise. Those barbarians, or Indians, or Africans, aren't really *human* in the same sense as me and my kids; surely, we can find a rationale for enslaving them. Those enemy civilians have made themselves complicit by failing to rise up against their tyrant; that means it is moral to carpet bomb them so we can shorten the war for our soldiers. Those land-hungry peasants or disobedient workers are sabotaging our progress toward a perfect, classless utopia; the voice of History tells us to remove them. And so on, through the centuries.

The central principle of solidarity in practice is simple and timeless: the Golden Rule. "Do unto others as you would have them do unto you." This ethical maxim, which Jesus quoted from the Old Testament, exists in some form in every culture on earth. It is so ubiquitous that it is easy for us to assume that it is universally accepted—at least in theory—although far too rarely practiced. But in fact things are darker than that.

Another maxim has crept into Western culture via worldly philosophers such as Machiavelli and Hobbes, who deeply influenced the modern frame of mind. It is the principle of the "consenting adult." According to the worldview underpinning this phrase, none of us is the least bit responsible for the decisions made by others; if they make stupid choices, that is not our problem. Even if we have led them to make the choice—if we have exploited them personally, economically, or sexually—we are still immune from responsibility: He or she was a "consenting adult." He should have known better, we tell ourselves.

In the place of an ethic that rests on a deep reciprocity and a care for the human value of each person based solely on his status as our fellow human, we embrace a heartless, pragmatic ethos that shrugs at suffering and confusion and is more than willing to take advantage of other's mistakes. So "consenting adults" work in sweatshops overseas making our iPads or resort to "abortion providers" when boyfriends abandon them. No individual rights are violated, no crime committed or contract broken, and secular modernity has nothing meaningful to say. Attempts by Marxists, feminists, and others to discuss "structural injustice" ring hollow, built as they are on borrowed Christian premises—the sanctity of life—that those activists reject. Only a comprehensive morality constructed on human solidarity can fill this empty core at the center of modern life.

Solidarity is the only solid ground on which social policies can be made that respect the humanity of each person we say we are trying to help, that deal with them as our moral and metaphysical equals, and that aim at empowering and lifting up the poor rather than buying off our consciences by treating poverty as a problem much like pollution.

Alongside the myth of the consenting adult, one of the most commonly cited reasons for rejecting solidarity is self-ownership, the principle promoted by radical libertarians, which claims that none of us owes anything to anyone unless we have freely agreed to give it to him as either a gift or an exchange. We are self-made men and women, creators of our destinies, unbeholden to anyone or anything, rugged individualists who have carved out all that we have and are from the rough-hewn stone of unforgiving nature, with a clear title to everything we attain or acquire. This is the picture of man popularized in the perennial best-selling novels of Ayn Rand, but it is echoed throughout popular culture in works in which the misfit, the loner, the outcast is held up as a hero for refusing to be cowed or seduced by the crowd. Philosopher Edward Feser summed up the underlying theory as follows:

> For many libertarians, the thesis of self-ownership is the foundation of their political philosophy. Natural rights to life, liberty, and property— the protection of which is, according to the libertarian, government's sole legitimate function—derive from self-ownership, in particular one's ownership of his body and its parts, of his capacities and labor, and, by extension, of whatever he can acquire by his non-coercive exercise of them. . . . [G]overnment cannot legitimately interfere with an individual's use of his body, abilities, etc., where that use does not involve the infringement of the rights of others, even when that

individual's use is otherwise immoral. Even if, for example, one decides to use narcotics or to drink oneself into a stupor night after night, the state has no right to stop him from doing so.[1]

Conversely, for the libertarian, if the state has no right to stop someone from destroying himself, it also has no responsibility to rescue him. People who make themselves unemployable or sick through their own bad habits will have to deal with the consequences on their own, or with the help of voluntary charity. Indeed, even those who through no fault of their own are too poor to afford housing, food, or medical care must be provided for through voluntary, private sector efforts; the state has no business redistributing income in pursuit of the vision of social justice imposed by those in power.

This vision of the proper limits of government action has broad appeal because it is, on many crucial matters, correct. Certainly, the modern welfare state with its nearly confiscatory taxes routinely violates the property rights of better-off citizens (see Chapter Ten), even as it serves to enable and reinforce self-destructive behaviors among the poor. Citizens of every social class are held back in their moral development when the state steps in to take over duties that rightly belong to individuals—such as saving for their retirements, caring for their aging parents, funding their kids' educations, and purchasing insurance. The crucial habit of thrift and the difficult skill of delaying gratification are constantly undermined when inflation or easy credit goads citizens to become spoiled consumers. The motive for amassing savings against a rainy day is removed when the government stands at our elbow, waiting, like P. G. Wodehouse's Jeeves, with an umbrella.

So when it comes to policy, the libertarians are much closer than the liberals to getting the answers right. There is an important core of truth in the principle of self-ownership that is worth emphasizing after a century that saw the rise of totalitarian dictatorships and total war. Certainly, the past hundred years of history ought to make us sympathetic to a presumption that each of us owns himself. A strong dose of self-ownership thinking in 1914 might have stopped the rulers of Europe from forcibly drafting millions of men to fight a brutal war over frivolous causes. Had self-ownership prevailed in Russia, millions of peasants would not have been deprived of religious freedom, thrown off their land, deported thousands of miles to Gulag camps, starved to death, or simply shot. Had Germans respected self-ownership, they would

---

1 Edward Feser, "Self-Ownership, Abortion, and the Rights of Children," *Journal of Libertarian Studies,* Volume 18, no. 3 (Summer 2004): 91–92.

not have "Aryanized" (that is, looted) the property of Jews, deprived them of civil rights, and finally exterminated them in camps. Had Japan respected self-ownership, it would not have sent its soldiers to China to engage in mass rape, organized pillage, and slaughter, and to use Chinese prisoners as human guinea pigs for biological weapons. Self-ownership might have prevented the death by shooting or starvation of up to 80 million people in Mao Zedong's Communist China. And so on. As we have already noted, R. J. Rummel estimates in *Death by Government* that in the twentieth century states were responsible for 133.1 million intentional homicides—not including soldiers or civilians accidentally killed during wartime. Every one of those deaths was a murder. Those of us who defend the need for a state after all that organized, state-based slaughter have got some explaining to do.

But so do libertarians. Although the government of China is indeed responsible for millions of forced abortions, most of the uncounted tens of millions of preborn children in the free world who died in surgical or chemical abortions were killed with their mother's consent, while the state stood by and watched. That is the libertarian Holocaust, brought on by the sick implications to which "self-ownership" can be taken. It is a bitter irony that modern liberals defend this one exercise of a principle that they otherwise hold in contempt; as they impose their degraded notions of the Common Good, and trample on the rights of individuals to work, trade, speak, and pray, they defend this single instance of radical, libertine self-ownership. A woman is free, in today's America, to abort her nine-month-old fetus—but not to buy a health insurance plan without pediatric dental care.

Some might step in at this point and say that they are pro-life libertarians, who recognize the implicit right to "self-ownership" of the preborn child. But the brute, biological fact of the human fetus's utter dependence, for nine long months, on the flesh and blood of another human being will strike most libertarians as an outrageous imposition on the liberty of the mother, who has every right to expel this "intruder" from the sanctuary of her womb. That was the position of Murray Rothbard, whose version of libertarianism (anarcho-capitalism) has attracted a surprising number of otherwise pro-life religious believers—no doubt because of its appearance of philosophical rigor and its justified rejection of the intrusive secular state. But let us listen to Rothbard on the subject of preborn children:

> The proper groundwork for analysis of abortion is in every man's absolute right of self-ownership. This implies immediately that every woman has the absolute right to her own body, that she has absolute

dominion over her body and everything within it. This includes the fetus. Most fetuses are in the mother's womb because the mother consents to this situation, but the fetus is there by the mother's freely granted consent. But should the mother decide that she does not want the fetus there any longer, then the fetus becomes a parasitic "invader" of her person, and the mother has the perfect right to expel this invader from her domain. Abortion should be looked upon, not as "murder" of a living person, but as the expulsion of an unwanted invader from the mother's body. Any laws restricting or prohibiting abortion are therefore invasions of the rights of mothers.[2]

Self-ownership, as the ruthlessly consistent Rothbard construes it, has other implications for the rights and duties of parents, extending far beyond the intimacy of the womb. He writes later in the same chapter,

Applying our theory to parents and children, this means that a parent does not have the right to aggress against his children, *but also* that the parent should not have a *legal obligation* to feed, clothe, or educate his children, since such obligations would entail positive acts coerced upon the parent and depriving the parent of his rights. The parent therefore may not murder or mutilate his child, and the law properly outlaws a parent from doing so. But the parent should have the legal right *not* to feed the child, i.e., to allow it to die. The law, therefore, may not properly compel the parent to feed a child or to keep it alive. (Again, whether or not a parent has a *moral* rather than a legally enforceable obligation to keep his child alive is a completely separate question.) This rule allows us to solve such vexing questions as: should a parent have the right to allow a deformed baby to die (e.g., by not feeding it)? The answer is of course yes, following *a fortiori* from the larger right to allow *any* baby, whether deformed or not, to die. (Though, as we shall see below, in a libertarian society the existence of a free baby market will bring such "neglect" down to a minimum.)[3]

So self-ownership, as a principle, prevents the state from intervening when parents starve their children. At this point it is tempting to simply toss the very concept aside as toxic, to decide that any theory that cannot

---

2 Murray Rothbard, *The Ethics of Liberty*, Chapter 14, mises.org/rothbard/ethics/fourteen. asp.

3 Ibid.

account for and defend the most basic unit of society, the family, can hardly be trusted on larger and more complicated questions. But self-ownership is not entirely wrong. But it is radically incomplete, an important piece of the truth which when ripped out of its living context leaves a bloody trail.

Private property and its protection from arbitrary confiscation or control are implications of human dignity—because property is at its heart the fruit of our labors, which ought to be free. In that sense, we do own ourselves. But let's ask a few pointed questions about what that ownership really means, how far it extends, and in what ways that ownership is conditioned by what we have ourselves received.

It is clear that no human being is really "self-made." We are born to parents, without whose care we would quickly die. Human beings are dependent on the constant protection of parents for longer than any other creature. Nor, once we reach adulthood, can most human beings survive alone. We are physically and emotionally dependent on cooperation with others. Our very consciousness is constituted and formed into fullness through the mediation of language, of words and grammatical structures that we learn from others, who have themselves inherited them from their ancestors. Likewise, we are the beneficiaries of the hard work done by our ancestors to establish an orderly society that protects individual rights and creates the infrastructure for education and technology. Think of the immense advantages in lifespan, opportunity, health, and wealth that a modern American or European enjoys over a persecuted Nuba tribesman or a Brazilian living in a favela. Can any of us rightly take credit for these? No, these are gifts that we have been given, and without them we would not have the knowledge, skills, freedom, or physical safety that make possible our efforts at creating wealth. Two people with similar talents and comparable work ethics will fare very differently if one of them is born on New York's Upper East Side and the other in an aboriginal community in Australia. The discrepancy between the opportunities offered to these two people ought to show us the measure of how much we owe to others and how little of the selves that we have become we can take sole credit for.

We do not give birth to our bodies, nor create ourselves. We take a vast array of inherited gifts and opportunities and do our best to steward and make good use of them. Given that fact, our ownership of our labor and our wealth is not complete and absolute. That ownership is conditioned by what we owe to others who came before us. For that reason, adults are expected to care for their aged parents. But even more than paying back the care and opportunities we have received, we are expected to pay them forward, to offer the next generation the best chance to thrive in its own right. This debt is more than a moral truth; it is a fact of mammal biology, of a race whose young are born from the bodies of parents, not hatched from abandoned eggs and left to fend for themselves.

In light of these social, biological, and moral realities, we can see that we do not own ourselves outright, free of any liens or claims. We owe the most to those who are closest to us— our parents and our children, and our direct benefactors. We owe a little less to those in our local community, and proportionately less to total strangers who are faraway fellow citizens. Our debt is least to people who live in distant countries, with whom we interact little except to buy the fruits of their labor. However, we still owe them something, a debt that may seem to materialists intangible or meaningless, but that in times of crisis can mean the difference between peace and war. We owe every human being, by virtue of his membership in the human family, respect for his intrinsic dignity (see Chapter Seven). We owe even distant strangers the recognition that their equal humanity is not affected by differences of wealth, race, or religion. We owe them the debt imposed by the Golden Rule: Do unto others as you would have them do unto you.

If it is ever hard to accept and internalize this truth, here is a helpful mental exercise: When you see a desperate refugee on television, waving an emaciated hand to keep the flies away from his eyes, do not compare him to yourself as you live now, in relative comfort and safety. Remember instead that you and he were once exactly the same, tiny fetuses nestled inside another person, utterly dependent on her protection and goodwill and completely incapable of making any efforts on your own behalf. Then think of all the things that must have happened in his life and yours to land you in such very different places, and how little you really did to end up so much better off than he is. That is the cold, unvarnished truth, and it isn't a comfortable one. That is why we work so hard to hide it from ourselves.

Perhaps if you try to extend your empathy to every human being on earth from conception to natural death you will fail. There's not enough butter on earth to spread across that much bread. But if you limit your moral concern only to those with whom you feel empathy, you will act like a moral monster. The answer lies elsewhere: outside the emotions, in the solemn and timeless rational truths that compose the natural law. Whatever your gut pretends, the fact remains that every human being on earth, regardless of age, is starkly your moral equal. That's true in the same sense that gravity and mathematics are true, and true regardless of how you feel about it. So act accordingly, and maybe your heart will catch up with your brain. Or maybe not. Do the right thing anyway: It's called being an adult.

The people of the pro-life movement, from those who work on Capitol Hill to those who operate pregnancy shelters, offer us hope. They challenge the lies we tell ourselves, the evasions we depend on, and the barriers we cobble together against our wholesome natural instincts. The most natural response in the world for a mother to have toward her child is to care for it. We know, deep down in our soul, that this is the "right" decision. We must in our day-to-day lives, and political action, hold this fundamental human truth in mind. No society that rests on falsehoods can long endure. It will sink into chaos, crime, and poverty.

Incorporating solidarity into our worldviews and our lives cannot be limited to people like abandoned single mothers, whom we rightly view largely as innocent. We would prove ourselves no better than Pharisees if we were to pretend that our common humanity only matters when we are speaking of fellow Americans whom we consider victims.

Solidarity is a universal principle that extends to embrace every member of the human family, and its most important function is to force us to take seriously the rights and human dignity of the people we are tempted to write off as threats to our comfort and safety. Those are the people whose very lives may depend on our practice of solidarity, who otherwise might become collateral damage.

Other proper subjects for our solidarity include, in America, prisoners, who in too many places are relegated to subhuman living conditions. According to Just Detention International,

> Sexual assault behind bars is a widespread human rights crisis in prisons and jails across the U.S. According to the best available research, 20 percent of inmates in men's prisons are sexually abused at some point during their incarceration. The rate for women's facilities varies dramatically from one prison to another, with one in four inmates being victimized at the worst institutions.[4]

The death penalty as we now know it in America is disproportionately applied to killers who lacked proper legal representation, to the point where it no longer upholds its old societal function: as a secular sacrament of public

---

4 "Sexual Abuse Behind Bars: A Human Rights Crisis in New York Detention Facilities," Testimony of Cynthia Totten, program director, Just Detention International, New York UPR Human Rights Consultation Criminal Justice Panel, February 26, 2010.

order, imposing on the worst of criminals the ultimate punishment. Instead it has become just another extension of poverty and inequality, including radically unequal legal assistance when people's very lives are on the line.

Within our own nation's borders, there are millions of people whom we routinely treat as less than fully human: illegal immigrants. These fellow members of the human family lack many of the protections of law that the rest of us take for granted. They are grossly exploited by unscrupulous employers, who can intimidate them with threats of deportation. Their presence in the labor force, in turn, enables the exploitation of native-born, legal workers—by driving down their wages or simply handing their jobs to more compliant illegal workers who will not form unions or report safety violations.

As Jason Jones has written before:

Any sovereign country needs to control its borders. Currently, the U.S./Mexican border is controlled—by drug gangs, human traffickers, American-based gun smugglers, and other criminal elements who are ravaging whole cities throughout Mexico. No American, Latino or otherwise, should favor this chaos. It is mostly Latinos who suffer as a result—who are gunned down by narco-terrorists, packed into Mack trucks to suffocate, or left in the desert to die. If America is ever to manage a comprehensive reform of immigration, securing the border must come first. If that means fencing it off and patrolling it, then that needs to happen, for the safety of citizens on either side, and would-be migrants themselves.

We need to end the underground economy, where workers are treated as they were in 1870, and extend the protection of law to every worker in America. That means (as part of immigration reform) imposing controls on employers, improving and making mandatory a program like E-Verify, by which employers can (in minutes) check the legal status of any new employee. They will have no more excuses for their sweatshops. This was the feature of the 1986 amnesty that broke down—thanks to complaints from businessmen to the Reagan Administration.

As pro-life activists, we move in conservative circles. Sometimes we hear otherwise humane people—who raise money to save the preborn babies of Latino mothers—switch gears to speaking of immigrants as if they were aliens landing from some hostile planet. We have met people who pray to Mexican saints like Miguel Pro speak from the other side of their mouth about "invasion" and "*reconquista.*" We have even met dogged supporters of mass deportation who employ illegal workers—explaining this away as "a reality of doing business." Conservatives need more integrity and a deeper sense of common, human solidarity with the people whose actions have left them trapped in the underground economy. It has been a long time since any of us have used rhetoric like "welfare queens" to describe impoverished Americans. It is long past time for discussions of immigration to reflect a similar courtesy and decency.

Immigrants who came here illegally have certainly benefited from America's order and prosperity. They have gained untold opportunities, used public schools and hospitals, and sometimes collected government benefits. But Americans have also benefited from their presence. Employers have prospered using cheap labor, consumers have enjoyed lower prices, and countless Americans have had their houses built, grounds maintained, meals cooked, and children or elders cared for, by workers who did not enjoy the protection of law. Large elements of America's market economy used these people to evade the costs imposed by the New Deal. We have enjoyed for decades a two-tier system: twenty-first-century labor and safety laws for legal workers, and nineteenth-century "robber baron" conditions for illegal immigrants. As we impose order on the border and in the workplace, we must acknowledge the fact that the people already here are not some looming threat to national security, or a tumor to be removed. They are neighbors, co-workers, friends, fellow parishioners, even family members of millions of Americans. They have earned through sweat equity a place at our national table, and it's time to bring them up out of the underground economy. The way to do that is to offer a path to citizenship to otherwise law-abiding migrants—as the final phase of a comprehensive approach to controlling the border and enforcing our workplace laws. No path to citizenship can (or should) be passed until the U.S. border is fully secured and mandatory workplace verification is in place. To offer an amnesty without such measures would simply invite millions more would-be migrants to risk their lives. We would be advertising the fact that human trafficking works. Thousands more would die in the desert.[5]

---

5 Jason Jones, "Conservatives Can Learn Latinos," *The Blaze*, November 30, 2012, www.theblaze.com/contributions/conservatives-can-learn-latinos/.

Solidarity might motivate us to secure the U.S. border and ensure the just treatment of every worker within it, but the principle extends far across national boundaries, to embrace every human being regardless of citizenship, race, or religion. Our foreign policy and military doctrine will be morally bankrupt if they do not reflect this fundamental human truth.

It is not the American way to disregard the sanctity of human life. During the most bloody war of the last century, American troops wished their German POWs a "Merry Christmas" at the Battle of the Bulge, and our media immortalized this inspiring story, letting all the world know that, as Americans, we recognize the dignity of even our bitterest enemies. Our sensitivity to violence and our abhorrence of cruelty have led us to put our trust in the most advanced techniques when it comes to war. We favor intelligence over brute force, and careful precision over ballistic attacks.

For these reasons, we have placed high hopes in the U.S. drone program. But the facts say that our hopes may have been cheated. The Bureau of Investigative Journalism (TBIJ) reports that in the course of 390 drone strikes over five years, American forces had killed "more than 2,400 people, at least 273 of them reportedly civilians." According to TBIJ, other strikes include the use of cruise missiles:

On December 17 2009 a US Navy submarine launched a cluster bomb-laden cruise missile at a suspected militant camp in al Majala, southern Yemen.

The missile slammed into a hamlet hitting one of the poorest tribes in Yemen. Shrapnel and fire left at least 41 civilians dead, including at least 21 children and 12 women—five of them were pregnant. A week earlier President Obama had been awarded the Nobel Peace Prize. He used his acceptance speech to defend the use of force at times as "not only necessary but morally justified."[6]

Such killings are committed via remote control, and those who pull the triggers are always safe on American turf. Drone pilots see the footage that the American media will never see fit to broadcast (as they were never willing to show pro-life films like *The Silent Scream*): unarmed men, women, and

---

6 Jack Serle, "More Than 2,400 Dead as Obama's Drone Campaign Marks Five Years," *The Bureau of Investigative Journalism*, January 23, 2014, www.thebureauinvestigates .com/2014/01/23/more-than-2400-dead-as-obamas-drone-campaign-marks-five-years/.

children running for their lives, hiding beneath cars, against the walls of shops, and even cowering in their own homes before being gunned and bombed to pieces.

What will we say if America's enemies, whose innocent children we have left dead with no memorial, develop the technological capacity to pilot drones into our country? What will be the tone of our reports when innocent children are struck down in the streets of New York or Washington, DC? What moral high ground could we claim?

Solidarity offers the only sound, universally appealing answer to the logic of those who would bomb civilians in the name of the "greater good," whether that good is defined by Islamist ideologues or unreflective Americans. Solidarity asserts the intrinsic dignity of every human person, especially of children, even the children of our enemies. As we noted in Chapter Eight, even in war, positive law must always strive to conform to the transcendent moral order. This is especially important when it comes to the state's use of lethal violence.

If solidarity helps hold the state back from using its monopoly of force excessively or unjustly, this principle also demands that sometimes the state swing into action in defense of those who would otherwise be utterly helpless. When "states rights" failed in the post-Reconstruction South, and local governments showed themselves unable or unwilling to defend the rights of African Americans, it was the duty of the federal government to step in and override the unjust decisions of local officials through legislation such as the Civil Rights and the Voting Rights Acts. It's an enduring American shame that it took almost a century after the end of slavery for blacks to gain the full rights of citizenship.

Likewise, solidarity imposes limits on our attempts to pare back government. Although we can and should resist the imposition of unjust or burdensome laws and crippling taxes, we know that there is a line beyond which libertarian, antigovernment rhetoric ceases to be reasonable. Certainly we want the government's powers to be as limited and localized as possible without sacrificing justice or denying the common good. But when shrinking the state endangers those core values, it undermines the order that makes real liberty possible and creates the chaos that historically has always yielded to tyranny. Sometimes these evils coexist. So today there is chaos in the womb as the laws refuse to protect the rights of preborn children, and tyranny in the lab, as hundreds of thousands of embryonic human beings languish in the freezers of fertility clinics. There is chaos on the Internet, as pornography of the vilest kind is pumped onto the tablets and phones of America's youth—

and tyranny in the dens of the sex industry, where women who are often the victims of human trafficking are exploited in the most dehumanizing ways.

No one who accepts the core principles we advocate here can be an outright anarchist, precisely because in the absence of government there can be no reliable way of ensuring that solidarity is taken seriously. The human person deserves better—it deserves ordered liberty.

Precisely because solidarity is so essential and so demanding, each era needs prophets of solidarity, who rise up and outrage the powerful by pointing out the nakedness of the emperor. In the sixteenth century, Fr. Bartolomé de Las Casas awakened the Spanish Crown about the savage abuse of native Americans. In the eighteenth century, William Wilberforce stirred the conscience of the British empire about the profound evil of slavery. (Thousands of Christian preachers would do the same work in America.) In the nineteenth century, Pope Leo XIII demanded that employers treat their workers as men, not cogs in their machines.

And in the twentieth century, by some strange movement of Providence, it was in Poland that three such prophets arose. A nation that had for centuries been divided by foreign conquerors, Poland would gain its fragile independence in 1917, and then have to defend it against a Soviet invasion, which sought to spread communism throughout Europe. It was on the Feast of the Assumption in 1920 that Polish armies defending Warsaw rallied, counterattacked, and saved Western Europe from Lenin's secret police.

But Poland would not be spared for long; the infant regime soon found itself trapped between two aggressive, totalitarian states—each of which denied the human dignity of people who stood in its way. As Timothy Snyder documents in *Bloodlands*, by 1939, Joseph Stalin had already shot or starved to death more than three million Soviet citizens for the "crime" of owning land or belonging to untrustworthy ethnic groups. Hitler's genocides still lay in the future, although the planning for them was under way. The Poles were an obstacle to each dictator's utopia, so Hitler and Stalin allied in 1939 to jointly overrun Poland and carve up the country. Each sent its secret police to murder Polish intellectuals and educators, in order to "decapitate" the nation and reduce its people to a leaderless horde of timid serfs. Most of the Jews of Europe lived in Poland and western Russia; the historic Kingdom of Poland had welcomed Jews expelled from other European countries. So when Hitler betrayed his ally, it would largely be on Polish soil that millions of "subhuman" Jews (along with Gypsies, Slavs, and others) would be murdered by killing squads, starved in ghettos, or gassed in camps. Almost six million Polish civilians—one out of four of the people who lived there in 1939—would be dead by 1945. That is when the Soviets marched in to impose a second totalitarian regime, which aimed (as Anne Applebaum documents in *Iron Curtain*) at completely absorbing every social institution into the Communist Party or state.

Against this backdrop of mass murder and tyranny, where human lives seemed as expendable as the bullets used to end them, arose three men whose witness shines like a light in the darkness and the silence. The first was Maximilian Kolbe, a fervent apostle of Franciscan spirituality and a pioneer of Catholic publishing and radio. So influential was he in prewar Poland that Kolbe was a prime candidate for either one of the totalitarian allies to liquidate. The Germans captured him in 1941 and imprisoned him for the crime of sheltering refugees (Jewish and gentile alike). It sent him, as it would send thousands of other priests, to Auschwitz. Kolbe had been there for two months when an escape by three prisoners provoked a savage German reprisal: ten other inmates would be starved to death. It hardly mattered that these prisoners had done nothing to flout authority; Poles were interchangeable units of brute slave labor, and the camp could afford to "spend" the lives of ten to better subdue the others. When one of the chosen victims, Franciszek Gajowniczek, cried out, "Oh, my poor wife, my poor children. I shall never see them again!" Kolbe bore witness to the truth of solidarity by stepping forth to starve in that prisoner's place. In a place where human life is given no value, the only way to assert the truth was to offer up his own. Through two weeks with neither food nor water, Kolbe led the prisoners in prayer and in singing the Psalms, until only he was left alive. The guards "humanely" killed him through lethal injection, and cremated his body on August 15, the Feast of the Assumption.[7]

The story of the second prophet of solidarity, Karol Wojtyła (Pope John Paul II) is too well-known to need much retelling. During the Nazi occupation, while he worked as a manual laborer, Wojtyła strove against the Nazi effort to lobotomize Polish culture, for instance risking a death sentence by running an underground theater troupe and staging plays that reminded viewers of humane values that were disappearing around them. He also helped Jewish citizens escape deportation to death camps, all the while pursuing his studies for the priesthood at an underground, illegal seminary. It was his experience of what he called the "bestiality" of the Nazi regime and the subsequent, suffocating Soviet puppet state imposed by Stalin

---

7 "St. Maximilian Kolbe: Priest Hero of a Death Camp," www.catholic-pages.com/saints/st_maximilian.asp.

that would drive Wojtyła to explore in his philosophical and theological work the central importance of human dignity and freedom. Indeed, at the Second Vatican Council, Wojtyła would be one of the voices raised in favor of *Dignitatis Humanae*, the document in which the Church recognized religious liberty as a fundamental human right. His writings on the dignity of labor (*Laborem Exercens*) and the need for solidarity to inform even profit-making enterprises (*Centesimus Annus*) have reshaped the way Christians think about economics.

Most famously, it was the choice of Wojtyła as pope, a veteran of countless struggles with communist authorities in Poland on behalf of workers' rights and religious freedom, that gave courage and hope to the founders of the first independent trade union in the Soviet bloc. It was named for the principle it embodied, Solidarity. Instead of the class struggle preached by Marxist determinism and materialism and aimed at an earthly utopia of economic efficiency, Catholic social teaching prizes individuality, variety, private property, and initiative, as well as the fruitful, willing cooperation of rich and poor in building the common good. These values emerge from the organic connections that unite men in society—family, friendship, church, and even work—and cannot thrive under a coercive system like socialism or communism.

It took the third prophet of solidarity to keep the Solidarity movement alive in its deadliest crisis and offer his own life as a testimony to the truths on which it was founded. Although John Paul II provided enormous moral support, he was no longer present in Poland to offer guidance, help the workers negotiate, or answer their daily concerns. This role fell to Father Jerzy Popiełuszko, a young priest whose health had been ruined by cruel treatment imposed during his mandatory military service because he refused to take off his rosary. Father Jerzy did not seek out the limelight; he merely wished to do his job by ministering to workers in Warsaw. He began with small-scale acts of defiance—transmitting illegal messages after martial law imposed by the communist government had outlawed the union, giving sermons at workers' Masses—but his witness proved so contagious that Father Jerzy became the spokesman for a national freedom movement that shook an empire to its foundations. As Filip Mazurczak wrote in *First Things*:

> In 1980 [Popiełuszko] began serving the St. Stanislaus Kostka parish in the Zoliborz district of Warsaw, just as Poland's Solidarity labor union started to challenge Soviet hegemony in Eastern Europe. During Solidarity's early success in 1980 and 1981 and the crackdown by

General Jaruzelski's military regime from 1981 to 1983, Fr. Popieluszko held monthly "Masses for the Fatherland" in which he decried the Communist government's human rights abuses and defended workers' rights, urging above all nonviolent resistance. He frequently quoted St. Paul, urging his faithful to "defeat evil with good." Tens of thousands of Poles attended these Masses, including secular dissident intellectuals such as Adam Michnik and Jacek Kuron, and Radio Free Europe regularly broadcast Fr. Popieluszko's sermons.[8]

President Reagan's Radio Free Europe turned a local phenomenon into an international sensation by rebroadcasting the sermons not just in Polish but in all the local languages of Eastern Europe, and they awakened workers and citizens of other captive nations to the fact that resistance was possible. In fact, it was happening—month after month after month, and Father Jerzy was still alive and speaking. His sermons were not angry calls for political resistance, but profoundly Christian statements about the proper dignity of man and what is owed him, delivered in the context of the Eucharist. They reached back behind the seventy years of barbarism and brutalist ideologies that had swept the West since 1914 and tapped into the common Christian, humanist heritage of Europe. Workers and intellectuals alike could see that the faith of their grandmothers, scorned by SS eugenicists and quashed by commissars, was still relevant for their own children. Just as the Nazis' nightmarish utopian project had come to an end, so could the Communists'. There was, as John Paul would write in *Memory and Identity*, a "limit to evil" imposed by human nature itself— the kind of limit that Winston Smith despaired of in *1984*, because he did not believe in God.

The grim subhumanism preached by a bad economist, Karl Marx, inspired few disciples by 1980, especially among those who lived beneath its leaden cloak. Only Western academics, it seemed, were true believers in Marx—and there were fewer of those since *The Gulag Archipelago* had exposed the slave empire where the Marxist regime disposed of dissidents. But there were still tens of thousands of bureaucrats and soldiers whose access to power, to a larger ration of bread and some extra vodka, depended on the supremacy of lies. And there were Soviet armies, under leaders who'd taken part in crushing other dissident movements in Budapest and Prague, who might well march

---

8 Filip Mazurczak, "Interview with Paul Hensler on Fr. Jerzy Popieluszko," *First Things*, November 2012.

into Poland if things spiraled out of control. And so there were men whose job it was to silence Father Jerzy.

The ordinary priest, committed to serving his people in the face of mounting harassment and even death threats, provoked an international crisis in the nations of the Warsaw Pact. This became clear when an issue of Russian *Pravda* specifically named him as an instigator of terrorism. The Soviet's puppet rulers in Poland knew how to read between the lines; they must silence him or face the consequences. So on October 19, 1984, three agents of Polish security stopped Father Jerzy's car, beat him to death, and disposed of the body—just as their forerunners in Stalin's secret police had disposed of 60,000 Polish officers and intellectuals in 1939. Stalin had gotten away with it; he'd even convinced the Western Allies that the crime should be blamed on the Nazis. Surely this "necessary murder" would do its work, too, and teach the sullen populace that they could not choose their leaders, that anyone who emerged from their midst and tried to resist would be mowed down and forgotten.

But too many minds and hearts had absorbed Father Jerzy's lessons. As Paul Hensler, who documented Fr. Jerzy's life in the film *Father Jerzy Popiełuszko: Messenger of the Truth,* recounts,

> The entire country was united by his message, so much so that when he was murdered, almost a million people gathered in Warsaw for his funeral, the largest gathering for a funeral in the history of Poland. They were saying, "We will not leave this place until you tell the truth." And the government was forced to put the murderers of Fr. Popieluszko on trial and send them to prison—the first time government agents had been put in prison in the history of the Soviet Bloc.[9]

Think of that. In almost seventy years, where tyrannical socialist governments had disposed of millions of citizens with impunity, there had never been a moment's accountability, until Father Jerzy refused to be scared into silence, even refusing a kindly offer by Cardinal Glemp to send him to safety in Rome. An interview in the film reveals that the priest would have regarded that as turning away from the cross.

What animates men like Jerzy Popiełuszko, like Maximilian Kolbe, like Karol Wojtyła? Citizens of a nation defeated, occupied, and enslaved, still all of them found the strength to face down the soldiers of subhumanism, to insist on living with dignity even when the price was likely death. The

---

9 Mazurczak, "Interview with Paul Hensler."

greatest natural virtue, Aquinas teaches, is magnanimity, or greatness of soul. A spirited man or woman bubbles over with an energetic love for the good things of life. He loves his own life, and other people's lives, far more than comfort or quiet. He is ready to fight injustice, to suffer but not in silence, and be ready to face the consequences. He knows that God is just, that the human soul is constant, that men can always choose death before slavery. And deep in that heart is a knowledge that all men are brothers. Each of us is a kind of miracle. And a man really should be ready to die rather than deny that.

Suggested Reading:

Carl Anderson, *A Civilization of Love* (New York: HarperOne, 2008).

Anne Applebaum, *Iron Curtain* (Harpswell, ME: Anchor Publishing, 2013).

André Frossard, *"Forget Not Love"*: *The Passion of Maximilian Kolbe* (San Francisco: Ignatius Press, 1991).

Pope John Paul II, *Centesimus Annus*, www.vatican.va/holy_father/john_paul_ii/encyclicals/documents/hf_jp-ii_enc_01051991_centesimus-annus_en.html.

———, *Laborem Exercens*, www.vatican.va/holy_father/john_paul_ii/encyclicals/documents/hf_jp-ii_enc_14091981_laborem-exercens_en.html.

———, *Memory and Identity* (New York: Rizzoli, 2005).

Paul Hensler, *Jerzy Popiełuszko: Messenger of the Truth* (video), directed by Paul Hensler (Jacksonville, FL: Jerzy Film, DVA, 2013).

C. S. Lewis, *The Abolition of Man* (New York: HarperOne, 2009).

Jacques Maritain, *The Person and the Common Good* (South Bend, IN: University of Notre Dame Press, 1973).

The Second Vatican Council, *Dignitatis Humanae*, www.vatican.va/archive/hist_councils/ii_vatican_council/documents/vat-ii_decl_19651207_dignitatis-humanae_en.html.

George Weigel, *Witness to Hope: The Biography of Pope John Paul II* (New York: Harper Perennial, 2005).

Chapter Eleven

A Humane Economy

Private property is the natural and necessary implication of the dignity of the human person, since wealth is the outcome of human labor intelligently admixed with the bounty of nature. This definition of wealth seems like plain common sense to most modern people. It was most memorably asserted by the political philosopher John Locke, and it was subsequently endorsed by Pope Leo XIII, giving it the imprimatur of the moderate Enlightenment and of the Catholic Church alike.[1] But this description of wealth is in fact the fruit of thousands of years of reflection and debate. In the ancient world, philosophers and theologians conceived of wealth quite differently, seeing the fruits of the earth and natural resources largely as a fixed supply of the necessities of life, which man essentially gathers without increasing or improving it. So the task of sages and saints was to convince us to distribute this God-given, finite amount of wealth wisely and fairly, taking account of the needs of the state and the wants of the poor. In the zero-sum game that ancient thinkers believed mankind is doomed to play, one man's accumulation could only come at his neighbor's expense. And indeed, the ancient economy was largely based on agricultural production, much of it done by slaves. The value added by tradesmen and bankers—who perform the vital work of distributing goods and capital from places where they are not needed to sites where they can be used more productively—was poorly understood and often dismissed, and merchants and moneylenders condemned as economic parasites. From Aristotle to St. John Chrysostom, you will look in vain for influential thinkers who recognized how economic exchanges could yield mutual benefits and increase the general store of wealth by allocating it more efficiently and serving human needs more effectively.

Late medieval Scholastics, especially a group of Dominican friars in Spain, would advance the understanding of wealth by studying empirically the nature of economic exchanges, and the mutual benefits they conferred on both parties in any honest trade. These friars—themselves sworn to poverty—

---

1 Joe Hargrave, "How John Locke Influenced Catholic Social Teaching," *Crisis*, November 5, 2010, www.crisismagazine.com/2010/how-john-locke-influenced-catholic-social-teaching.

were encouraged in this endeavor by the explosion of wealth that marked the high Middle Ages, which was driven both by technological improvements in agriculture (such as more effective plows and crop rotation) and the explosion of trade with the Middle East in the wake of the Crusades. The medieval guilds, composed of producers and tradesmen who had organized along religious lines under patron saints, formed interest groups that spoke up for the moral legitimacy of profit-seeking ventures and the social usefulness of commerce—even as they used their guild privileges to choke off competition. The economic power of urban elites began to threaten the dominance of aristocrats, allowing burghers to purchase exemptions from strangling feudal laws, and cities to establish themselves as sanctuaries from serfdom, where common people could succeed or fail based on their merits, rather than staying fixed in the caste in which they had been born.

The expansion of economic liberty helped to create a base of support for political freedom, and demands grew for representation of citizens in government, for instance in institutions such as the English House of Commons. This thrust toward representative government would clash with the efforts of princes to subjugate nobles and commons alike in the pursuit of "absolute" monarchy. Conflicts such as the English Civil War and the "Glorious Revolution," and the successive Swiss wars of independence against absolutist France and Austria, ensured the survival of the principle of representative government and the expansion of the kind of economic and political freedom that American civic leaders would rally to defend in 1776 (see Chapter Twelve).

The implications of private property are not primarily political or even economic but moral. When we accept this principle, we see that the gap between a patch of fertile dirt and a loaf of bread is bridged only through the work of human beings, each of whom is a unique and irreplaceable creation. Each person in the chain of production—from the farmer who plants the seeds to the investors in John Deere Worldwide, whose factories made the tractor—has the right to dispose of his own labor and wealth and to be its primary beneficiary.

Every man-hour of work that a person performs, whose fruits are taken away from him by force, amounts to forced labor. So when we seize the wealth of one person to spend it on someone else, we ought to admit to ourselves what we are doing: conscripting people to work against their will for someone else's benefit. A just society will try to avoid conscripting people's labor, or seizing part of their wealth, first of all out of deference to their human dignity and freedom of action. Taxes that take part of one person's wealth—that conscript his labor—will only be imposed when their use is demanded by one of the core principles essential to human flourishing, such as the sanctity of life or the transcendent moral order. The wealth of citizens should be seen not as a common pool to be dipped into at the discretion of their rulers, but as an extension of their liberty, which should not be trespassed lightly. The preferences people express through supply and demand, which reach producers through the supple communications network that we call the price system, are an expression of human dignity. People have the right to make imprudent decisions, to make mistakes; using the government's coercive power to corral people into making "healthier" choices entails treating citizens not as responsible adult human persons, but loveable, wayward pets.

There are certain types of transactions (for instance, sales of nuclear weapons) that the state can and should refuse to permit, some contracts (such as the sale of human embryos) the community can simply refuse to enforce. Of course we should impose pollution and safety regulations that protect innocent third parties from toxic side effects, which often are not accounted for in the prices of goods or services. But our interventions will be fewer, more prudent, and more reluctant, if we remember that the price system and the market are, at heart, the source of economic order, an exquisitely subtle organic system that we no more wish to distort and destroy than we do the human reproductive system.

It is possible to overemphasize private property rights, to absolutize them in a way that indeed distorts their crucial role in the function of a free and fair society. Nineteenth-century laissez-faire economists were sometimes guilty of neglecting the moral and social preconditions that make private property a worthy concept in the first place. Rather than deal with the usual exceptions offered to the sanctity of private property—such as Aquinas's observation that a starving man may justly steal a loaf of bread—we think it is more useful to consider property as simply an outgrowth of liberty. Where solidarity, or human dignity, or the transcendent moral order would place limits on the individual's claim to "self-ownership," it may also lay claim to some control over his use of property. Insofar as a person has only been able to accumulate wealth because of the efforts of others, he owes them or their society some share in the wealth he has won. Hence store owners who benefit from functioning roads and police protection must contribute through their taxes to the support of such government services. Businesses whose products undermine true human dignity can be subject to restrictions, and those that violate the transcendent moral law may be prohibited altogether—although we must carefully weigh the evil side effects of increasing government power.

The starting point is and must remain liberty, and every proposal that would limit the liberty or impinge on the property of a person should be subject to the strictest scrutiny—given the fact of human dignity, and the ugly habit majorities have of coercing and bullying minorities, particularly when the latter enjoy greater wealth. Remembering the humiliating restrictions, repeated confiscations, and ultimate persecutions that harried Jews in Christian Europe, Armenians in Turkey, and Chinese through much of Asia, we should be wary indeed of economic measures that unduly target the prosperous.

If we use the same scale of moral indebtedness that sets the limits on self-ownership (see Chapter Ten) to judge the limits of private property, the economic structures we promote will be much more natural, just, and unintrusive than those prescribed by modern ideologies. Yes, our property is our own because our labor is our own. But to whom do we rightly owe some part of our labor? First of all, to those who made that labor possible—our parents, and the local communities that have provided a safe infrastructure in which we live. We also owe some of our labor to those whom we have promised support, such as our spouses. We are also obliged to pay forward to future generations—especially to our own children—the love and care we received from our own parents. This chain of moral obligation extends beyond what the law can make explicit and enforce; indeed, the law is a clunky and blunt instrument that we should use only when people utterly fail to meet the most essential moral obligations—for instance, when "deadbeat dads" neglect their minor children. Likewise, the moral duty imposed by solidarity demands that we provide some safety net for those in our community who cannot care for themselves. The best means for meeting those needs (see Chapter Nine) are usually the voluntary efforts of private charities, and subsidiarity calls on us to build up a robust network of such initiatives, rather than turn to the state to use coercion to channel wealth where it is needed.

A political and economic system that starts with the freedom of the human person and allows him to meet his natural obligations willingly— only employing coercion when real injustices cannot be resolved in any other way—deserves a better name than "capitalism," a term that Karl Marx invented to describe a system that he believed privileged property over people. We propose a term coined by the great free-market economist and social philosopher Wilhelm Röpke: a humane economy. The word "humane" conveys what we mean, both in its literal meaning and in the connotations of kindness that it carries: man's dignity demands an economic system that provides for his needs, enables his efforts, and takes account of both his self-centered drives and his fundamentally social nature. It is in the context of the family that man first lives in society, and the family is the crucible in which basic selfishness is refined into something nobler—a concern for the welfare of other human beings, first of all those with whom one has shared upbringing and blood, and then for those people we choose to marry, and then those whom we bring into this world through procreation. The family is the school of unselfishness, or rather of a higher selfishness that stretches and extends the circle of empathy, expanding one's love and work to a circle of other people. The habit of altruism can then be applied to neighbors and fellow citizens, and finally to every member of the worldwide human family. Our concern for others will be diminished, of course, in proportion as we move further out from the circles in which we really interact with people, but the principle of solidarity teaches us that it should never fall to zero. To treat even distant foreigners as less than fully human is to invite once again all the murderous hatreds and atrocities that marked the twentieth century.

The way for modern subhumanism and genocide was paved in the nineteenth century, when people in the very same nation, often of the same race, treated members of lower social classes as less than human. The historical reality of capitalism was marked by profound moral blots, moments when business owners took unfair advantage of desperate workers, when laws protecting the basic human dignity of laborers were not in place and employers used the power of the state to coerce their workers or close out free competition. American slavery, for all the feudal and paternalistic pretensions of plantation owners, was a firmly capitalist institution, providing cheap, reliable labor to large-scale farmers who engaged in the speculative enterprise of international commodity production. Likewise, in the nineteenth century, immigrants from Asia were marched at gunpoint from place to place as "coolie" gangs to do the dirtiest, most dangerous jobs that slave owners would not risk their human "property" doing. Irish laborers who had come to escape the Potato Famine were thrown into deadly working conditions; child labor helped keep down adult workers' wages— and left uneducated young people suited for no other kind of work outside the factories.

The necessary reforms that marked the late nineteenth and early twentieth century probably saved the market economy from the excesses of capitalism by enacting legal restrictions and guarantees that recognized the true humanity of workers and prevented employers from treating them interchangeably with machines. Had such reforms not been passed, it is likely that workers' revolutions would indeed have swept the West and subjected Europe and America to an economic system that was in the long run even less compatible with human freedom and dignity: socialism. That system pretends that political systems and cultural reconditioning can remake man himself, purging him of the inborn urge to first look out for himself and the people he loves, and forcing on him altruistic self-sacrifice on behalf of a class or race.

In fact, we naturally empty and even deny ourselves for the sake of our families, and are proportionately willing to make lesser sacrifices for others, our willingness generally diminishing the further away people are from what rightly remains our vital center—our selves. Each of us is first and foremost the steward of his own being, with the right and the duty to preserve himself and the unique human dignity with which he was born. In this context, where we speak of legitimate self-interest (psychologists call it "healthy narcissism"), we may echo Rabbi Hillel's famous question: "If I am not for myself, who will be?" However, the self that we rightly champion is not the angry monad imagined by Ayn Rand, but the person whose life and loves are shaped by a profound exchange of love and service in human families and other communities. We should never deny those real relationships in the name of a misguided quest for total autonomy, nor pervert and replace them with a coerced community imposed on pain of imprisonment.

One of the classic texts written in defense of political and economic freedom is Frederic Bastiat's *The Law*. Probably the best-known essay by Bastiat is "What Is Seen and What Is Not Seen," in which he points out what economists call the "broken window" fallacy. A dry and gracious stylist, Bastiat recounts this concept in what sounds like one of Aesop's Fables, but it boils down to this: Certain economists seem to think it a good idea to run around breaking windows in order to create jobs for glassmakers. Such thinkers fixate on what is seen—the newly employed glassmaker— and completely ignore what is not seen: the other, more prudent uses of the money that was wasted fixing the window. Once you have smashed the window, you can see with your own two eyes the friendly glassmaker who is happy to earn some money fixing the thing; what you will never see is the person who might have been hired to plant the garden if the window hadn't been broken, or the roses that never grew there.

Bastiat's logic here is unassailable and applies throughout the economy. Critics of value-neutral economics have noted that every divorce increases the Gross Domestic Product, by creating jobs for attorneys and day-care center workers. Likewise, cases of lung cancer create new jobs for doctors, nurses, and hospice workers. The term in introductory economics classes for the wasted window-fixing money is "opportunity cost," since the broken window costs the homeowner other opportunities for spending the money more usefully. But more important is the key distinction between what is seen and what is not seen, especially when we move from questions of productivity to those of justice.

Kindhearted people, in reacting to political and economic issues, have the bad habit of fixating on what is seen and ignoring what is not seen. They do so most commonly in conflicts between employees and employers, or members of designated "victim" groups and nonmembers who dispute their claims. We can see the outraged public employee picketing the statehouse, and hear his concrete, specific claims of why he needs more money. We can feel his pain. We do not typically see the millions of taxpayers who share the cost of employing these workers or imagine what else they might have done with the money if the government had not confiscated it.

The case gets even more poignant when what is seen is a person who is palpably poor, demonstrating outside the statehouse asking for benefits. It is all too easy (and common nowadays) to airily dismiss the people who are not seen—the overtaxed working-class people who cannot afford parochial school, or SAT prep classes, or other worthy uses of their own money, which they have worked to earn. The same thing applies to policy issues such as affirmative action: We see the hopeful face of the black or Latino kid who got a boost into a state university, but we do not see the lower-income white kid who was turned away to give the other kid a place. The language typically used by social justice advocates to champion what is seen includes stock phrases like "a concrete, living, needy image of God," while they dismiss the interests of the person who remains unseen as "mere abstractions."

In such cases we are no longer considering productivity, like pointing out that smashing windows to make new jobs is wasteful. When we are discussing the government using coercion to confiscate someone's wealth and transfer it to somebody else, we are talking instead of justice. Is it just to force this taxpayer over here to fund the benefits of that tax-taker over there? Is it fair (or wise, or free) to construct a value-neutral bureaucracy, managed by a distant federal government over which each one of us has only the tiniest influence, and allow it to confiscate more than one-third of everyone's paycheck, to use as its hired managers see fit? Subsidiarity and solidarity dictate that in certain matters only the government, and in a few cases only the federal government, can remedy grave injustices or prevent the commission of new ones. But is that really true of one-third of life?

When Christians speak of a "preferential option" for the poor, do they really mean that in every case in which a person wants something funded by someone else who has more money, the former should get it? Is the right of private property, the freedom to harness the fruits of your labors and spend them as you think wise—including on charitable giving that you freely choose—so faint and tenuous that any claim at all by someone poorer must always prevail?

In the name of a pseudo-Christian paternalism, we would have in fact embraced the suffocating, managerial state that Pope John Paul II warned against in *Centesimus Annus*. Worse yet, since the modern state is secular, by giving it one-third of our wealth (and, hence, one-third of our work), we have surrendered vast arenas of life to value-neutral, utilitarian managers. In overtaxed New York City, the Catholic schools are closing because parents cannot afford the tuition, while thousands of dangerous, less effective public schools are lavished with funds. In how many other areas of life are our individual choices taken away from us and handed over to strangers with alien values, who use the coercive power of government to redirect our money as they wish?

But this habit of choosing the seen over the unseen has even darker implications; it is, in fact, at the heart of the pro-choice mentality. Those who are addicted to choosing the seen over the unseen look at the issue of abortion with the same unthinking concreteness of the window-smashing economist. They hear the distress of women with unintended pregnancies, they see their desperate situation, they can picture themselves in their place and empathize with their suffering. What they don't see, can't hear, and will not imagine are the merely "abstract" rights of the preborn child who waits in the darkness. And so, in the name of compassion, they side with what they think are the best interests of the person they can see.

Not every destructive economic distortion can be blamed on politics or the government. A healthy, humane economy depends on healthy humans, whose level of character and civic virtue determines whether the complex, sensitive mechanism that is a free economy can actually function, or whether it will collapse into poverty, tyranny, and war. Economic reality is not the DNA that forms the social organism, dictating which poems will be written and which constitutions amended. Marx's vulgar materialism, predicated on an a priori rejection of God, refuted itself over seven blood-soaked decades from Königsberg to Cambodia, as the world relearned this truth: It is culture that drives politics, and it is the dance between the two that produces the kind of economy that emerges in a country. Leave aside "black swan" events like the Potato Famine or the Black Death and you can trace a people's economic fortunes to the social values that motivate them and the institutions those values have built. Of course, there is a constant feedback loop among these human realities, since economy, politics, and culture shape, form, and sometimes distort each other. As Peter Viereck documents in *Metapolitics*, ninety years of increasingly vehement and irrational romantic nationalism in Germany prepared the way for World War I. Defeat in that war brought with it crippling reparations, which the desperate Weimar Republic attempted to deal with through hyperinflation. That economic tactic had a profoundly destructive impact on German society, as Sebastian Haffner's memoir of that period, *Defying Hitler*, recounts. Inflation that could make a morning's wages almost worthless by dinnertime punished the thrifty by wiping out life savings and rewarded the worst kind of reckless gambling, both in economics and in politics. So economic collapse, brought on by a culturally driven war, prepared the way for the deepest kind of social, political, and moral corruption.

Scholar Robert Reilly points to a similar, centuries-long feedback loop in the contemporary Islamic world, suggesting that the stagnation, instability, and lack of technological infrastructure that plague so many Muslim countries can be traced to Islam's creedal rejection of reason and even causality in understanding nature: According to orthodox Islam, a rock falls not because of gravity, but because God happens to will it, and it is perfectly possible that any given rock might hang in midair forever, should He wish it.[2] Accepting such a doctrine has consequences that ripple all through culture, discouraging rational analysis, long-term planning, and the willingness to compromise—and, in times of crises, fomenting extremist solutions.

In Western Europe and America, we face a persistent economic malaise that has proven so grave and intractable it has spawned a cottage industry among those who wish to explain where we went wrong. Some suggest that we are witnessing a general failure of the free-market system. Others point to big government gone wild, printing money to fuel artificial economic growth that rests on "irrational exuberance" and reckless investments. Financial industries engaged in shuffling money from place to place have become major economic and political players, replacing invention and entrepreneurship as the source of the wealth of our top "one percent." American manufacturing has collapsed, with industries fleeing to former Third World countries, where people are willing to hazard long hours and harsh conditions and sacrifice

---

2 Robert Reilly, *The Closing of the Muslim Mind* (Wilmington, DE: ISI Books, 2011).

their present happiness (and sometimes their health) for the sake of their families' futures.

However serious each of these problems is, each is also a symptom of something deeper. A common cultural cause underlies the decline of so many Western nations. We are eager to spend, reluctant to pay for our spending with taxes, and perfectly willing to shift the cost of our own present comforts into a deficit that will weigh down our descendants. In effect, we are deadbeat grandparents.

Our forefathers may have lapsed from time to time into foolish, self-destructive acts of hedonism, but the culture in which they lived and the faith they followed called things what they were: They knew sin as sin, and knew the need for repentance and reparation. These people knew that we live not only for ourselves, but at the very least for the sake of our children. Italians planted olive trees that their distant descendants would some day profit from; now they have ceased even to plant the children, attaining one of the lowest birth rates now on earth. (They compete with the Spaniards and the Québécois for that honor.) Even free-spending, big-government, American Democrats such as Franklin Roosevelt built their policies on the classic assumption that the basic unit of society was not the individual but the family. As Allan Carlson documents in his classic *The American Way*, for all the flaws of the New Deal (it centralized power in Washington, wasted money, starved the private sector, was largely unconstitutional, and probably prolonged the Depression), at least its policies were driven by a deeply wholesome agenda: to let men be the breadwinners for their families so that women could raise healthier, smarter, more productive citizens. That common-sense, instinctual principle is now considered so radically retrograde and offensive that simply stating it is enough to drive a politician out of public life. (A manifesto that Senator Rick Santorum published asserting such things, *It Takes a Family*, probably helped him lose his seat in the Senate.)

Since the Sexual Revolution and its angry stepsister, feminism, overturned our assumptions about what sex means and what it's for, we have almost forgotten how to form families, or what they are. Divorce laws have made the contract of marriage tragically easy to escape from, even as we have tightened up bankruptcy laws and canonized student loans as sacramental covenants. Judges and voters alike have redefined marriage in many states to include homosexual unions. Single people can adopt children, and couples can cook them up in petri dishes, discarding the "surplus" embryos or sending them up to Harvard to be cannibalized for parts. What agenda is served by all these bizarre acts of rebellion against the plain nature of things and the immemorial structure of human society? Nothing so elevated or insane as Marxist-Leninism. Nothing so cool and mathematical as capitalism. The philosophy underpinning our current crisis, which explains our Keynesian politics and addiction to credit card debt, Europe's falling and our own flat birth rates, our willingness to tax our children (via deficits) instead of ourselves, is a simple creed known to every teenager: "We want the world and we want it now," in the words of Dionysian rock-god Jim Morrison, who died a bloated shell of a man at age twenty-eight, leaving behind no acknowledged children, but at least twenty paternity suits filed by women he had abandoned.

Repulsed by the gray "organizational men" who toiled without credit or creativity inside massive corporations, the young (who are now middle-aged) took as their creed a vulgar hedonism, papered over for some by New Left politics. Even when hippies cut their hair and got "real" jobs, the creeds they had popularized changed our economy and politics, all across the Western world. Gone was the stern frugality of the Depression generation, the optimistic fecundity of those who birthed the Baby Boom. In its place came a cleverly calculating Epicureanism, a breed of men who lived for pleasure but knew how to avoid overdoses and V.D., who relied on now-legal abortion to clean up the unintended consequences of pleasure, who looked to vacant New Age spirituality or endless acquisition for its own sake, with endorphin rushes from risk buffered by the certainty that their banks were "too big to fail." When the focus of life becomes not pursuing the good, or even transmitting life so someone else has the chance to, and descends instead to the accumulation of diverse, amusing experiences, man as an organism ceases to function as he was built to. His machines, lazily tended, break down and fall apart. His governments, overburdened and underfunded, welsh on their debts. His countries are either depopulated or colonized by fertile foreigners. He looks around, and he shrugs. If he majored in English, he might remember Eliot's line from "Ash Wednesday": "This the way the world ends / Not with a bang, but a whimper."

If we are to restore effective government and prosperous economies throughout the West, the first step will have to be averting our gaze from the funhouse mirror into which most of us have been staring for much of our lives. We must start to think as members of families first, and as individuals second. We need to see our fertility not as a toxic waste that sometimes spills, but a primary purpose of life—perpetuating the human family. Our parents made real sacrifices to put us on this earth. Are we too weak or feeble to act like human beings and replace ourselves? But there is the rub. Having children is ipso facto proof that each of us is replaceable—for here are the little ones ready to replace us. That means we are mortal. And who wants to admit something like that?

One of its noblest and most balanced scholars of economics is Röpke, the author of the classic book from which we took this chapter's title, *A Humane Economy*. Röpke was a many-faceted figure: a courageous soldier in World War I who rejected the nationalism and militarism that caused it; a lifelong Lutheran who imbibed the deepest insights of Catholic thinkers such as Chesterton, Belloc, and Pope Pius XI; a defender of the free-market economy who nonetheless saw its limits and potentially self-destructive tendencies; an embodiment of the best of liberal Weimar who, in the post-war cultural tussle, became the most eloquent spokesman in Europe for the timeless principles of Christian humanism.

Röpke was also a man who knew how much his principles are worth: As a low-level (though highly talented) university professor in the late 1920s, he was one of the first to appreciate the threat posed by the National Socialists, and he used his own modest salary to print anti-Nazi pamphlets he had written, then distributed them personally to voters at the polls. Fittingly, he would be the first professor fired by the Nazis for his views. Refusing a Nazi offer to "adjust" his views to the new regime, he fled Germany one step ahead of the Gestapo, working in exile first in Turkey, then in Switzerland. It was there that Röpke wrote his two greatest works, *The Social Crisis of Our Time* and *The Moral Foundations of Civil Society*, books that were smuggled into the Third Reich and read in secret by future Christian Democrats such as Ludwig Erhard, whose policies sparked the postwar German "miracle."

Röpke knew that economics is neither a "hard" science, like physics, nor a matter of arbitrarily chosen premises and approaches, like literary criticism. We cannot reduce human wealth-seeking behavior to a set of deterministic rules, like the movement of subatomic particles; nor can we treat it like a poem, which can have an indefinite number of mutually exclusive but equally "valid" interpretations. Instead, in economics as in the ancient discipline of political philosophy, we lay down general principles based in the observed truths of human nature, as seconded by history, and try to make predictions about what men are likely to do under a wide variety of conditions. Given those predictions, we attempt to offer policies grounded in justice and guided by prudence.

However, no economic system, however wisely constructed, can function if men lack either temperance or fortitude. And while certain evil economic arrangements can sap men of these virtues, no system can supply them. The survival of a free economy and free society, as Röpke wrote, depends on such extra-economic virtues, which men acquire through philosophical reflection, religious practice, and virtuous upbringing. What is refreshing is that Röpke views all economic questions through the lens of this broader, more holistic view of man, one well suited to pursuing the vision of the good society.

Röpke honed his vision of the good by contrasting the healthy, rural community in which his family had lived for generations with the social chaos that emerged with World War I. As a classical liberal with a cosmopolitan education, he was repulsed by the vicious nationalism that convulsed most European countries in the buildup to that war, and even more by the militaristic regimentation of society that was imposed in the name of attaining victory. A winner of the Iron Cross for bravery at the front, Röpke reacted very differently from many German veterans of that war; instead of feeling nostalgia for the camaraderie of the trenches and simmering rage at his country's defeat, Röpke rejected the militarism that had brought the mass slaughter about, and flirted with both socialist and pacifist ideas, searching for a solution to prevent another such war.

Thus far, Röpke followed the trajectory of many English and French survivors of that catastrophe. But his path was diverted when he encountered the work of Ludwig von Mises, a pioneering economist of the Austrian School whose books and essays debunked the shining promise of the Soviet experiment. Specifically, Mises explained that the destruction of private property and competition were not merely immoral but enormously impractical—since a complex modern economy relies for its power to meet human needs on the "votes" cast by consumers through their spending. Restrict or dictate the prices that producers of goods could charge, and you muffle the voice of consumers to ask for the products they want. Instead, manufacturers are ordered by bureaucratic managers to produce what they think the common people really need. The economic chaos that erupts in the absence of the crucial information provided by prices becomes the pretext for still more coercion by the state, which eventually takes over management of ever more aspects of human life, in the vain attempt to re-create artificially the spontaneous order that a free economy—respectful of man's right to work and spend as he chooses—had once generated.

In other words, socialism amounted to militarizing the whole of society, subjecting the lives of civilians to the dictates and blind obedience demanded of frontline soldiers. As Röpke wrote,

> Life in the army had shown what it meant for the individual to exist as part of an apparatus whose every function assumed lack of freedom and unconditional obedience. . . . [P]hysical degradation was also

accompanied by a spiritual one that worked to the total debasement of human dignity in mass existence, mass feeding, mass sleep—that frightful soldier's life in which a man was never alone and in which he was without resource or appeal against the might (inhuman but wielded by man) that had robbed him of his privacy. . . .

War was simply the rampant essence of the state, collectivity let loose, so was it not absurd to make one's protest against the dominance of man over man take the form of collectivism? Not all the pacifist, antimilitarist, and freedom-demanding statements of even the most honest socialists could obscure the fact that socialism, if it was to mean anything at all, meant accepting the state as Leviathan not only for the emergency of war, but also for a long time to come.[3]

Instead of taking as a model the Kaiser's defeated army, or the punitive socialist dictatorship that Lenin was even then imposing on Russia's people (see Chapter Four), Röpke looked to the home of his youth and the wholesome, complex human relations—including the free exchange of goods and services—that welded its people together without the need for coercive micromanagement. As one of his American students, Patrick Boarman, recalled, Röpke's vision of the good was forever formed by

life in the small German village on the edge of the Lüneburger Moors in which he grew up. The simplicity and naturalness of this village existence left the sensitive youth with a host of memories which were to influence the whole cast and direction of his professional work in economics and social theory. The warmth, the love, the stability, the small joys and sorrows of this rural childhood, in which family, church, school, parents, friends and nature were melded into an organic whole.

Röpke himself recalled,

People helped each other with labor and with tools, wherever and however the opportunity arose, whether in the fields, at slaughtering time in the Winter, or on other occasions, and each was generous with what at the moment he happened to have a surplus of. It would have occurred to no one in this giving and taking to make a precise

---

3 Wilhelm Röpke, "The Economic Necessity of Freedom," *Modern Age*, Summer 1959, excerpted in *The March of Freedom*, ed. Edwin J. Feulner (Dallas: Spence Publishing, 1998), 305–6.

calculation of how he would come out in the deal. Everybody knew when or where a birth had occurred, or was imminent. We all took part in weddings, at least to the extent that, with the help of a scarf spread in front of the marriage coach, we kids exacted the tribute of a few pennies from the groom. When the funeral bell sounded from the old church tower, everyone knew for whom it tolled this time, and whoever could manage it walked the last mile with him.[4]

Röpke knew the life in modern cities across the world was radically different, partaking in none of the aspects of communal life that made life so rich and humane in an organic village. Industrial workers cut adrift from extended family and ancestral traditions were culturally impoverished and economically dependent on the unpredictable vagaries of the world economy. The very free economy that made it possible for Europe to support hundreds of millions more human beings than it had in the Middle Ages—with greater freedom, better health, and longer lives unmarked by famines—also presented ordinary workers with a new form of insecurity. Their livelihoods depended not merely on their willingness to work, but on the fluctuating demand in distant nations for the product that they produced, which could plummet when cheaper competitors in other countries entered the market. In other words, even in 1920 workers were suffering from the effects of what we now call globalization. Those workers, whose only asset was the labor that they could offer, had been turned into what Marx called proletarians. In what they perceived as self-defense, they joined socialist movements that offered not just political advocacy but festivals and meeting halls, anthems and rituals designed to replace the Christian rites that so many workers had abandoned when they moved to industrial centers. Socialism offered secular salvation, enlivened by parodies of sacraments.

What these workers sought was sufficient economic security to plan out decent lives for their families and a modicum of economic independence, and some safety net that would catch them if the plant where they were working suddenly slashed their wages or shuttered its gates. In the past, such security had been offered by extended families, and most simple yeomen had a patch of land where in hard times they could grow enough food to survive, without becoming a ward of the state. The ideal situation, Röpke believed in common with distributist thinkers such as G. K. Chesterton, was for large

---

4 Patrick M. Boarman, "Apostle of a Humane Economy: Wilhelm Röpke," *Humanitas* Vol. 13, no. 1 (2000): 47–48.

swathes of society to own their own small farms or businesses, and thereby keep their independence both from the government and from large economic enterprises. A sturdy class of yeomen, shopkeepers, and artisans had been the backbone of movements for political and religious liberty in England as in Switzerland, and without that class Röpke feared for the future of freedom.

An urban worker had none of the traditional social or economic props on which to rely, and it was no great surprise to Röpke that socialist movements offered to furnish them through the state. The bitter irony, he pointed out in subsequent books such as *A Humane Economy* and decades of columns for the influential *Neue Zürcher Zeitung,* was that the growth of government actually stifled the prospects of people obtaining their own land, running small businesses, or otherwise keeping their economic independence. As we have seen in America, agricultural subsidies and regulations are invariably turned to the advantage of multinational corporations with the budgets to hire lobbyists and loophole-hunting lawyers, while small organic farmers find their products regulated right off store shelves. Small businesses find it much harder and comparatively more expensive than big corporations to comply with the countless regulations that rain down on business owners, demanding "diversity" hiring quotas, handicapped-accessible facilities, and insurance plans that violate employers' consciences and break their modest budgets. The more power the central government acquires, the stronger large corporations become, and the less economic and personal liberty every citizen can enjoy. Churches and other units of civil society must yield the functions and sometimes their freedoms to agencies of the state, and the magnificent hodgepodge that is a truly free society is ever more homogenized into a massive collection of atomized individuals whose primary relation is to the federal government— which offers them health insurance, unemployment insurance, a regulated (i.e. "Common Core") education, old-age pensions, and a ready-made ideology that underlies and unites all such efforts: that lowest common denominator of post-Christian life, utilitarian hedonism (see Chapter Six). We will find that the state that takes up to half of our wealth to spend for our own benefit is training us to think along its lines, to go along so we can get along, to make a tolerable place for ourselves in the gray, subhumanist future.

Given that few of us live in large and supportive extended families, and that only a small minority of Westerners either own family farms or independent businesses, what are the prospects for making our economy more humane? Are we doomed to lean ever more heavily on the secular, centralized federal government—with its profoundly ingrained and subhumanist view of man—to confiscate large segments of our wealth, in return for making its safety net ever more comprehensive? In that case, society's future is clear. As reporters like to say, "Follow the money." An ever-increasing portion of the nation's wealth will be redirected toward the only kind of goal that could motivate a centralized government in a nation this large and diverse: the utilitarian hedonist ideal of a long, comfortable, painless, and meaningless life. The state might crack down harshly on churches and other dissident groups that advance a different philosophy of life—as the U.S. federal government has in its mandate that Christians who own businesses must fund medical abortions (see Chapter Nine). But the state really need not be in such a hurry. The Obama administration arguably overplayed its hand when it enacted the HHS mandate, trying too quickly to liquidate religious institutions that were already withering in the hostile atmosphere of a growingly secular culture, starved of funds and increasingly hobbled in practice by the state's encroaching burden of tax and regulation. Even a Jacobin mayor of New York City, for instance, would hardly need to pass a law attempting to close down Catholic schools, which are already collapsing, as parents crumple under the double burden of school taxes and tuition.

Must we, as some "crunchy" dreamers insist, attempt to impose a distributist regime via legislation to restore the economic independence of citizens from the state by mandating the break-up of large corporations and farms, confiscating and redistributing the means of production into the hands of family farmers and small businessmen? Let us leave aside for the moment the immense practical, legal, and political hurdles that stand in the way of any such effort. The primary objection to imposed distributism is a moral one: Although we might agree that the ideal state of affairs is one in which many small businesses and farms support a thriving yeoman class that fights for freedom, no one has an intrinsic human right to own his own business or farm such that the state can justly seize his neighbor's (larger) property and hand it over to him. Nor is it morally wrong, per se, to operate a large business or farm. To assert that the state should violate the property rights of citizens merely in order to pursue an "ideal" state of economic affairs is to lurch into utopianism and to violate the human dignity and autonomy of one's neighbors. Is it right for one group of citizens, which happens to prefer farmers' markets and mom-and-pop shops, to use the bayonets of the state to force other citizens to adopt their shopping preferences? Would the seizure of farms by a distributist regime be any more moral than the seizure of farms by the Bolsheviks—and if so, why? A noble, or even transformative, end does not justify evil means. Furthermore, it is unclear that a government-sponsored regime of distributism would in fact promote the economic independence that its partisan claims to champion. As David Deavel writes,

> The corporatism favored by distributists involves massive intervention by the government in every consumer's economic choices. . . . In Belloc's *Essay on the Restoration of Property* he advocated not only the re-establishment of guilds, but also the following long list of state interventions in the economy:
>
> * subsidies for artisans;
> * progressive or "differential" tax schemes applied to wholesalers—whose money would be put into credit unions, which the guilds would use to finance small businesses that could compete with them;
> * rules and taxes that made it hard to sell smaller pieces of real estate or to buy up farmland;
> * rules for leasing property that include an automatic right to purchase by installment; and
> * a series of state-created credit unions.
>
> The distributist embrace of big government tinkering with everyday economic activity has long outlived Hilaire Belloc. Many distributists advocate that the government buy out failing banks and industries and then redistribute their assets according to "justice."

When you run the economy through the government, the results are easy to see; we have seen them again and again throughout history: Government agencies will take their share off the top, and funnel wealth into the coffers of the state. The bureaucrats who direct the funds toward one business rather than another will effectively control them—as federal agencies now exert enormous power over Catholic colleges and hospitals, for instance. Worst of all, the continual fiddling with markets, wages, and prices, with no foreseeable end, will result in economic chaos—as government mandates, rather than the choices of consumers, set the costs of goods and services. This is no recipe for freedom.[5]

---

5 David Deavel, "What's Wrong with Distributism?" *The Intercollegiate Review*, August 5, 2013, www.intercollegiatereview.com/index.php/2013/08/05/whats-wrong-with-distributism.

A much better option than hitching the wagon of liberty to the interventionist state, whose utilitarian ideology will always win out in the end, is to simultaneously fight for the reduction of government power and the expansion of free, private efforts to accomplish the same civic goods that the welfare state claims to offer. The same conservatives who rightly decry high taxes should be involved in supporting soup kitchens, private schools that serve the poor, crisis pregnancy centers, and scholarships and job training efforts that serve the underprivileged. The only plausible means for reducing the size and scope of government—apart from total fiscal collapse, which for entitlement programs such as Social Security may already be unavoidable— is to make its functions redundant. If we see that the government's safety net has turned into a kind of intergenerational poverty trap, we must reweave the network of free, voluntary organizations that once provided alternatives to the vulnerable, before we try to dismantle what the state has put in place. This is not just a political but a moral imperative.

For Further Reading:
Allan Carlson, *The American Way* (Wilmington, DE: ISI Books, 2003).
Alejandro Chafuen, *Christians for Freedom: Late Scholastic Economics* (San Francisco: Ignatius Press, 1986).
Samuel Gregg, *Wilhelm Röpke's Political Economy* (Cheltenham, UK: Edward Elgar, 2010).
Henry Hazlitt, *Economics in One Lesson* (New York: Three Rivers Press, 1988).
Pope Leo XIII, *Quod Apostolici Muneris,* www.ewtn.com/library/ENCYC/ L13APOST.htm.
———, *Rerum Novarum,* www.vatican.va/holy_father/leo_xiii/encyclicals/ documents/hf_l-xiii_enc_15051891_rerum-novarum_en.html.
Pope John Paul II, *Centesimus Annus,* www.vatican.va/holy_father/john_ paul_ii/encyclicals/documents/hf_jp-ii_enc_01051991_centesimus- annus_en.html.
Leonard Read, "I, Pencil," www.econlib.org/library/Essays/rdPncl1.html.
Wilhelm Röpke, *A Humane Economy* (Wilmington, DE: ISI Books, 2014).
———, *Economics of the Free Society* (Grove City, PA: Libertarian Press, 1994).
———, *The Social Crisis of Our Time* (New Brunswick, NJ: Transaction Publishing, 1991).
John Zmirak, *Wilhelm Röpke* (Wilmington, DE: ISI Books, 2001).

Chapter Twelve

The Road to Subhumanism: How We Got Here

Where did subhumanism come from? That's easy: It came from us; we fathered it. It grew out of Christian failures, and post-Christian movements of "liberation" arose to subsist as parasites on the vast moral capital accumulated over centuries in which the humblest beggar was affirmed as the moral equal of an emperor—until it was at last exhausted.

Most of the arguments presented by believers in one or another variety of subhumanism are not based on a positive love for the goods those philosophies affirm. Instead, subhumanists are moved by an angry, bitter, or heartbroken response to the failures and hypocrisies that litter our Christian and humanist past. The subhumanist arguments we outline in this chapter are those that advocates of the Whole Life principles we outlined in Chapters Seven through Eleven are sure to encounter. They lie behind and beneath the anger of the "pro-choice" activist, the false compassion of the euthanasia doctor, the cold calculation of the social engineer. Subhumanists reject far more than a single religious tradition. They lop off and toss away the cumulative knowledge gained in thousands of years of civilized life and philosophical thought, in favor of a dark and cynical set of debaters' points. Humanists will need to answer the actual arguments offered, but to do that they need to know the real historical grievances that underlie those who fight against a culture of life.

The theologian Henri de Lubac wrote an incisive treatise, *The Drama of Atheist Humanism*, that with careful fairness looks at the founders of major antireligious movements, such as Ludwig Feuerbach, Auguste Comte, Karl Marx, and Friedrich Nietzsche, trying to understand what human goods those thinkers thought religion imperiled, and which they meant to rescue. Speaking broadly, that generation of "Promethean" thinkers, whom de Lubac calls "heroic humanists," asserted that Western man had for many centuries engaged in one or more of the following errors:

157

1. *We had projected onto God virtues (such as wisdom, love, and providence for the future) that man must cultivate. We "alienated" the best that was in man by locating God as the source, summit, and telos of all our earthly efforts—which must seem tainted and futile compared to His imagined unearthly perfections.*

2. *We had ceded to God control over human destiny, embracing passivity instead of energetic activism. We used a fantasy of divine justice meted out in the next life to assuage the effects of injustice in this life, thus blunting the impulse for change.*

3. *We allowed human life to be stunted, cramped, and ridden with guilt and fear of an invisible, all-powerful, punitive father-figure.*

The heroic humanists who advanced these critiques got support from outside their ranks, from men who claimed no such broad philosophical project, but merely claimed to report on the outcome of their empirical scientific research—employing a method that for centuries had been gradually displacing religion and speculative thought as the source most people looked to for intellectual certainty. (Indeed, the very word "science," which once referred to every mode of knowledge, including theology, had by the late nineteenth century been narrowed in common use to refer mainly to strictly empirical studies.)

So when Darwin's theory offered an alternative explanation for the rise of life, even human life, his assertions provided explosive ammunition to those who wanted to free mankind from the shadow of God. Freud's explanation of the workings of the human psyche—an idiosyncratic, highly anecdotal account based on an appallingly limited sample of wealthy Viennese—passed as science on the same model as Darwin's. Freud's insights, however, were powerful, and offered a compelling new explanation for the perversities and frustrations of human life. His theories displaced, for many, what had been the dominant explanation: a scheme of sin, grace, and repentance that Augustine had developed from the writings of St. Paul.

Each of the salient points raised by the heroic humanists that de Lubac cited has some historical validity, in the sense that deformations of Christianity did endorse or practice it, and so deserves our attention.

1. *We had projected onto God virtues that man must cultivate. We "alienated" the best that was in man by locating God as the source, summit, and telos of all our earthly efforts—which must seem tainted and futile compared to His imagined unearthly perfections.*

This is the core of Ludwig Feuerbach's *The Essence of Christianity*, and one might say that it stands at the core of the heroic humanist charge against Christianity. It implies that the package of divine perfections attributed to God by the Western tradition is a mere collection of human attributes such as knowledge, power, goodness, and foresight, all of which are combined and inflated to infinity by a simple logical sleight of hand affirming each of these attributes, then specifying that it is limitless. So God has perfect knowledge, eternal existence, absolute power, pure goodness, et cetera. Even if this were a fair description of how Christian philosophers proceeded, that would not prove that such divine perfections were a myth; it might merely explain how finite, limited minds fumble when they try to express conceptions of the infinite. Few of us can adequately understand or explain quantum physics, but only an anti-intellectual would use that as proof that quantum physics is nonsense.

To make Feuerbach's charge stick, secular thinkers have to assert that positing such a perfect Being, and conceiving him as separate from ourselves, is inherently demeaning to human beings—that by inventing an impossible criterion of absolute perfection, Western man has debased human dignity and generated a self-reinforcing psychological mechanism that diminishes his best efforts, disparages his noblest accomplishments, and takes away his rightful pride as the apex of the natural order, replacing it with a false and destructive humility before the realm of the unseen. This is indeed what contemporary "new atheists" such as Richard Dawkins claim.

But is it true? Does our common experience tell us that holding to ideals that exceed our grasp must lead to despair and cringing self-abasement? Is this true, for example, in athletics, where young people dream of joining professional teams and breaking records? Is it true in romantic love, where young people look to mythic examples of mutual devotion like Shakespeare's *Romeo and Juliet*? In political and military life, when we invoke fallen heroes, are we dooming the next generation to despair because they probably cannot equal Nathan Hale or Joan of Arc?

Perhaps the poison lies not in the fact that an ideal is practically unattainable, but in the very essence of ideals that are *by definition* out of our grasp. Although one likely will not outperform Hank Aaron or Abraham Lincoln, in theory it is *possible*, whereas God's perfections are not even theoretically within reach. Maybe that is what makes it so degrading to man to believe in God, as Jean-Paul Sartre asserted. This argument makes a little more sense, but it fails to explain how perfectionist goals in other areas of life actually function. Physicists seek an ever more perfect knowledge of how the universe works; political idealists try to achieve perfect justice; economists seek to maximize wealth and productivity; artists strive for a beauty that they cannot even conceive before creating it. Does the "infinite" horizon toward which all these people strive in fact work to lower their standards, undermine their efforts, and turn them—as new atheists argue—into timid, breast-beating serfs?

Conversely, what results have we seen in social and artistic life as a result of lowering standards, trashing ideals, "defining deviancy down," and preemptively surrendering our vision of the good particular to that art or science? Corruption, mediocrity, and despair more often emerge from such cynicism. What is more, there is no evidence that before the rise of Christianity, Western man treasured ideals of higher perfection that were attainable by human means—only to encounter the inflated perfections attributed to God, then respond by throwing out such human efforts and sinking into despair. The late Roman Empire, where Christianity took hold, took for granted and morally yawned at slavery, infanticide, aggressive war, the slaughter of enemy civilians, authoritarian government with no code of individual rights, prostitution, and gladiatorial entertainment. It was only the rise of Christianity that encouraged serious moral reflection—outside of Jewish or Stoic elites—on evils like these and efforts to limit or abolish them. It took an Augustine to codify the principles of a "just war"; no philosopher would have dared to raise such concepts with Julius Caesar, whose ruthless conquest of Gaul was fueled by personal ambition and national aggrandizement. He returned to Rome triumphant, with thousands of hostages and slaves whom he marched through the streets, and was not greeted with questions by Greek or Roman moralists. There was never a pagan Ambrose, ready to confront an all-powerful emperor with the fact that he had violated the rights of his subjects. These concepts would have been impossible to convey in pagan terms. They emerged on a broad scale only with Christianity, and we have good reason (thanks to the events of the twentieth century) to wonder whether they could really outlive it.

For all the flaws in this atheist argument, there were reasons why it emerged. The notion of a morally perfect, omnipotent God who sits in judgment on our every action does indeed exert a strong psychological pressure. It can produce quite healthy outcomes, such as humility; penitence and amendment; forbearance toward the faults of others; even a rueful, ironic sense of human existence as fundamentally comic, which we find in authors such as Chaucer and Cervantes. Magnificent personalities such as

Francis of Assisi, Teresa of Ávila, and John of the Cross emerged from the crucible of painful awareness of personal sin judged against the goodness of God. Other people with different personalities, who embraced distorted theological modes of dealing with sin or followed certain ideas well beyond their logical conclusions, did indeed emerge from the encounter with human limits and God's perfection with a crippling sense of guilt that goaded them throughout their lives. Some theological conclusions that have been drawn from Augustine's analysis of sin and grace have seemed monstrous to most— among them the Calvinist-Jansenist doctrine of double predestination, which explains the persistence of evil in the world and reconciles it with God's omnipotence by concluding that God has only chosen a tiny number of souls whom he will save, that he saves them without their free will, and that the rest of the human race is irretrievably lost no matter what they do. That version of Christianity, embraced by the American Puritans, proved so repugnant to reason that much of New England by the early nineteenth century rejected orthodox Christianity altogether for the vague uplift of Unitarianism. It's hard to blame them.

Another disturbing side effect of the idea of divine perfection is the phenomenon of messianic utopianism, which emerged again and again in Europe during the Middle Ages and Reformation. As Norman Cohn documents in *The Pursuit of the Millennium*, the praise lavished on the poor throughout the Gospels and the promises of a perfect "New Jerusalem" on earth to be found in Revelation served as highly combustible fuel for radical preachers, disgruntled tradesmen, and displaced intellectuals, who sometimes attracted followings of thousands to violent movements to eradicate every trace of evil and construct the perfect society here and now. The Flagellants began by doing penance to ward off the plague but ended by calling for the destruction of the "corrupt" Catholic Church. The "People's Crusade," when it proved unable to fight the Muslims in the Holy Land, settled for persecuting the Jews at home in Europe. Such movements wreaked havoc in dozens of cities and claimed the lives of many thousands. In the annals of historical anti-Semitism, these were among the worst events recorded before the Holocaust. Some rulers invoked utopian themes when they promised to root out "evil" in their realms, which for them meant forcibly converting or driving out religious minorities. (The Jews were expelled, at one point, from every major country in Europe, except for Poland.) Church leaders, although they regularly and firmly condemned such utopian movements, were sometimes powerless to prevent the actions of mobs led by half-educated or unbalanced self-proclaimed prophets.

The violent events that marked the Reformation—from the brutal, and brutally subjugated, Peasants' Rebellion to the general slaughter of the Thirty Years' War, wherein whole cities full of "heretics" were burned or put to the sword—surely gave plenty of fodder to worldly thinkers who wished found find more "realistic," mundane philosophies. Following on the work of precursors such as Marsiglio of Padua and Niccolo Machiavelli, Hobbes reacted to the savage English Civil War (fought between Puritans who wished to remake English society and Anglicans who wished to crush out their dissent) by replacing a distant, infinitely demanding God with a concrete, finite, tangible source of order: Leviathan, the secular state invested with absolute power over the lives of individuals in order to protect them from each other and themselves. John Locke rejected such grandiose claims for the state, and instead focused his energy on "demythologizing" Christianity, fudging its supernatural claims and trying his best to convert it from a faith with stark metaphysical claims and extensive moral teachings into a scheme of interpersonal kindness, which would lubricate the interactions between sovereign individuals who contracted with the state to protect their lives, liberties, and property.

These and later "moderate" Enlightenment thinkers came to a tacit agreement: that Christianity made too much of God and of man alike, and asked too much of man for his own good. Whether or not some perfect, divine goodness existed, they taught, it is out of our reach, and we will only deform ourselves and wreck our earthly lives by constantly grasping for it— either the knowledge of it through religious orthodoxy, or the practice of it through the traditional Christian virtues.

To spare society the violent clashes that often emerged over dogmas, these early modern thinkers urged on people a more distant, disinterested (Deist) God and a less demanding, more practical moral standard. Man would not be the fallen image of a perfect God, but a rational actor negotiating with his fellow men, haggling (mostly) nonviolently over the good things to found in this life. The next life could take care of itself.

2. *We had ceded to God control over human destiny, embracing passivity instead of energetic activism. We used a fantasy of divine justice meted out in the next life to assuage the effects of injustice in this life, thus blunting the impulse for change.*

This idea was best and most famously expressed by Marx, who built on his reading of Feuerbach when he declared that religion is the "opium of the people." In Marx's day, "opium" did not have all the pejorative force it does today; although opiate drugs were known to be addictive, they were also considered almost miraculous in their pain-blocking effects: for the first time in human history, surgery patients and wounded soldiers did not have to howl in agony until they recovered (or most likely died). Here is Marx's statement in context:

> Man, who has found only the *reflection* of himself in the fantastic reality of heaven, where he sought a superman, will no longer feel disposed to find the *mere appearance* of himself, the non-man [*Unmensch*], where he seeks and must seek his true reality.
>
> The foundation of irreligious criticism is: *Man makes religion*, religion does not make man. Religion is, indeed, the self-consciousness and self-esteem of man who has either not yet won through to himself, or has already lost himself again. But *man* is no abstract being squatting outside the world. Man is *the world of man*—state, society. This state and this society produce religion, which is an *inverted consciousness of the world*, because they are an *inverted world*. Religion is the general theory of this world, its encyclopaedic compendium, its logic in popular form, its spiritual *point d'honneur*, its enthusiasm, its moral sanction, its solemn complement, and its universal basis of consolation and justification. It is the *fantastic realization* of the human essence since the *human essence* has not acquired any true reality. The struggle against religion is, therefore, indirectly the struggle *against that world* whose spiritual *aroma* is religion.
>
> *Religious* suffering is, at one and the same time, the *expression* of real suffering and a *protest* against real suffering. Religion is the sigh of the oppressed creature, the heart of a heartless world, and the soul of soulless conditions. It is the *opium* of the people.[1]

Thus for Marx, religion is a form of mass delusion produced as a psychological mechanism for masking and mitigating a world that some men have made unbearable for other men through political and economic exploitation. Religion serves to distract serfs or industrial workers from the wealth that their employers are stealing from them; to sanctify and make untouchable

---

1 *A Contribution to the Critique of Hegel's Philosophy of Right, Deutsch-Französische Jahrbücher* (Paris), February 7 and 10, 1844, found at www.marxists.org/archive/marx/works/1843/critique-hpr/intro.htm.

unjust social and political structures; to pacify and make obedient men who would otherwise revolt; to divert the energies needed for pursuing earthly good into an entirely imaginary arena. Thus, as a necessary part of rectifying these injustices and achieving what the masses *really* want (earthly justice), it is essential to discredit what they *think* they want—eternal happiness. On this model, the masses of men (especially in Marx's time) are akin to an alcoholic leaning against a bar with a bottle in his hand. The socialist is the temperance crusader who barges into the bar with a hatchet, smashes the bottles, and drags the dipsomaniac to a rehabilitation clinic. If bartenders or bouncers try to prevent this rescue, of course they too must be subdued by force—since they are essentially poisoners, working on behalf of systematic thieves.

Hence the mass persecutions of unarmed priests, nuns, and religious folk which had already been seen in history—for instance, in the French Revolution's genocide in the Vendée, which killed between 150,000 and 300,000 religious peasants—were entirely justified. So too, by plain logical deduction from Marx's theory, would be the mass persecutions conducted against ordinary Christians and their clergy in revolutionary Mexico, Spain, Russia, Ukraine, China, Vietnam, Cuba, North Korea, and other nations caught up in socialist revolutions. A level of savage coercion that Islam prohibited its armies from using against Christians at the height of the Arab conquests, that no bishop or pope would have endorsed against pagans in the Spanish conquest of the Americas, is here implicitly called for by a humanist philosopher and social reformer.

What is easy to overlook in Marx's statement is the flabbergasting paternalism with which he views the common man. While hundreds of millions of souls have held a wide array of religious faiths all around the world, Marx's coterie of secular Europeans can safely dismiss in advance their arguments and experiences, without even troubling to examine them, because they know the real reason that the masses believe—and the masses do not. They have been swindled, snookered, beguiled by their landlords and employers into glumly accepting a grim earthly fate in return for . . . pie in the sky when they die. Marxists know this; the masses do not. It is incumbent on Marxists to use whatever means necessary to drag these enslaved souls to the sole oasis of freedom that Marx discovered. What is more noteworthy here than Marx's cynicism is his hubris—which he shared with many other political philosophers, right and left. Indeed, we must cite a trenchant observation by the French libertarian thinker Frederic Bastiat, from his 1850 work *The Law*:

Present-day writers—especially those of the socialist school of thought—base their various theories upon one common hypothesis: They divide mankind into two parts. People in general—with the exception of the writer himself—form the first group. The writer, all alone, forms the second and most important group. Surely this is the weirdest and most conceited notion that ever entered a human brain!

In fact, these writers on public affairs begin by supposing that people have within themselves no means of discernment; no motivation to action. The writers assume that people are inert matter, passive particles, motionless atoms, at best a kind of vegetation indifferent to its own manner of existence. They assume that people are susceptible to being shaped—by the will and hand of another person—into an infinite variety of forms, more or less symmetrical, artistic, and perfected.

Moreover, not one of these writers on governmental affairs hesitates to imagine that he himself—under the title of organizer, discoverer, legislator, or founder—is this will and hand, this universal motivating force, this creative power whose sublime mission is to mold these scattered materials—persons—into a society.

These socialist writers look upon people in the same manner that the gardener views his trees.[2]

In *The New Science of Politics*, Eric Voegelin diagnosed the temptation of intellectuals to arrogate to themselves this kind of all-encompassing insight as a modern revival of the ancient attitude of the Gnostics. These early competitors with Christianity held that salvation from a world of suffering and alienation was possible—but only through the attainment of a *set of secret insights* that an intellectual and spiritual elite would pass on among themselves. Of course, the ancient Gnostics were never keen on sharing their private revelations with the masses. They sought not political power but status as a spiritual elect. The democratizing impulse of Christianity, exercised over many centuries, in which ignorant peasants were just as likely to attain eternal salvation as mitred abbots or kings, influenced those with Gnostic aspirations in quite a different direction. They would not separate themselves from the ignorant hordes in private reverie, but instead organize to spread their privately decanted doctrines to the masses, by force if need be—and enjoy, instead of splendid isolation, the heady satisfaction of seeing

---

2 Found at bastiat.org/en/the_law.html#SECTION_G037.

their own ideas reshape the lives and even the souls of millions of other men. Instead of elitism, they would be practicing broad-based benevolence, by freeing the ignorant many through the brilliant insights of the few.

Now that we have briefly critiqued both the outcome and the motives that lie behind Marx's assertions, it remains to ask how much objective truth they might retain. Just the fact that an assertion can be used in an evil way, or that the man who made it had suspicious intent, does not necessarily make the statement false. To give an example: Black activists in apartheid South Africa pointed to the injustices of its racist political system. The white authorities tried to discredit them by pointing to the fact that some of them belonged to the Communist Party—which was true, and an effective rhetorical tactic, but also quite irrelevant to the fact that apartheid itself was evil.

So how much truth is there in the assertion that Christian faith encouraged the mass of men to become political quietists and economic victims? Will the evidence we find be sufficient to support Marx's solution—which is to dismiss the religious impulse as a secondary side effect of political economic oppression, so that we must first make men atheists before they can be free? Or will we find that Christianity, like every other movement that has existed for thousands of years, has operated in a wide variety of ways—sometimes supporting, sometimes opposing, sometimes in cool coexistence alongside the structures of power? The Church was founded, of course, by a victim of judicial murder—thanks to the collusion of Roman occupiers and a cabal of collaborating Jewish high priests—on the false charge that Jesus was leading a political revolution. Its most effective apostle, Paul, was the first important voice to advise Christians to focus on changing men's hearts instead of their system of government. In a statement that would bedevil the victims of tyrants in subsequent centuries, he wrote,

> Let every person be subject to the governing authorities. For there is no authority except from God, and those that exist have been instituted by God. Therefore he who resists the authorities resists what God has appointed, and those who resist will incur judgment. For rulers are not a terror to good conduct, but to bad. Would you have no fear of him who is in authority? Then do what is good, and you will receive his approval, for he is God's servant for your good. But if you do wrong, be afraid, for he does not bear the sword in vain; he is the servant of God to execute his wrath on the wrongdoer. Therefore one must be subject, not only to avoid God's wrath but also for the sake of conscience. For the same reason you also pay taxes, for the authorities are ministers of God, attending to this very thing. Pay all of them their

dues, taxes to whom taxes are due, revenue to whom revenue is due, respect to whom respect is due, honor to whom honor is due. (Rom. 13:1–7)

On the face of it, this sounds like an injunction to absolute passivity in the face of civil power. And certainly, rulers used this passage when they sought the support of clergy and believers in repressing every kind of revolt. If Paul's advice were all encompassing and applicable to every exercise of authority, then Christianity really would have served the purpose that Marx attributed to it—as a political and civic anesthetic.

The first great historic challenge to such a compliant attitude to the demands of political power came when Roman persecution of Christians began—in Paul's own lifetime, under the emperor Nero. (Indeed, Paul would die a martyr in Rome, having used all the legal resources available to him as a Roman citizen.) If a Christian was asked by the legitimate Roman authorities to turn over sacred books, reveal where other Christians were hiding, or worship the emperor as a god—was he forbidden to resist them? Looking to Jewish precursors such as the Maccabees, Christians began to distinguish between just laws (which must always be obeyed) and unjust ones (which might be resisted), and assert the superiority of conscience to public authority.

Indeed, while we moderns take for granted the notion that marriage is a purely voluntary institution requiring both parties' consent, that was not the case in pre-Christian Rome. A father's absolute authority over his children (which could include putting one of them to death) also entailed the power to bestow one of his daughters on a man of his own choosing. The first organized resistance to this custom came from Christians—especially Christian women who had made vows of virginity. The lists of Roman martyrs are full of stories (some of them spruced up with legendary details) of young women like Agnes and Cecilia, who held their faith as higher than the commands of a father or magistrate; and the Church incorporated in its early canon law the absolute requirement that a marriage must be consensual or it was invalid. (The consent of the bride would be challenged again, by a different secular power—the Germanic barbarians who considered abduction and consummation sufficient to seal a marriage.)

So from the most basic unit of society, the family, to the highest apex of power, the emperor, Christians almost from the beginning have discerned where obedience to authority is demanded, where it is merely allowed, and where it is outright forbidden. Just as Antigone became a bone in the throat of the tyrant Creon because she insisted that piety outweighed the commands of the king (see Chapter Eight), Christians facing a wide variety of overreaching governments over the centuries have consistently held the private conscience as a higher authority than the state.

Augustine offered the most enduring reflections on the relations between Church and state. In *The City of God*, he clarified Paul's observations on slavery, contradicting Aristotle's claim that some men are slaves by nature; no, the existence of slavery is, like the existence of war, the side effect of sin in the world. Augustine wrote that God "did not intend that His rational creature, who was made in His image, should have dominion over anything but the irrational creation,— not man over man, but man over the beasts."[3] This passage, by noting that slavery is contrary to God's creative intention, planted the seed of the Christian critique of that institution. However, Augustine was neither a pacifist nor an abolitionist; his main concern was not the political arrangements of the earthly city so much as their relevance for our journey as "pilgrims" to the heavenly city. So he warned masters to treat their slaves with justice and with the same Christian love of neighbor that they treasure toward members of their families; he also noted that slavery to sin is far worse than economic or political subjugation. One could assert that here Augustine was endorsing political passivity, urging people to ignore their "objective" enslavement in favor of merely "subjective" internal states. That is precisely what Marx would say.

Or was Augustine offering the weak a different kind of power—a power that the rich and the strong could never take away? He pointed to the spiritual freedom that believers would treasure in every kind of evil situation, from ancient slavery to modern prison camps managed by Marxists. In prizing the inner life as more important than external circumstances, he in fact was igniting an inextinguishable spark of hope in the millions of people who would find themselves trapped in situations that are really, objectively, beyond any earthly remedy. It was precisely this sense of a higher purpose immune to material suffering that Viktor Frankl reported in *Man's Search for Meaning* was what kept his fellow prisoners from killing themselves at Auschwitz. A spark of spiritual dignity was the difference between life and death. The same can be true for entire societies, as the grim progress of subhumanism through the twentieth century shows.

---

3 *The City of God*, 15, trans. Marcus Dods, in *Nicene and Post-Nicene Fathers, First Series*, Vol. 2, ed. Philip Schaff (Buffalo, NY: Christian Literature Publishing Co., 1887), found at www.newadvent.org/fathers/120119.htm.

On the broader issue of Christian obedience to civil governments, Augustine said that an organized government of society is just as vital as the organization of the body, and that Christians are obliged to be better citizens than pagans, since they accept not only just civil laws but a higher standard imposed on them by their faith. He did not directly address the issue of civil (or non-civil) disobedience to unjust laws, but he approved of the martyrs' refusal to obey Caesar by worshipping him, and he had learned the faith at the feet of the bishop Ambrose, the man who rebuked the Christian emperor Theodosius for his massacre of a crowd and denied him entrance to his church or reception of the sacraments until he repented. This is the model the Church employed through most of its history for resisting unjust governments: using ecclesiastical sanctions to threaten the ruler with eternal punishment for his temporal misdeeds. This power was enough to stop the Holy Roman emperors from appointing their cronies as bishops and to force the English kings to give the Church her independence throughout the Middle Ages. But papal power was overused and misused during the Renaissance to serve the temporal quarrels of morally dubious popes. It lost its force entirely after the Reformation taught kings a dangerous lesson: If the Church proved an obstacle to their agglomeration of power, they could take their whole nation (as Henry VIII did) out of the Catholic orbit, with the additional bonus of the Church's accumulated property, which could be seized from the unarmed monks and nuns who had used it for centuries to support higher learning and social services for the poor. At that point, popes lost any power to restrain Christian rulers, and the Church ceased to serve as a counterbalance against the growing, centralizing power of the early modern state.

What neither Augustine, nor any political or theological thinker, came up with before the seventeenth century was a theoretical basis for citizens' organizing to resist the demands of the state. Intellectuals do not like to admit it, but most theories we ponder in history books emerged from historical practice—and not the other way around. It's not so much that ideas have consequences. Institutions do. Political ideas emerge when defenders of existing institutions find that they need to support, explain, and improve their practices. Ideas on their own are frail and forgettable things; the constitutions of Latin American nations that followed the American example and threw off their colonial masters were full of the same rhetoric of liberty as the documents crafted in Philadelphia in 1776. What the Latin American nations lacked were the institutions and precedents of limited, decentralized government that could have made such ideas effective. So they ended up as empty rhetoric, and most of those liberated nations descended into dictatorships not much different than the Spanish colonial governments they had replaced.

Institutions have consequences, and the fact that one institution in the West, the Church, outlived a collapsing Roman empire guaranteed a certain practical independence for the Church. (Compare this with the Church in the Christian East, which was quickly subordinated to the power of the Byzantine emperors and the Russian tsars.) Likewise, it was crucial that Rome was conquered by mostly Germanic invaders; unlike the suffocatingly centralized, authoritarian Roman Empire, the German tribes had deep-seated customs that limited the powers of their kings and granted extensive rights of resistance to noblemen. These limits of royal power and rights of resistance were periodically asserted in the form of revolts against kings—one of which resulted in the English Magna Carta. The common law tradition emerged from this milieu of leftover Roman law, longstanding tribal custom, and weak kings dependent on the cooperation of their nobles. The weakness of kings gave concrete power to Parliament in England, to the electors in the Holy Roman Empire, and to imperial "free cities" all through Germany and Italy.

As Russell Kirk explained in *The Roots of American Order*, it is in these medieval political realities—not Enlightenment pamphlets—that we find the seeds of modern, Anglo-American liberties. The result of historical accidents and cultural conditions, these rebellions and refusals laid the groundwork in reality for rights that would later be defended philosophically, using Christian and classical arguments that went beyond tribal custom to ground liberties in the dignity of the human person, and to extend the rights of noblemen to every citizen. In countries where centralizing kings succeeded in quashing the nobles and imposing royal rule—such as Russia, Spain, and France—we even today see a much higher degree of centralization and a higher value placed on order than liberty.

Sadly, the Church did become dependent on the good auspices of kings, at much the same time that many rebels against the injustices of those kings began to embrace secular arguments about the nature of power from the pens of men like Machiavelli and Hobbes. So for several centuries after the Reformation, and especially in the wake of the brutally anti-Christian, implicitly totalitarian French Revolution, Christian leaders (Catholic and Protestant alike) ranged themselves almost exclusively on the side of authority rather than liberty. The biggest exception can be found in England, where the ecclesiastical compromise that was Anglicanism used the power of the state to persecute Catholics and ultra-Protestant "dissenters" and Puritans. In

England, Catholics drew on the writings of Robert Bellarmine, who refuted the "divine right of kings" invented to bolster the Anglican throne, and argued for the right of citizens to overthrow a tyrannical ruler; the Puritans, with greater practical effect, cited medieval and common-law precedents and used the medieval institution that was Parliament to hamper and resist the attempts of the Stuart monarchs to impose an absolute, centralized monarchy in England. What few of us realize today is that, viewed politically, the Puritans were acting as conservatives—clinging to ancient privileges that "modern" political thinkers of the day considered archaic holdovers from the dark days of feudalism. From a theological perspective, however, the Puritans were citing Christian precedents and practices against the revived, essentially pagan Roman law that modern monarchs were using to bolster their seizure of absolute power. When the American founders imitated their Puritan ancestors and cited "the rights of Englishmen" against the English parliament and king, they were likewise using a medieval weapon to resist a modern invention—the centralized state.

Sadly, in almost every Catholic country, such states had successfully subjugated the Church, granting monarchs the power to appoint every bishop in their country, control the Church's finances, even prevent the publication of encyclicals with which they disagreed. (The last twinge of such throne and altar absolutism emerged in Franco's Spain, where the generalissimo disapproved of the liturgical changes after the Second Vatican Council and forbade their implementation for several years.) The state "rewarded" the Church by repressing and even persecuting Protestants—sometimes over the protests of the popes. (The Spanish Inquisition against the Jews and Louis XIV's vicious assault on the Huguenots were both conducted in defiance of papal disapproval.) When dissenters arose against these unaccountable, inequitable regimes, they came not in the form of religious sects that cited medieval liberties for limitations on the state, but of *philosophes* who called for radical, often utopian schemes that would liquidate the Church, keep or even increase the power of the central state, and use that power in the service of "enlightened" ideals. The best example is, of course, Rousseau, who saw a renewed, revolutionary state as the tool for enforcing virtue and "freedom" on every citizen, replacing all the free institutions of Church and community with agencies of the state.

The cruelties, wars, and ideological extravagances of the French and related revolutions drove most churchmen even further into the arms of authoritarian monarchies, even as thinkers who saw the legitimate Christian principles of moral equality and human dignity lurking behind the Enlightenment rhetoric of some revolutionaries—for instance, Hugues-Félicité Robert de Lamennais—were subject to condemnation by popes who feared the return of the anticlerical mobs. The peoples of Catholic nations under foreign occupation—such as Poland and Ireland—were appalled when popes supported their "legitimate," non-Catholic rulers against popular, national revolts.

But there were exceptions. Christian thinkers whom we can place squarely in the classical liberal—in modern American terms, we might say "moderate libertarian"—tradition did emerge and exert significant influence. Edmund Burke, whose family members were persecuted Catholics in Ireland, looked at the British constitutional tradition and saw in it rich resources for defending the freedom of individuals and nonstate institutions against both grasping rulers and tyrannical majorities. His philosophy of slow, organic change that maintains the continuity of social institutions would become an important theme for moderate conservatives ever after. Charles Carroll, the only Catholic to sign the Declaration of Independence, drew on his Thomist training to philosophically defend the nascent representative government in America and to advocate the free market in terms strikingly close to those used by Adam Smith in *The Wealth of Nations*. Carroll would set the tone for an American Catholicism that was vigorous, faithful, and apostolic, in a democratic and pluralist context. The success of the Church in America, and its almost entirely positive experience with liberty, would prove a major influence on the development of Catholic political thought; an American thinker, the great Jesuit John Courtney Murray, would provide much of the framework and most of the arguments supporting the Church's (too long belated) embrace of religious liberty as a basic human right at Vatican II.

Most important among thinkers in the broadly Catholic tradition was Alexis de Tocqueville, who had seen the collapse of the autocratic monarchy restored after the French Revolution and had traveled to America to see how humane values might be preserved in the rough-and-tumble world of free elections and an untrammeled free market. Without noblemen and state-empowered churchmen, would there be anyone left to care for those goods—such as public charity, liberal education, and the preservation of culture—that have no native constituency in a market economy? Or would those goods be neglected until a powerful state arose to organize them, on the Jacobin model?

What Tocqueville found—and recorded in *Democracy in America*—was that Americans did not need a native aristocracy or an established Church to nurture these noncommercial values. Civic-minded Americans, organized through their freely chosen churches or any of thousands of voluntary service organizations—which, he noted, Americans were constantly founding—seemed eager to take on the tasks of education, philanthropy, and civic improvement. The urge to organize freely into groups whose activities transcended their narrow self-interest created a uniquely vigorous sphere that Tocqueville called "civil society." Such "intermediate institutions" that stand between the naked individual and the power of the state, the "little platoons" (as Burke called them) that range from the extended family to the parish to the philanthropic society, are the barriers that protect freedom in the long run. They are institutions with consequences. To protect them from co-option and control by the state, the Church has embraced the principle of "subsidiarity" (see Chapter Nine), which asserts that it is a sin against justice for the state to absorb an activity that it is possible for civil society to accomplish on its own. This principle, long inherent in Catholic political theory, was something that Pope Pius XI found it needful to enshrine in an encyclical, *Quadragesimo Anno*, as a rebuke to the totalitarian governments all across Europe that were swallowing civil society and centralizing power over every level of culture through the state's coercive muscle.

It would shock the loyal reader of Marx to realize how many of these institutions, whose actions belie mere selfishness or the will to power, found their origin in the churches. If we move beyond the narrow question of how much Christianity encouraged political resistance, and look instead at how Christians responded to social and economic injustice, we see how blind and time-bound Marx's perspective really was—for all his pretensions of laying out universal, "scientific" laws of history. Christians began their social activism in the earliest days of the Church: it was Christians who joined Rome's Jews at the city walls to rescue unwanted infants exposed and left to die; Christians organized the first real charities for the Roman poor; Christians who asserted the equal spiritual dignity of slaves and masters. After the fall of Rome, Christian monks famously collected and painstakingly recopied the works of pagan literature and opened schools to teach the neglected poor. Monks and nuns honeycombed Europe in the Dark and Middle Ages, opening schools at every level, organizing relief during famines, and operating hospitals. Reforming friars emerged during the first days of budding capitalism to denounce those moneylenders who preyed on the poor and to open low-interest credit unions for workingmen and peasants. It was only with the Reformation and its wars that much of this civic infrastructure was smashed, as religious orders dissolved or were driven out, Church lands were seized by the state, or Church offices were co-opted by Catholic monarchs and used as means of exerting state power. Even then, in foreign missions and the new territories opened up after 1492, it was typically friars and sisters who ministered to natives abused or dispossessed by conquering Europeans, and who championed their rights against the greed of land-hungry colonists. In the eighteenth century, Methodist laymen in England founded the abolitionist movement, which would take fire with Christian preachers across America. In the twentieth century, we have seen the civil rights movement, the pro-life movement, and the Solidarity movement in Poland all emerge from Christian milieus to challenge the consciences of the powerful through nonviolent, moral witness.

In short, although there have been historical periods in which clergymen found it necessary to counsel against the common people organizing revolts against their rulers, it is grossly false and misleading to portray Christianity as a force that favors repression and social stasis. Indeed, the rapid rate of social, political, and economic change in the West, compared to the much more stable, hierarchical societies that existed throughout Asia in the same centuries, suggests that Christianity is, if anything, a force for disruption and innovation. Its principles are so radical and its message so demanding that no status quo is ever safe.

3. *We allowed human life to be stunted, cramped, and ridden with guilt and fear of an invisible, all-powerful, punitive father-figure.*

This critique of patriarchy itself has many fathers. It recurs with some regularity, suggesting its enduring power, and the fact that it is based on real abuses. We see its first outlines in the writing of French Enlightenment figures such as Voltaire, who let his legitimate outrage at the rigidly authoritarian French monarchical system extend to the theology that the regime leaned on for legitimacy. The top-down, patriarchal theory of royal authority, wielded without any constitutional limits or court of appeal, gave moral force to a regime that had indeed become tyrannical. As we have noted, the "modern" theory of absolute monarchy that the Church rejected in principle was thriving in practice in a number of Catholic countries. The Church's power to push back against the state had collapsed with the Reformation, and monarchs were using pagan Roman theory to revoke and override the Christian common law principles that had provided restraints on royal power through the Middle Ages. Except in England, whose extreme religious division had aided supporters of Parliament, assemblies that once had given voice to the nobles and commons were losing their power to legislate or restrict taxation. In Spain, the Habsburgs revoked the venerable *fueros*, or local constitutional restrictions on royal fiat, and throughout the sixteenth century imposed a rigidly centralized monarchy on the vast Spanish Empire. The Estates General in France were left unsummoned for hundreds of years in the wake of the bloody Fronde (1648–1653), the civil war in which King Louis XIII broke the back of the aristocracy. Although the monarchy nominally backed the Church in Spain and France—and proved its loyalty by persecuting helpless Jews and Protestants—in fact such Catholic kings gained almost complete control over the clergy in their countries. The king of France might not have the power to pick the pope (as he had through the Avignon period), but he could and did prevent the pope from choosing the bishops in France, from collecting all the revenues due the Church from her own lands, and sometimes from publishing documents that the king found uncongenial. Monarchs could even promote or stymie the development of doctrine. Much as we might be grateful for the Church's firm condemnation of the ugly Jansenist heresy, it gives us pause to learn that Pope Innocent X only issued his bull denouncing the heresy under pressure from the king of France, or that subsequent persecutions of Calvinist Frenchmen would be provoked when a pious mistress of King Louis XIV had a fit of conscience over the persistence of heresy in her lover's kingdom. It was over the fierce objections of Pope Innocent XI that Louis XIV revoked the religious freedom of French Protestants and drove hundreds of thousands of them into exile— in some cases, seizing their children so they could be raised as obedient Catholic subjects. There is even a heresy known as Gallicanism, which asserts that local authorities (namely, the king) ought to reign supreme over Church affairs, without Rome's interference. This heresy was sponsored and promoted by the kings of France.

In England, the Anglican bishop Robert Filmer developed a comprehensive theory of royal, patriarchal authority over Church and state, tracing the absolute rights of the monarch back to Adam's paternal dictatorship over his sons. Hobbes would radically secularize this argument in *Leviathan*, arguing that the ceaseless war of "all against all" would rage throughout society if any authority existed that could push back against the king.

Even as the Church and Scripture were being corralled into support for modern regimes marked by unchecked centralized power, the philosophical supports for faith were being radically undermined by new philosophical systems. Although we cannot do a fair summary of centuries of intellectual history in just a few lines, put briefly, the movements were these:

Nominalism, which began with William of Ockham and profoundly influenced such figures as Luther, denied that human reason could speak with any authority over matters that elude human experience. God, whatever he is, and all matters supernatural, are beyond even our power to speak by analogy. So that when we say that God is "just," it need not mean anything like our human idea of justice; it could even be the opposite. Such a notion was very well suited to theologians like Calvin, who wished to assert that it was perfectly just for God to punish for all eternity unbaptized infants and the millions of souls whom he had predestined for hell. The only knowledge we have about God comes from revelation—from the Bible itself, and from the guidance God gives believers in reading it. Of course, in the absence of any higher authority to interpret that complex and sometimes puzzling document, the result of this position is theological anarchy; hence the hundreds of divisions into which the Church was shattered after Luther. Over time, the violent clashes between these sects and the remnants of Roman authority would bring religion itself into disrepute, and make it necessary for states that wanted civil peace to treat religious faith as an arbitrary, private set of beliefs that ought to have no influence in society. There is no accounting for taste, or faith, and the only way to stop people fighting over it is to agree that it really isn't that important.

Rationalism asserted that man can only be sure of what he knows by logical and mathematical deduction. This movement was launched and is still best represented by René Descartes, who admitted that he sought to make himself the progenitor of all future philosophy and science. He attempted this task by crafting a brilliant rhetorical weapon—his systematic doubt of every assertion that could not be proved by the mind reflecting upon itself. No sense data, no history, no tradition or authority could have any probative value; the only thing the mind really knows is itself. From that self-regarding foundation Descartes built a philosophical system that rendered religious truths irrelevant, that ruled out of court any opinion or doctrine that was passed along by tradition, and that encouraged each solitary intellectual to view the opinions of his fathers or his community through a jaundiced hermeneutic of suspicion. Like a modernist architect, each thinker arrives with a bulldozer to knock down the ancient temples and dusty museums to clear a vacant lot on which he will build from scratch something utterly new that he has conceived from scratch. While few today still agree with the system Descartes built, he radically redefined the role of a philosopher (and hence of an intellectual); instead of being a link in a chain of transmitted wisdom that reached back through history and reflected on difficult questions, each ambitious young man was challenged to create philosophy ex nihilo. In other words, each philosopher felt the pressure to act as God.

Subsequent rationalists included Baruch Spinoza, who developed a pantheism that reduced God to simply an empty title for everything, and Immanuel Kant, who followed the conclusions of nominalism even further, to assert that we can have no rational knowledge even of earthly things in themselves, but only of those fragments that our limited minds perceive. How much less can we presume to know anything of God or divine precepts? Instead we must build a purely human world upon what moral system best accords with the moral rules we derive from reflecting upon the nature of human reason.

While the best minds of Europe were casting corrosive doubts on the rational basis for accepting Christianity, in Protestant countries the results of nominalism were becoming all too clear: Religious thought split into two opposing but complementary tendencies, each of them based on the premise that our rational minds can know nothing certain about the supernatural:

Fideism asserted that we must accept the content of divine revelation, even when it appears to outrage the tenets of logic and the voice of our moral sentiments. This impulse is first associated with the Church Father Tertullian, who countered the objections of pagan philosophers with the (in)famous quip: "I believe because it is absurd!" The more predominant strain in Christian thinking, however, belonged to Augustine, who urged his readers to "believe in order that you may understand." The tension between these two responses to rational challenges continued for a thousand years, as Etienne Gilson documents in *Reason and Revelation in the Middle Ages*. With the rise of nominalism and the rejection of Aquinas's attempted synthesis of reason and faith, Tertullian's answer began to prevail among those who chose to believe as an act of will—in the teeth of what they thought was the verdict of their reason.

Tertullian's choice prevailed in the Reformation. Apart from a willful, fideistic rejection of reason's authority, there is no other way for the human mind to choke down the implications of Luther and Calvin's core doctrine— namely that man has no free will, that God chooses whom to save or damn with absolute, arbitrary freedom, then overpowers such souls with his grace, which they cannot reject or resist. Other souls whom he chooses not to save will follow their sins into hell. All this is just, and even merciful, because . . . the Bible tells me so. If reason rebels against assertions like these, then reason is, in Luther's words, a "whore." The fideistic approach to faith and reason has the advantage of bolstering a creed against the shifting winds of philosophical opinion—at the price of making it brittle. Returning to the humanist objection we are examining here, it is certainly fair to characterize such a God as an "invisible, all-powerful, punitive father-figure." In fact, to most of us, that kind of God would be a wicked and cruel father, whom we would be relieved to discover did not exist.

One of the ugliest strains to emerge in Christian rhetoric fed into this image of God: the "substitutionary" theory of Jesus's redemption, which asserted that God the Father was full of wrath at human sin—including original sin, which applied even to infants—and that the only means by which the human race could be saved was for Christ to take on himself the full burden of that wrath and to suffer hideously on man's behalf until his father's wrath was fully appeased, at which point man could be offered mercy. This theory was widely held in Catholic and Protestant circles—though it was never affirmed dogmatically—and it no doubt performed its intended task of instilling a proper awe for divine justice and gratitude for Christ's redemption. But the image of God it fostered was indeed of a punitive, vindictive father, whose attitude toward his creatures was exactly that pictured by Jonathan Edwards in his justly infamous sermon, "Sinners in the Hands of an Angry God":

> The God that holds you over the pit of hell, much as one holds a spider, or some loathsome insect over the fire, abhors you, and is dreadfully provoked: his wrath towards you burns like fire; he looks upon you as worthy of nothing else, but to be cast into the fire; he is of purer eyes than to bear to have you in his sight; you are ten thousand times more abominable in his eyes, than the most hateful venomous serpent is in ours. You have offended him infinitely more than ever a stubborn rebel did his prince; and yet it is nothing but his hand that holds you from falling into the fire every moment. It is to be ascribed to nothing else, that you did not go to hell the last night; that you was suffered to awake again in this world, after you closed your eyes to sleep. And there is no other reason to be given, why you have not dropped into hell since you arose in the morning, but that God's hand has held you up. There is no other reason to be given why you have not gone to hell, since you have sat here in the house of God, provoking his pure eyes by your sinful wicked manner of attending his solemn worship. Yea, there is nothing else that is to be given as a reason why you do not this very moment drop down into hell.[4]

---

4 Found at www.ccel.org/ccel/edwards/sermons.sinners.html.

Other theological traditions, of course, co-existed with this one on both sides of the Tiber. One apostolic metaphor for Christ was the "divine physician" (or "wounded healer"), which emphasized Christ's willingness to endure on our behalf our earthly sufferings, which are the inevitable effects of human sin. In the Catholic tradition, the devotion to the Sacred Heart was particularly important in counteracting the harsh, forbidding image of God that was popularized by Jansenism. Believers were encouraged to meditate on Christ's human nature as much as on his divine personhood, to see their own sufferings and acts of charity as directed toward Jesus himself. As priests used to say to encourage the use of the sacrament of confession, when a sinner repents it removes a nail from Jesus's crown of thorns.

Pietism, which also developed in Protestant lands, represented another means of refiguring God and the divine economy. Like nominalism, it gave little credence to what reason had to say about matters of faith. But instead of focusing efforts on disciplining the mind to humbly accept the inscrutable dictates of God, pietists chose to fight for the human heart. Theological orthodoxy was a starting point for internal exercises aimed at training one's emotions along Christian lines—developing a lived, felt friendship with Christ through humble reading of the Bible and fellowship with other Christians. The current Evangelical Protestant emphasis on a personal relationship with Christ can be traced to the pietist movement; so can the mainline, liberal Christian tendency to pare Christianity down to a mild ethical creed emphasizing kindness and solicitude on behalf of the poor and the marginalized (which can come to include those whose marginal status derives from their moral choices, i.e., active homosexuals). Pietists did not intend it, but their powerful emphasis on the affective, instead of the rational faculty, helped prepare the ground for "romantic" Christianity, as crystallized in the writing of Friedrich Schleiermacher, who held that the essence of true Christian faith was to be found in the human heart, which felt profoundly its dependence on Christ's redemption. Faith consisted of this feeling, and the Church was the collection of those who shared it.[5] This assertion nicely shunted aside all questions of dogma or other assertions about divine reality that could not be sustained by modern men who had abandoned the effort to use human reason to know about God. Christianity became a thing like poetry or music—a nonessential means for moral and

---

5 John L. Murphy, "Modernism and the Teaching of Schleiermacher," www.catholicculture .org/culture/library/view.cfm?recnum=3016.

"spiritual" uplift, rather than a fighting creed that made implacable claims about the nature of the universe. On this view, the Christian God was, far from being a cruel and vindictive father, something much more like what C. S. Lewis called a "senile grandfather in heaven," who nods at all his progeny's fumbling efforts and pins them to the divine refrigerator.

A final, and culturally potent, source of the perception that the Jewish-Christian image of God is a crippling, fantasy father-figure is, of course, the work of Sigmund Freud, whose speculative interpretations of culture and psychology—labeled as clinical science—made their mark on the twentieth-century perception of religion. In *Moses and Monotheism*, *The Future of an Illusion*, and *Totem and Taboo*, Freud applied his theories about infantile sexuality and father/son rivalry to biblical narratives. In essence, he concluded that the divine father pictured in orthodox theology and Scripture was an internalized, transformed image of one's earthly father, who represented the punitive aspect of the "superego," that psychological mechanism that restricts and controls the potent instinctive urges that goad all human behavior. Put in his bluntly shocking and deeply resonant terms, the son's Oedipal desire to possess his mother sexually is inhibited by the jealousy of the father, whose threat of violence teaches the son to control and sublimate his impulses. One approved way to sublimate such desires is to project them into the "imaginary" realm of religion—which also provides more potent curbs against the free, destructive play of instinct than any external authority ever could. So religion serves not just as an opiate, but as a kind of chastity belt. Once feminist authors began to ring their own changes on Freud, they developed elaborate theories of how patriarchal religion was invented to control female sexuality and keep intact the unequal structures of the heterosexual family, private property, and other cultural institutions that inhibit the free play of female desire.

There is much truth to the objections raised by humanists of various stripes, who note how Christian rhetoric has been abused in the service of all-too-human agendas and been hijacked by the strong for use against the weak. But how much does that prove? Is there any set of ideas that is not prone to being appropriated by the smartest, the richest, or the most politically savvy segment of society? Certainly not Marxism, as any survivor of seventy years of Soviet rule would attest. What of the loudly egalitarian feminist movement? Feminism, at least, does not have a gulag or terror famines to its credit. Or does it? What else can we call the tens of millions of fetuses destroyed under cover of law in the past forty years? Those unborn children are surely the "kulaks" of the feminist revolution. Nor were their deaths incidental. The core feminist project of leveling the playing field for women, granting them the same erotic and economic freedom enjoyed by "emancipated" men, is simply unachievable without abortion. Every large, well-funded feminist organization considers abortion non-negotiable; women's studies departments nationwide are univocally "pro-choice." Well-meaning attempts by faithful women to foster a "pro-life feminism" are doomed to fail, unless feminism is completely recast and purged of its corrosive fixation on power imbalances as the operative factor in every human relationship. That seems unlikely.

The jaundiced "hermeneutic of suspicion" fundamental to Marxist, Freudian, feminist, or other reductionist theories of religion proves too much, if it proves anything at all. Christianity is subject to their critiques precisely because the ethical standard it sets for itself is so very high— inhumanly high, as Jesus's listeners in the Gospels were keen to point out. Impassioned movements for human rights arose in the West—as they did nowhere else—to challenge the hypocrisies and imperfections of Christian practice *because of* Christian theory and the infinitely high value it places on every human being's ultimate worth. We look in vain for conscientious objectors in the armies of Genghis Khan, for Shinto priests shaming samurai for conducting unjust wars, for an Aztec Bartolomé de las Casas denouncing human sacrifice. As Thomas Sowell has pointed out, human slavery has been practiced across the world throughout human history; only the Christian West produced any abolitionists.

For Further Reading:

Augustine, *The City of God,* trans. Marcus Dods (Peabody, MA: Hendrickson Publishing, 2009).

Frederic Bastiat, *The Law* (New York: Tribeca Books, 2012).

Norman Cohn, *The Pursuit of the Millennium* (Oxford: Oxford University Press, 1970).

Edward Feser, *The Last Superstition* (South Bend, IN: St. Augustine's Press, 2010).

Ludwig Feuerbach, *The Essence of Christianity,* trans. George Eliot (Amherst, NY: 1989).

Etienne Gilson, *Reason and Revelation in the Middle Ages* (New York: Scribner's, 2000).

Peter Hitchens, *The Rage Against God* (Grand Rapids, MI: Zondervan, 2011).

Russell Kirk, *The Roots of American Order* (Wilmington, DE: ISI Books, 2000).

Leszek Kolakowski, *God Owes Us Nothing* (Chicago: University of Chicago Press, 1998).

Henri de Lubac, *The Drama of Atheist Humanism* (San Francisco: Ignatius Press, 1995).

Donna Steichen, *Ungodly Rage: The Hidden Face of Catholic Feminism* (San Francisco: Ignatius Press, 1991).

Alexis de Tocqueville, *Democracy in America* (Chicago: University of Chicago Press, 2002).

Eric Voegelin, *The New Science of Politics* (Chicago: University of Chicago Press, 1987).

Epilogue:
The Great Campaign

Having read through this survey of modern ideologies that claimed almost 200 million innocent lives and the virtues that could have saved those lives, you might well feel dispirited. You and I are no match for demagogues who craft "big lies" that turn ordinary people into genocidal mobs. We cannot take down all the sophists who weave from fashionable half-truths a silk shroud to mask our everyday evils. Even the stories of heroes who risked all they had in the fight for human dignity can seem impossibly out of reach. We can tell ourselves that we are not made of the same kind of stuff, the fiber that lets a man defy his nation's government, its ruling elites, its secret police. We are just regular Joes and Janes, and life will not ask us to make this sort of sacrifice. It had better not, because we will fail.

But that is a lie. It's the same kind of lie that subhumanism tells us about each other, about our neighbors and spouses and children, and especially about strangers who look or think or pray just a little bit different.

The heroes among us prove that this simply isn't true. The texture of their lives, and the sacrifices they made, prove that each and every one of us can do more. We can be better. Neither Jérôme Lejeune, nor Mary Anne Yep, nor Jerzy Popiełuszko was born with special powers, wearing a halo, or in a manger. Ordinary human beings like me and you, they were confused and frightened and tempted. Each one of them could have made very different choices, could have trundled along and averted his eyes from the truths that were being trampled.

Subhumanism, for all the intellectual or political masks it wears, says just one central thing: That man doesn't really matter all that much. That there is nothing in us that exceeds or transcends the ugliness of Darwinian competition, the limits of biology, the inevitability of death. That is a lie.

We can treat people as if they were robots, ghosts, or beasts. We can starve, enslave, imprison them, or kill them. But that doesn't change the reality. If we look up, and also within, we will find the mysterious image and likeness of God. We will discover the truth that we and our neighbors have an incomparable beauty and worth. A dignity that no one can take away.

Our thousand-year reichs, our workers' paradises, our brave new worlds, are ghastly fantasies that human beings create, and that history duly comes along and exposes. And what is left behind, bruised and battered but still unbowed, is the face of Man—as noble and as beautiful as Adam reaching out his hand to the God who made him. We will remember that, and we will do what is needed. We will feel from the depths of our hearts to the highest flights of our imagination a love of the good, a hatred of cruelty and smallness of soul, and a loyalty to each and every member of our family, the human family. We will fight to enshrine the basic principles of decency in our political, economic, and personal lives. We will have courage. We will prevail.

Acknowledgments

First and foremost, I have to thank my beautiful wife, Alexandra. On our first date I bored her with the plan for this book. Through our courtship and marriage she has been my audience of one as I have pontificated on the whole-life principles or railed against ideologies of evil. Now, eight years and five children later "the book" has become a reality. Profound gratitude to my wonderful family, especially my children, Micah, Marion, Maximilian, Jacob, Eva Marie, Isabella, and Andrew. This book is my feeble effort to help cultivate a peaceful, humane society for you and your future children.

I thank the Human Rights Education & Relief Organization (HERO) for the generous grant to support the book's completion, and the HERO family, our staff, volunteers, and donors. Andrew Breitbart would always remind me that I have "the coolest posse in Hollywood." To wake up every day and have a team that shared my vision of promoting the incomparable worth of the human person has turned a lonely vocation into a joyful quest. Thanks to Josef Lipp, who has grown from my right-hand man to my full partner. This book would not have been possible without his willingness to shoulder more than his fair share of the burden at Movie to Movement. His humility, strength, and commitment to mission inspires me to strive to be not only useful but Holy.

Yvonne and Rich Seeman: You have been with me from the beginning. I am so confident in your friendship that I fear I take you for granted. All of our successes are the fruit of your trust and sacrifice.

Eustace Wolfington: You are an exemplar of the power of long-range planning, patience, and generosity. Wolfhounds!

Jennifer Cadena: Thank you for your years of selfless commitment to the cause of Life. You truly are the co-founder of HERO. You planted the trees that are now bearing fruit.

Jeannette Angulo, Ashley Alquist, and Danielle Lipp: There can be no more difficult job in the world than being the assistant to an obsessively driven man with raging ADHD and an abundance of energy.

Megan Drapa: Whenever I am down, I think of the night Matt and I were drinking beer and eating pizza in a Chicago hotel room, when you appeared on the evening news with frozen fingers and toes, clipboarding for a candidate with no chance of winning. Thank you for always being willing (and often eager) to tilt at windmills with me. I especially love how you seem to become more joyful the more certain defeat appeared: You truly are Irish.

Michael Centanni, Rick Hocking, and David Miller: Knowing that you are a phone call away is the only reason I can sleep at night.

Sam Curphy and Mary Lindstrom: The best lawyer and accountant money can buy. ("Can you send the invoice again? I've seemed to misplaced it.") Thank you for investing in HERO and for not billing by the minute.

John J. Jakubczyk: You truly are the Godfather of the whole life movement.

Bob Atwell: Thank you for believing in me even when cool-headed reason tells you not to. All I've ever needed to know about being a man I've learned from you.

Ann Hocking, Marti Gillin, and Lenore Miller: The grace from your prayers is ever present.

Kim and Tom Bengard: Thank you for being funny, cool, and not strange. Thank you for modeling civic duty, kindness, and humility. Tom, you give me hope that even with all my raging ADHD I can one day make something of myself. Kim, I am overwhelmed at your servant's heart. Your hospitality would inspire Dolley Madison.

Mickey O'Hare: You are one tough hombre. You are the model of constancy and fortitude.

Keith Mason: You are not as tough as Mickey but I wouldn't want to meet you in a dark alley. You are tenacious and a relentless innovator.

Kate Zhou: You are a tireless advocate of liberty.

Andrew Breitbart: You truly are "The White Plume over the battlefield."

My heroes: Steve McEveety, Matt Schoeffling, Brad Philips, Rep. Chris Smith, and his wife, Marie.

Special thanks to Joseph Farah, Brad Thor, Roxanne Phillips, Shelia Liaugminas, James Perry, Sam Brownback, the Yep family, Richard Viguerie, Alveda King, Dick Bott, Keet Lewis, Eduardo Verastegui, Kristan Hawkins, Abby Johnson, Lila Rose, Bryan Kemper, Fr. Frank Pavone, Joni and Stephen Abdalla, Lou Bremer, Thomas Cook, Bear Woznick, Kristan Hawkins, Theodore Baehr, Mark Joseph, John Sullivan, Josh Walsh, Nick and Kevin Costello, Joe Giganti, Aimee Murphy, Brian Lohmann, Lesley Burbridge, Pattie Mallete, Courtney Abernethy, Khadine L. Ritter, Mia Reini, Chevonne O'Shaughnessy, Patrick Novecosky, Angela Grey, Barrett and Mary Moore, Zip Rzeppa, and Deby Schlapprizzi.

And thank you to the 260,000 supporters and volunteers for Movie to Movement and *IamWholeLife.com*.

—Jason Scott Jones

My thanks to Faye Ballard, and to Susie and Franz Josef Zmirak for their incessant help and support. Without you none of this would have been worthwhile, though it still might have barely been possible.

—John Zmirak

We jointly wish to thank Faye Ballard for her invaluable advice, Jane Cavolina for her careful copyediting, and Gwendolin Herder of The Crossroad Publishing Company for keeping this project on track.

About the Authors

Jason Scott Jones is a filmmaker and human rights activist. His film projects include *The Stoning of Soraya M., Bella,* and *Crescendo.* He was national grassroots director of Sen. Sam Brownback's presidential campaign in 2008, and is president of Movie to Movement and the Human Rights Education Organization (H.E.R.O.). He lives in Hawaii. This is his first book.

John Zmirak is an editor, college teacher, screenwriter, and political columnist. He is author of the popular Bad Catholic's Guides, *Wilhelm Röpke,* and *The Grand Inquisitor* (graphic novel). He is a former editor at *Investor's Business Daily.* His work has appeared in *Aleteia.org, The Blaze, National Review, The Weekly Standard, First Things, The American Spectator, USA Today, Commonweal, The American Conservative,* and *The National Catholic Register;* and he has contributed to *The Encyclopedia of Catholic Social Thought* and *American Conservatism: An Encyclopedia.* He has been a commentator on Fox News and the Christian Broadcasting Network. He edited a number of popular guides to higher education and served as press secretary to Louisiana governor Mike Foster. His columns are archived at *www.badcatholics.com.*

You Might Also Like

Tea Party Catholic

The Catholic Case for Limited Government,
a Free Economy, and Human Flourishing

By Samuel Gregg, Foreword by Michael Novak

272 Pages, Paperback, ISBN 9780824549817

"If you don't know Samuel Gregg's writings, you don't know one of the top two or three writers on the free society today." — Michael Novak, bestselling author, *Washington's God: Religion, Liberty, and the Father of Our Country*

Over the past fifty years, increasing numbers of American Catholics have abandoned the economic positions associated with Franklin Roosevelt's New Deal, ideals upheld by Ronald Reagan and the Tea Party movement but also deeply rooted in the American Founding. This shift, alongside America's growing polarization around economic questions, has generated fierce debates among Catholic Americans. Can a believing Catholic support free markets? Does the Catholic social justice commitment translate directly into big government? In Tea Party Catholic, Samuel Gregg draws upon Catholic teaching, natural law theory, and the thought of the only Catholic Signer of America's Declaration of Independence, Charles Carroll of Carrollton—the first "Tea Party Catholic"—to develop a Catholic case for the values and institutions associated with the free economy, limited government, and America's experiment in ordered liberty.

*Support your local bookstore or order directly
from the publisher at www.CrossroadPublishing.com.*

*To request a catalog or inquire about
quantity orders, please e-mail
sales@CrossroadPublishing.com.*

 The Crossroad Publishing Company

You Might Also Like

Against the Grain

Christianity and Democracy, War and Peace

By George Weigel

352 Pages, Hardcover, ISBN 9780824524487

Cutting against the grain of conventional wisdom, New York Times bestseller, George Weigel, offers a compelling look at the ways in which Catholic social teaching sheds light on the challenges of peace, the problem of pluralism, the quest for human rights, and the defense of liberty. In this major contribution one of America's most prominent intellectuals offers a meticulous analysis of the foundations of the free society as he makes a powerful case for the role of moral reasoning in meeting the threats to human dignity posed by debonair nihilism, jihadist violence, and the brave new world of manufactured men and women.

Support your local bookstore or order directly from the publisher at www.CrossroadPublishing.com.

To request a catalog or inquire about quantity orders, please e-mail sales@CrossroadPublishing.com.

The Crossroad Publishing Company

You Might Also Like

Open Mind, Faithful Heart

Reflections on Following Jesus

By Pope Francis (Jorge Mario Bergoglio),
Edited by Gustavo Larrázabal,
Translated by Joseph Owens

320 Pages, Hardcover, ISBN 9780824519971

"The secret of Pope Francis is found in this book." —Bishop Martínez Camino

Before Pope Francis was elected pope he had faithfully submitted this resignation to retire as is customary for bishops when reaching 75 years of age. In preparation he asked his editor at the Claretian publishing house of Buenos Aires to work with him on gathering his most principal texts and speeches. Open Mind, Faithful Heart is the result of their collaboration. The spiritual foundation for much of what Pope Francis has surprised the world with since his election, radically reframing the Catholic contribution, is found in these texts. The book clearly outlines the inspiration needed to address the urgent challenges to our world and human living today.

Support your local bookstore or order directly
from the publisher at www.CrossroadPublishing.com.

To request a catalog or inquire about
quantity orders, please e-mail
sales@CrossroadPublishing.com.

The Crossroad Publishing Company